Surviving the Demise of Solo Practice: Mental Health Practitioners Prospering in the Era of Managed Care

Surviving the Demise of Solo Practice: Mental Health Practitioners Prospering in the Era of Managed Care

Editors

Nicholas A. Cummings, Ph.D., Sc.D.
Michael S. Pallak, Ph.D.
Janet L. Cummings, Psy.D.

PSYCHOSOCIAL PRESS
Madison   Connecticut

Library of Congress Cataloging-in-Publication Data

Surviving the demise of solo practice : mental health practitioners
  prospering in the era of managed care / editors Nicholas A.
  Cummings, Michael S. Pallak, Janet L. Cummings.
      p.   cm.
    Includes bibliographical references and index.
    ISBN 1-887841-03-2
    1. Managed mental health care—United States.   2. Psychiatry—
  Practice—United States.   3. Psychotherapy—Practice—United
  States.   4. Clinical psychology—Practice—United States.
  I. Cummings, Nicholas A.   II. Pallak, Michael S., 1942–
  III. Cummings, Janet L.
    [DNLM: 1. Mental Health Services—organization & administration.
  2. Group Practice.   3. Managed Care Programs—organization &
  administration.   WM 21 S963 1996]
  RC465.6.S87   1996
  616.89'0068—dc20
  DNLM/DLC
  for Library of Congress   96-14756
                                                                  CIP

Manufactured in the United States of America

Contents

Appendices
   Compiled by Dennis P. Morrison

About the Authors

Daniel Berman, Psy.D., M.H.A., R.N. A nationally recognized healthcare consultant, Dr. Berman writes a monthly column on managed care issues and practice. Doctorate 1990, Newport University; M.H.A., Columbia Pacific; R.N., Armstrong State College.

Charles H. Browning, Ph.D. President and Director of Practice Development & Marketing Consultants Group, a division of Duncliff's International. President and Clinical Director of Browning Therapy Group, Inc., a multidisciplinary brief therapy group practice in Southern California. Doctorate 1975, University of Nebraska.

Janet L. Cummings, Psy.D. President, The Nicholas & Dorothy Cummings Foundation, Inc. Former staff psychologist, American Biodyne (MedCo, now Merit Behavioral Care). Doctorate 1992, School of Professional Psychology, Wright State University.

Nicholas A. Cummings, Ph.D., Sc.D. President, Foundation for Behavioral Health and Chairman, The Nicholas & Dorothy Cummings Foundation. Founding CEO, American Biodyne (MedCo, now Merit Behavioral Care). Former President, American Psychological Association. Founder of the four campuses of the California School of Professional Psychology. Chief Psychologist (Retired), Kaiser-Permanente. Founder: National Academies of Practice, Washington, D.C. Founder: American Managed Behavioral Healthcare Association. Former Executive Director, Mental Research Institute, Palo Alto, CA. Founder: National Council of Schools of Professional Psychology (NCSPP). Doctorate 1958, Adelphi University.

Richard S. Edley, Ph.D. Executive Vice President and Chief Operating Officer, Managed Networks of America. Former management at FHC Health Systems/OPTIONS, as well as American Biodyne (MedCo, now Merit Behavioral Care). Postdoctoral

Fellow at McLean Hospital, Harvard Medical School. Doctorate 1988, Emory University.

Bruce C. Gorman, M.C.R.P. Vice President for Public Sector Programs, Merit Behavioral Care Corporation (formerly MedCo). Previously, Vice President for Network Development, American Biodyne, and Administrator, Aetna Life Insurance Company. He holds a master's degree in City and Regional Planning and a B.S. (cum laude) in Economics from the University of Maryland.

Greg T. Greenwood, Ph.D., M.B.A. Vice President, Behavioral Health, Blue Cross and Blue Shield of Texas, Inc. Former Vice President and Northern Region General Manager; Indiana area director; center director; staff psychologist, American Biodyne (MedCo, now Merit Behavioral Care). Former staff psychologist, Gallabue Community Mental Health Center. Previously assistant professor, Indiana University School of Medicine. Doctorate 1985, Bowling Green State University. Master's of Business Administration 1995, University of Texas at Dallas.

Kristina L. Greenwood, Ph.D. Vice President of Clinical Development, CORPHEALTH, Inc. Former Vice President of Clinical Operations, ADAPT Healthcare, Inc. Former director of training and development; regional clinical director; center director; staff psychologist, American Biodyne (MedCo, now Merit Behavioral Care). Previously staff psychologist, South Central Community Mental Health Centers. Doctorate 1985, Bowling Green State University.

Scott O. Harris, Ph.D. Codirector, The Center for Behavioral Healthcare. Former Director of Outpatient Utilization Management Department, Managed Health Network. Author: *When Growing Up Hurts Too Much*. Adjunct professor, Pepperdine University and the California School of Professional Psychology, Los Angeles. Doctorate 1982, California School of Professional Psychology, Los Angeles.

Thomas D. Kalous, Ph.D. Psychologist and provider network manager, Merit Behavioral Care (MBC), Colorado Area. Founder, trainer, and consultant, Clinical Supervision Resources. Past Chair of the Interprofessional Committee on Clinical Supervision for the State of Arizona. Former faculty member and curriculum developer, University of Phoenix. Doctorate 1992, Ohio State University.

Dennis P. Morrison, Ph.D. Chief Executive Officer, South Central CMHC; consultant to behavioral healthcare industry on outcomes and clinical information systems. Former Director of Clinical Information Systems, MedCo (now Merit Behavioral Care). Previously Director of Marketing and Director of Business Development, National Computer Systems-Assessments. Doctorate 1984, Ball State University.

Michael S. Pallak, Ph.D. Vice President, Health Marketing & Management, Inc. Executive Vice President, Foundation for Behavioral Health. Former Executive Officer, American Psychological Association. Formerly the Vice President for Research, American Biodyne (MedCo, now Merit Behavioral Care). Former faculty, University of Iowa. Previously Dean, California School of Professional Psychology (Berkeley/Alameda). Doctorate 1968, Yale University.

Sharon A. Shueman, Ph.D. Director of Quality Management, PacifiCare Behavioral Health, Laguna Hills, CA. Principal, Shueman Troy Associates, Pasadena, CA. Former Director, APA/CHAMPUS Project and Quality Assurance Program, American Psychological Association. Doctorate 1977, University of Maryland.

Warwick G. Troy, Ph.D., M.P.H. Director, Division of Applied Research and Professional Services and Center for Behavioral Health, California School of Professional Psychology, Los Angeles. Chair, Presidential Task Force on Education and Training for Work in Organized Delivery Systems, American Psychological Association. Principal, Shueman Troy Associates, Pasadena, CA. Former Director of Mental Health, Southern Sydney Area Health Services, Sydney, Australia. Doctorate 1976, University of Maryland. Master of Public Health 1990, UCLA.

Introduction

This book is designed to serve as a guide to success for all those practitioners who avail themselves of an unprecedented window of opportunity. Not since the industrialization of healthcare in the early 1980s have practitioners been handed a means by which they can recapture control of healthcare delivery and thereby regain their autonomy, respect, and dignity. But this window of opportunity will be short-lived. For those who are willing to seize the moment, this volume is more than a survival manual; it is a road map to prosperity.

In 1985 Dr. Nicholas Cummings founded American Biodyne as the first clinically-driven managed mental healthcare delivery system. Key decision making positions were occupied by practitioners, and American Biodyne became the "boot camp" for the industry as these pioneers became the CEOs, presidents, vice presidents, and various executives in the many companies that followed Biodyne. Those who advanced, prospered and defined the future are represented here in the various chapters, along with their mentor. After those early years American Biodyne (later MedCo and now Merit), along with the industry, lost its clinical focus. Those who originally implemented that clinical focus reveal how it can be regained.

In the first three chapters Dr. Nicholas Cummings gives the origins of managed behavioral healthcare, describes where it is today, and predicts where it will be in the future. He remains optimistic, stating that for the provider, finally "the trend is our friend." If the appropriate response is forthcoming, he envisions the emergence of a Renaissance practitioner.

Cummings was the first mental health practitioner to warn of the impending industrialization of behavioral healthcare, and he is now the first to herald the new era of opportunity for the provider. He brings the perspective of several decades of practitioner activism. Almost 40 years ago he designed and implemented the first comprehensive psychotherapy benefit in an era in which the conventional wisdom was that psychotherapy could not be covered by health insurance. He predicted accurately that the day would come when most Americans would have health insurance, and if mental health were not a covered benefit, the behavioral health professions would not develop. Subsequently he accurately predicted the community mental health centers movement, the professional school movement in psychology, and eventually the industrialization of healthcare.

Dr. Cummings describes specifically the kinds of groups behavioral healthcare providers must form. He warns these are not the so-called "carve-outs" that most practitioners are looking toward, but what he describes as "carve-ins." If his voice at times is strident, no offense is intended. As a psychotherapist for nearly half a century, he is aware of the profoundly negative effect of denial and the need to confront it repeatedly. The professions have been in the grip of a severe denial, refusing to hear even the most shrill warnings. A number of myths and outmoded attitudes cherished by the professions have hampered their ability to meet the challenges of managed care. Cummings deftly delineates the paradigm shifts required to unleash the providers' potential to prosper.

Echoing Cummings' insights is a respected healthcare executive who, although not a provider, is sympathetic to the needs of practitioners. Bruce Gorman has vast experience in organizing networks for managed care, and then marketing their services. He has witnessed firsthand both successful and unsuccessful provider groups, and strongly believes that with a change in perspective practitioners have much to contribute as leaders of the new healthcare environment.

As the role of the practitioner has drastically changed, so have the roles of educators, trainors, and supervisors of practitioners. In the first of a trilogy, Dr. Warwick Troy and Dr. Sharon Shueman describe how graduate training must change to meet the needs of 21st century clinicians. Dr. Troy chairs the American Psychological Association's (APA's) new Task Force on Graduate Education, and Dr. Shueman is a nationally recognized expert on the creation and measurement of quality of behavioral healthcare services. Shielded even more from business demands than providers have been, educators comprehend little of what is happening in the industrialized healthcare world. They are uncomfortably becoming aware that students and consumers are demanding more relevant education and training, and this volume is invaluable in helping them with these challenges.

But as graduate education must change, so must undergraduate education. Otherwise, students will not be prepared for the medical courses attendant to training in prescribing medication, as well as the business and managerial aspects of future doctoral training in psychology. Dr. Janet Cummings is not only a recently trained and licensed psychologist, but she attended the APA's first and only cosponsored experimental training program in prescription privileges. Because of a previous career, she was well prepared for this curriculum, while her fellow students were not. She shares her insights into the need to begin the changes in curriculum before the student enters graduate education.

Dr. Thomas Kalous completes this section by enunciating the changes in the role of a supervisor in the new healthcare environment. As are all the chapter contributors, Dr. Kalous is writing about the very things he is doing in his everyday practice with a large managed care company. Supervision is significantly changed in its perspective and its demands.

In Part III the business aspects of practice are specifically addressed. Drs. Kristina and Greg Greenwood began their psychological careers as psychotherapists, and continued that role in a different fashion when they joined American Biodyne in 1986. They then began to advance as supervisors and managers, culminating in their present roles as successful, high-ranking executives in two different healthcare companies. They describe this transition step-by-step, along with the paradigm shifts they made in the process. Their story is an exciting one, told in such a manner that any ambitious mental healthcare professional can follow.

Dr. Charles Browning imparts invaluable practical information on how to successfully partner with managed care. He describes the best ways to be accepted in provider panels even when these are closed, how to garner the lion's share of referrals, and how to make a case manager your respected ally. He even presents the details of such specifics as successful sample letters and forms to the scripting of successful presentations and interviews. Dr. Browning has refined these practical tools over many years of successfully partnering his Browning Group with managed care.

A renowned expert who consults with providers who want to form their own "physician equity" groups, Dr. Richard Edley recounts the do's and don't's of a successful large regional group practice. As an executive with two managed care companies, Dr. Edley has had the experience of going into a new territory and creating a healthcare business where before there was no managed care.

The world of capitation, RFPs, case rates, and prepaid health is a strange and foreboding place for most practitioners. Dr. Daniel Berman, also a renowned consultant, makes these and the myriad of other managed care terms comprehensible and doable. At the core of his recommendations is his concept of the "dynamic balance" among clinical, business and consumer interests which, when achieved, results in satisfactions and conflict reduction among all three players.

Finally in Part III, Dr. Nicholas Cummings takes the reader comfortably and knowledgeably through the most foreboding world of all for the practitioner: that of acquiring the capital to form one's own successful group practice. Included are the do's and don't's of a business plan, the best ways to approach venture capitalists, when to acquire competitors or be acquired, and a host of other imperatives which are simply, but comprehensively presented. Of particular importance is the distinction between a company formed for eventual public offering versus one intended in perpetuity to provide a congenial place to practice.

Section IV introduces the importance of outcomes research and the puzzling and rapidly changing world of informatics, neither of which can be ignored in the current healthcare climate. Dr. Michael Pallak, formerly vice president for research at American Biodyne and one of the researchers on the Hawaii Medicaid Project, acknowledges that outcomes research may be the toughest transition of all for the practitioner. Accustomed to never having his or her clinical judgment questioned, the provider must now prove efficacy and efficiency. Dr. Pallak walks the reader through the most significant and practical forms of outcomes research and indicates what is really needed to obtain contracts and contract renewals.

As the practitioner struggles with the belated industrialization of healthcare, the remainder of society is entering the information age. Informatics are impacting on healthcare in rapid and dramatic ways, and Dr. Dennis Morrison opens this world to the practitioner. He clearly delineates the computerization needs of the provider, expanding these to meet the needs of growth, and sparing the uninitiated reader the inordinate complexities of informatics. His chapter is packed with valuable, concise and understandable information without which there can be no successful group practice today.

What of the practitioner who does not aspire to becoming a manager, supervisor or researcher, and simply wishes to remain a clinician? Dr. Scott Harris is such a practitioner who has successfully maintained that role in the current healthcare environment. He shares how he has done this, and what changes in attitudes and practice patterns are required to remain in what many practitioners would perhaps call the most desirable role of all.

A case example was chosen to demonstrate in vivo how changes in attitudes can improve one's therapeutic skills as well as one's efficacy in the healthcare system. Dr. Janet Cummings has chosen suicide, an area in which she has expertise, to show how the hazards involved in the inordinate cost of the treatment of suicidal patients can result from the deeply imbedded defeatism of the practitioners. Cost-effective treatment of the suicidal patient can also be the most appropriate therapeutically.

At the end of the book there are three Appendices that have been prepared by Dr. Dennis Morrison and have never before been compiled. The valuable information in these Appendices can be found nowhere else. Appendix A lists information system vendors; Appendix B contains the most frequently used clinical information systems and where to obtain them; and Appendix C has Internet addresses in which practitioners would be most interested. The information contained in the Appendices is finally concluded with a list of suggested readings in health informatics.

PART I

Resocialization, Paradigm Shifts, and Future Trends

1.

The Resocialization of Behavioral Healthcare Practice

Nicholas A. Cummings, Ph.D., Sc.D.

There is a strong wind blowing, and that
can bring imagination or a headache.
Catherine the Great

For the first time since managed care initiated the industrialization of mental health and chemical dependency treatment more than a decade ago, practitioners have the opportunity to recapture the field of behavioral healthcare. This window of opportunity is unprecedented, but it will be short-lived and probably will not recur within the lifetimes of most providers who are practicing today. It has resulted from the formation of purchasing alliances, described below, with which practitioner groups may contract directly, thus by-passing the managed care companies (MCOs). To take advantage of this reprieve, there is much that must be done.

The resocialization of behavioral healthcare is already well underway as mental health practitioners stampede into group practices. At the present time a sizable number of practitioners have changed their attitudes and modes of practice and are prospering under managed care. This segment is growing rapidly. There is another segment whose members have declared they will lose their practices before they will change. A rough estimate of these segments is about 20% each, of the total number of practitioners, leaving the overwhelming majority of practitioners, perhaps as many as 60%, who are unhappily accommodating to managed care. They hate managed care, are resistant to change, and pin their hopes on the "any willing provider laws," that have now been enacted in most states, which more or less mandate that networks accept any provider who is licensed and agrees to join the network. They covertly oppose change, resist acquiring an education in the growing arsenal of time-sensitive psychotherapies, surreptitiously attempt to treat patients in the traditional way, and anticipate legislation that will perpetuate their ability to make a living. From the small group that overtly opposes change, and from the large group that covertly resists change, will come the 50% of today's providers who will not be in practice by the end of the century.

In addition to those who will or will not be in practice, there is emerging a second dichotomy for those who will still be in practice: practitioners who will work for the "company store" versus those who will work for themselves as owners of their own financially capitated group practices. Although this book is directed toward survival, it is primarily directed toward those who will do more than just survive and who will be managers of managed care companies or owners of physician equity group practices.

THE PRACTITIONER ADVANTAGE

The American people like their doctors. Collectively the professions must learn to take advantage of the high degree of professionalism in the United States that has won patients' respect and loyalty. But there is a difference between utilizing this loyalty versus relying on it. Those practitioners who believe that patient loyalty does not also depend on other, mostly economic factors, are scheduled for loss of practice. Over and over again doctors have been shocked to hear from a departing long-time patient, "Doctor, I love you. But if I come to you there is a large copayment. If I go to the managed care plan my company has contracted with, there's no copayment."

Surveys repeatedly demonstrate overwhelming patient satisfaction with practitioners. In fact, most patient satisfaction surveys

GRADING THE HEALTH PLANS

An influential business group issued its annual report card on health plans and HMOs, based on a new survey of 20,000 employees and retirees. Here's how the plans measured up:

Health Plan/HMO	Overall Customer Satisfaction With Health Plan	With Doctor
Aetna HMO (Northern California)	C	A
CaliforniaCare (Blue Cross)	C	B
CIGNA	B	A
FHP/TakeCare	B	A
Foundation	B	A
Health Net	B	A
Kaiser (Northern California)	A	A
Lifeguard	A	A
MetLife	C	B
PacifiCare	C	A
PruCare	C	A

KEY: A+: 90% or more satisfied; A: 80-89% satisfied; B: 70-79% satisfied; C: 50-69% satisfied; D: 50% or less satisfied

Source: Pacific Business Group on Health

CHRONICLE GRAPHIC

Figure 1.1

conducted by health plans actually reflect attitudes toward the caretaker, not the insurer. When practitioner and health plan are separated, surprisingly the patients rate the doctor high even when they rate the health plan low. An excellent example is the survey conducted by the Pacific Business Group, one of the largest and most active purchasing alliances in the nation (Hall, 1995). This survey found, as is shown in Figure 1.1, that even when patients rate the health plan as unsatisfactory or marginally satisfactory, they rate the doctors very highly.

Now that purchasing alliances have made it possible to contract directly with practitioner owned/managed groups, thus by-passing the managed care companies, practitioners have the advantage of wide public acceptance along with the ability to better contain costs by eliminating the "middle man," the managed care organizations (MCOs). In spite of the obvious advantage of this, practitioner groups must learn to predict and control costs. Without this ability, one is not a player in the health system today.

THE RACE FOR SURVIVAL:
MCOS VERSUS PRACTITIONERS

The MCOs are well aware of this edge held by practitioners, and they are now relying on practitioner inertia and unwillingness to change to win the race that is evolving. Knowing that practitioners can now compete directly, the MCOs are frantically buying up group practices so they can proffer their own captives in the struggle for contracts. Many successful group practices are selling to the MCOs, unable to resist "cashing in" and erroneously believing they can maintain their autonomy under the new ownership.

The next two or three years will determine who will win this race. Practitioners who want to create a congenial career environment where they can practice with self-respect must act now to form practitioner-equity group practices.

CLINICIAN, HEAL THYSELF

Some authorities (Austad, in press; Wylie, 1995) have named the intransigent segment the "Old Guard." They are older practitioners who are comfortable in long-term practices and blindly resist change. Even though only approximately one out of every ten referrals becomes a long-term therapy case, in due time an established therapist will have accumulated a full caseload of long-term patients.

Unfortunately for the psychotherapy profession, the old guard is in control of the governance of the professional societies and insists on making open warfare on the new order. Psychology is a prime example, for professional psychology "Kevorkianized" itself by bringing in leadership that was willing to say what the old guard wanted to hear. The old guard paid handsomely to be told managed care was a passing fad, that it would go away, and that the old system would prevail. When most psychologists realized the suicidal path the profession had been traversing, they brought in new leadership which is taking an aggressive but pragmatic advocacy stance. Psychology has to accept its own responsibility: Dr. Kevorkian goes only to those who want assistance in their own suicide. Psychology's old leadership, which rendered the American Psychological Association (APA) irrelevant in the decision-making arena of healthcare, must accept responsibility for its willingness to take down the entire profession rather than change. There were many other alternatives available rather than suicide, but they were unacceptable to those in power as they required healthy changes. At the present time, this old guard is generating voluminous hate mail directed against the new leadership, continuing the suicidal course.

Up until now the influence of the old guard has been pervasive. Psychologists running for APA office had to declare a militant antimanaged care platform in order to be elected. The Council of Representatives has been in the grip of the old guard for more than a decade, with members leaving only to be later reelected from another constituency. One member of the Council even declares it a virtue that he has been a member of that body for 23 of the past 30 years. The members of the APA Council of Representatives who dared vote for the proposed Division of Managed Care had their names published and were privately threatened with political reprisal. The future of the profession was in the stranglehold of a tyrannical, suicidal old guard. The losers would be the young psychologists entering the field who would find psychology's voice diminished.

As Stearn (1993, p. 163) reminds us, "It is a familiar fact to all clinicians that patients are often ambivalent about making changes in their lives even if those changes are in some 'objective' sense, for the best. Many factors contribute to patients' resistances. . . . Patients often need to learn new skills before relinquishing old behavior patterns. . . . Many patients tenaciously cling to old behavior patterns to reaffirm a needed sense of connection."

If only we understood ourselves as well as we understand our patients.

ACQUIRING NEW SKILLS

Two recent surveys (Kent, 1995; Levenson & Davidivitz, 1995) have revealed that there is widespread disregard amongst psychologists servicing managed care for the responsibility to acquire training adequate to practice.

Brief psychotherapy is not simply a truncated version of long-term therapy. It has its own parameters and requires additional training requirements, a position that has been amply demonstrated (Bennett, 1994; Budman & Gurman, 1988; Cummings, 1992). Belar (1989) not only emphasizes the importance of brief therapy, but insists on specific training in what has been termed "HMO therapy" as the most relevant to current managed care. Hoyt (1995) found that most therapists entering the job market today get their short-term therapy training on the job, often in uneven and haphazard fashion. He calls for comprehensive training and experience in brief therapy models. Friedman and Fanger (1991) pointed out that it is easier to teach brief therapy to students and novices since they do not have to unlearn previously ingrained assumptions about long-term therapy. The importance of "unlearning," or a change in attitudes, has been emphasized extensively by Friedman and Fanger (1991) and by Cummings (1995b).

There is a growing arsenal of efficient and effective psychotherapies (Bennett, 1994; Bloom, 1992) that is unknown to most practitioners, and even more surprising, to those who educate and train graduate students. Balint (1957) first pointed out that effective brief therapy is the outcome of having been trained in brief therapy, a finding reiterated many years later by several authors (Bennett, 1994; Bloom, 1992; Budman & Bennett, 1983; Budman & Gurman, 1988; Cummings, 1977). Levenson and Davidivitz (1995) conducted a national survey and found that although 65% of the respondents were working with managed care, less than 30% had any training in brief therapy, less than 50% had ever read a book on brief therapy, and a staggering 94% responded that they had been inadequately trained and needed to learn more about brief therapy.

In his survey of 233 psychology interns, Kent (1995) found that only 39% had received even one seminar on brief therapy in graduate school, and only 37% were receiving any internship supervision in brief psychotherapy. Yet by an overwhelming 95%, these interns believed it was a valuable treatment, an equal 95% saw it as the most appropriate treatment in the real world, and 87% had already made up their minds to work in managed care after the completion of their internship. In the face of this career decision, the additional finding that only 15% had been formally taught anything about managed care is alarming.

When the nation's first managed behavioral health carve-out delivery system was established in 1985, the founders were so appalled by the disparity between training and the new practice expectations that they instituted at considerable expense a 130-hour, 2-week preservice intensive training with 4 hours per week of in-service training along with intensive supervision in brief therapy (Cummings, 1986; Cummings & Sayama, 1995). The finding that the level of training has improved only slightly in the past decade suggests that our profession may be teetering on the brink of moral irresponsibility.

SEGMENT FOUR: THE NEW GENERATION

The ultimate resocialization will occur with the emergence of a new generation of psychotherapists. This has already occurred in medicine, which experienced managed care several years before the field of mental health. The current generation of physicians are graduating from medical school with a different set of expectations from their elders. Rather than being in solo practice and oriented to a high income, they apply to the premier HMOs, such as Kaiser-Permanente, first. Inevitably we shall see this new practice ethic among our young colleagues.

In addition, the master's level psychologists, who will not experience a reduction in income and may even benefit from increased employment opportunities, will complete the resocialization of psychotherapists. For this fourth segment of colleagues, as well as those from the third segment, those who have accommodated with vast unhappiness but will decide to change, this book moves on to the attitudes and behaviors necessary for the change that will precede the regaining of autonomy and self-respect in practice.

This new generation of behavioral healthcare practitioners, like their medical colleagues who are preceding them, must be prepared to work in settings never before contemplated, as the following example will illustrate. An unexpected innovation that, if it catches on, will hasten the decline of the hospital is the concept of the "medical mall" (Tomsho, 1995). Now found in California, Florida and a handful of other states, medical malls reflect the healthcare industry's continued effort to keep patients out of the hospitals. The malls have lower overhead than traditional hospitals because they do not have emergency rooms, neonatal care units, or other services that require a great deal of staff and expensive equipment. Instead, they concentrate on primary care, diagnostic services, and outpatient surgery and therapy.

So far patients like the convenience of the one-stop shopping where they can obtain medical tests, meet doctors, have procedures done, and have their recuperation in the same place. Early results have prompted Continuum Care Corporation of Boston to begin building in West Palm Beach, Florida, a medical and surgical center with *outpatient* medical and surgical diagnostics and procedures which includes a 120 bed nursing home/recovery center (Tomsho, 1995). Such an innovation is doubtlessly only one of a number of surprising initiatives that will develop to the decline of the current hospital system, with expanding opportunities for outpatient behavioral healthcare.

In the meantime, what is happening with the current generation of practicing clinicians? A recent survey (Saeman, 1996) reveals that psychologists over age 50 are contemplating early retirement, young psychologists are looking for salaried jobs, and those in between are working longer and longer hours in an attempt to maintain a semblance of their previous incomes. Most state their practices are declining, while 25% report things are better. Although this is a decided minority, the figure is probably twice as high as it was two years ago, indicating more and more psychologists are adapting to healthcare industrialization and prospering. This essentially has been accomplished by self-determination and without the help of their professional societies which are finally showing signs of emerging from a decade of denial.

2.

The Impact of Managed Care on Employment and Professional Training: A Primer for Survival

Nicholas A. Cummings, Ph.D., Sc.D.

> *The illiterate of the future are not those who cannot read or write, but those who cannot learn, unlearn and relearn.*
> *Alan Toffler*

Psychotherapists have long been conditioned to believe that more is better, "self actualization" is the real goal of psychotherapy, and, consequently, the most prestigious practitioners are those who see a limited number of clients over a long period of time (Bloom, 1992). Managed care, with its emphasis on brief therapy, is changing all of this. There is a growing body of outcomes research demonstrating that efficient therapy can also be effective therapy (Bennett, 1994). For the past several years it has been argued that most psychotherapists must receive retraining to become skillful in the efficient–effective therapies (Budman

This article was first published in *Professional Psychology: Research and Practice, 26*(1), 10–15, 1995. Copyright © 1995, the American Psychological Association. Reprinted with permission.

& Bennett, 1983; Budman & Gurman, 1988). The author, who over the past decade has retrained literally hundreds of psychiatrists, psychologists, social workers, and counselors in a 130-hour module over a 2-week period, has observed that in order for retraining to be successful, there must be significant changes in the practitioners' attitudes and belief systems. This "enabling attitude" has only now begun to receive the attention of those who are engaged in retraining practitioners (Bennett, 1994; Friedman & Fanger, 1991).

Yet this point of view is not new. Balint (1957), in his monumental work, said, "A further reason for the failure of traditional courses is that they have not taken into consideration the fact that the acquisition of psychotherapeutic skill does not consist only of learning something new: it inevitably also entails . . . a change in the doctor's personality" (p. 23). Although Balint was speaking of training the general medical practitioner in psychotherapeutic skills, three and a half decades later Bennett (1994), in addressing the personality changes needed to retrain psychotherapists in efficient–effective interventions, stated that "ironically, much of this involves teaching psychotherapists to become more like general practitioners" (p. 30).

When Cummings and VandenBos (1979) described their "general practice of psychology" and argued that the psychologist should function as a primary care physician not subject to a gatekeeper, they had not anticipated how important these concepts would be in this era of managed care. Their formulations are more appropriate than ever:

> By combining dynamic and behavioral therapies into interventions designed to ameliorate the presenting life problem, using a multimodal group practice, professional psychology can define its own house in which to practice. This general practice of psychology postulates throughout the life span the client has available brief, effective intervention designed to meet specific conditions as these may or may not arise (p. 438).

And in further describing "brief, intermittent psychotherapy throughout the life cycle" they concluded:

There is a great need in our society for that now extinct person known as the family doctor, a caring human being who heard and responded to all of a family's therapeutic needs. Who is better equipped to be the family doctor in this age of alienation than the psychologist? (p. 439).

THE RESOCIALIZATION OF PSYCHOLOGY

There is currently underway the greatest resocialization of psychology to occur since the explosion of clinical psychology in the post-World War II era. It is being stimulated by the unprecedented growth of managed care, and it is occurring without (until very recently) the help and guidance of the American Psychological Association (APA). Professional psychology is rapidly changing itself to meet the demands of survival in spite of the short-sighted assurances of many of professional psychology's leaders over the past several years that managed care was paradoxically both a gimmick that would go away, or a threat that would be defeated. This seemingly overnight resocialization of professional psychology has five aspects:

The Stampede into Group Practices

Recognizing that solo practice is rapidly becoming an endangered species (Cummings, 1986; Cummings & Dörken, 1986; Dörken & Cummings, 1991), psychologists are forming multimodal group practices all over the nation and at an astounding rate. In many instances managed care companies have helped psychologists in their networks to identify exceptionally skilled colleagues and have encouraged their banding together and facilitated their transition from solo to group practices. The principles of the general practice of psychology (Cummings & VandenBos, 1979) are receiving new and intensive interest and the lines of demarcation among the various "schools" of psychology are blurring in favor of psychotherapy integration (Cummings, 1992). Among those practitioners so engaged there is a new vitality, while for those who desperately cling to solo practice or who have waited too long and find the networks closed to new applicants, there is a growing fear and depression.

Acquiring the Growing Arsenal of Time-Effective
Treatment Techniques and Strategies

Psychology's long-standing resistance to brief psychotherapy is being swept away in the rush to acquire new skills in time-effective interventions. Those who have long been associated with intensive, problem-solving approaches (Bennett, 1994; Budman & Gurman, 1988; Cummings, 1992) are suddenly in demand and new national companies have been formed in response to the clamor for retraining. The scores of brochures that come to practitioners through the mails show that for every seminar in long-term therapy there are literally dozens of offerings in time-effective, or brief therapy. The APA, which would be expected to lead the way in this conceptual revolution, is curiously aloof. Both the stampede into group practices and the rush to acquire new therapy skills are grass-roots phenomena by psychologists in the trenches.

A Shift in Values and a Fundamental
Redefinition of the Role of a Helper

Practitioners who have long enjoyed a steady, limited stream of fee-for-service clients coming through their comfortable offices will understandably lament the passing of this golden era of psychotherapy. Yet new payment methods such as capitation and prospective reimbursement free the practitioner to perform services needed by the client but heretofore not covered by fee-for-service. Ultimately, they make possible offices without walls, practices that avail all community resources right in the community itself, a frightening prospect for many and eagerly welcomed by others. Because the shift in attitudes and values is difficult, but fundamental to the practitioner who survives, changes required will be more fully described below.

The Ability to Demonstrate Efficiency and
Effectiveness through Outcomes Research
in One's Group Practice

Both practitioner and client are struggling with the new intrusions called utilization review and case management. Gone are the days when the third-party payer, mystified by what goes on in the inner sanctum of psychotherapy, accepted the word of the practitioner. Gone also are the days when practitioners justified their treatment by quoting gurus, originally those such as Freud, Jung, and Adler, and more recently, to name only a few, Haley, Erickson, Goulding, Masterson, and occasionally (to the dismay of the author) even Cummings. Organized settings make possible sophisticated outcomes research, and soon third-party payers (now the managed care companies) will know more about what goes on in the treatment setting than does the practitioner. Psychotherapists will have to demonstrate their effectiveness as well as their efficiency.

Confidentiality is for the protection of the client and must be zealously guarded. It was never intended to protect the practitioner from inefficiency or ineptitude, but many psychotherapists rationalize confidentiality as a refuge for themselves. As harsh as it may sound, not all practitioners are created equal. Fifty percent are below average by definition! As time-effective techniques continue to reduce the number of psychotherapists needed, managed care companies will want to draw from the upper half of the normal curve of providers. Practitioners will have to justify what they do in outcomes research. This will require a reformulation of confidentiality so that it continues to protect the client, yet yields aggregate data that permit research.

Psychologists with their knowledge and training in research will have the advantage over other professions which provide psychotherapy and who are not so highly trained. However, psychotherapy outcomes research is a difficult and highly specialized endeavor, and just as retraining in time-effective therapy is needed for most practitioners, the sharpening of research skills will be a must.

Regaining Autonomy by Qualifying as a Prime (Retained) Provider

Most psychotherapists who provide treatment services for managed care companies do so in networks of preferred providers. The industry is beginning to identify practitioners whom they call prime providers or retained providers. These are practitioners who have formed multimodal group practices through which a total array of treatment and diagnostic services can be delivered on a capitated or prospective reimbursement basis. Thus the group named as a prime provider is responsible for a defined population in a geographic area. Prime provider, or retained groups have demonstrated exceptional skills in time-effective therapies, and they further demonstrate their continued and growing effectiveness by conducting their own outcomes research. Internally, outcomes research is used to sharpen the focus and effectiveness of their own delivery system.

The innovative vitality of many psychologists has propelled them beyond the prime provider groups to regional group practices (RGPs) which are multidisciplinary, involve scores and sometimes even hundreds of practitioners, and serve a wide geographical area and diverse populations. The RGP is undoubtedly the wave of the future, and will require purchasing the legal, business, and management skills needed to succeed. Herein lies real autonomy: contracting with Managed Care Organizations (MCOs), these RGPs possess considerable clout. An MCO can readily replace an individual practitioner and even a small group. A delivery system utilizing a large regional group is not easily replaced, resulting in an increase in bargaining strength for the practitioners.

The advantage of prime provider groups to the managed care companies is in significant savings in utilization review and case management inasmuch as the retained provider group is case managing itself, individually and collectively. The advantage to the practitioner is that he or she regains autonomy, for now no one is looking over one's shoulder.

ESSENTIAL PARADIGM SHIFTS

These emerging regional group practices (RGPs) have a special attractiveness to managed care companies other than just the ability to serve large segments of the market, namely their ability to predict costs. This enables the RGP to enter into capitation agreements and to assume risk. It will not be long before group practices that cannot predict costs will be replaced by those that can.

To succeed as a prime provider will require a fundamental and even pervasive shift in values from the traditional approach, which is referred to as the "dyadic model," to the time-effective approaches which are referred to here as the "catalyst model." The author, drawing upon his experiences in retraining literally hundreds of psychotherapists over the past decade, has chosen to describe this imperative change in values as a series of paradigm shifts. He also acknowledges liberally incorporating the fertile ideas of Bennett (1994) and Budman and Gurman (1988) which, in turn, are based on their own extensive experiences in retraining.

The need for a fundamental shift in values is no more pronounced than in the expressed attitudes of Cantor (1993) who justified 11 years of semiweekly sessions by the nonsequitur that she had accorded the client a reduced fee, or by Kovacs (see Rosofsky, 1993) who acknowledges that he would accept a Woody Allen in 24 years of psychotherapy as the price to be paid for therapist autonomy. Society simply will no longer accept such blatant rationalizations, and since we have lost control over the delivery of our own services, such statements resemble "grandstanding" to our own constituency.

The extreme positions of Cantor and of Kovacs are not reflective of most psychologists who, nonetheless, understandably dislike managed care. Working within it is seen as akin to sleeping with the enemy (to quote the popular motion picture), not exactly a winning attitude, and one which has been nurtured by the unnecessarily strident stance of the APA (Zimet, 1994). It has not been easy for psychology, which struggled many years to attain autonomy only to see the rules of the game change just as it became the preeminent psychotherapy profession. All this underscores the importance of the following paradigm shifts.

Paradigm Shift 1

Dyadic Model: Few clients are seen, but for lengthy courses of treatment, usually individually.

Catalyst Model: Many clients are seen, for brief episodes of treatment, very often in nontraditional modes.

Outcomes research has already begun to demonstrate that many psychological conditions do better in brief episodes of problem-solving therapy (Cummings, 1994). Other examples are group programs designed to teach and facilitate independent living among the chronically mentally ill which maximize effectiveness, while continuous individual psychotherapy for these clients has only minimal impact. Many therapists have found that it is much harder work to see a large volume of patients in brief episodes than to treat a few patients several times a week continuously for several years.

Paradigm Shift 2

Dyadic Model: Treatment is continuous, often weekly or even more frequently.

Catalyst Model: Treatment is brief and intermittent throughout the life cycle.

Brief, intermittent therapy throughout the life cycle has now been empirically studied for more than 30 years follow-up (Cummings, 1992), and has been shown to be more efficient and effective than keeping the patient in treatment beyond the resolution of the life problem presented.

Paradigm Shift 3

Dyadic Model: The therapist is the vehicle for change, and emphasis is on treating psychopathology; the aim is "cure" in some form.

Catalyst Model: The therapist is merely a catalyst for the client to change, and the emphasis is on restoring the inevitable drive to growth that has gone awry.

This is decidedly a developmental model which regards growth as the striving of every living organism. The therapist acts as a catalyst so that the client resumes the growth cycle which was temporarily derailed. It broadens the client's repertoire of responses to conflict, stress, or anxiety beyond the typical mode acquired in childhood. The client may, in future years and under exceptional stress, temporarily resort to the old mode, but it is surprising how little intervention is needed to resume growth in these intermittent contacts.

Paradigm Shift 4

Dyadic Model: The therapy is the most important event in the client's life, and it is within the treatment span that the client changes.

Catalyst Model: The therapy is an artificial situation like an operating room, and significant changes occur and keep occurring long after therapy has been interrupted.

This is especially difficult for therapists who need the narcissistic supplies accorded by grateful clients. It is long-term clients whose dependency has been fostered that are grateful. In the newer model the client recalls the experience as something that was accomplished by oneself.

Paradigm Shift 5

Dyadic Model: Therapy continues until healing occurs, and the client is terminated as "cured" to some degree.

Catalyst Model: Therapy is yeast for growth outside therapy, and formal treatment is only interrupted. The client has recourse to therapy as needed throughout the life cycle.

The client does not remain in treatment, as many do, for insurance against the fear the problem or symptom will recur. Termination anxiety is diminished or eliminated inasmuch as treatment is only interrupted and the client is encouraged to return as needed.

Paradigm Shift 6

Dyadic Model: Individual and/or group psychotherapy in the office are the main modalities by which healing takes place.

Catalyst Model: Every healing resource in the community is mobilized, often as a better approach than office practice.

Rather than disdaining support groups or self-help programs, the practitioner cooperates with, and offers consultation to, these resources.

Paradigm Shift 7

Dyadic Model: Fee-for-service is the economic base for practice, and the therapist must constantly fight against limitations in benefits.

Catalyst Model: Prospective reimbursement or capitation frees the therapist to provide whatever psychological services are needed by the client.

House calls, imperative with house-bound agoraphobics and desirable with the chronic mentally ill as two examples, become standard. Prevention programs which include such things as stress management, assertiveness groups, healthy life-style programs, parenting groups, and vocational and marital counseling can be provided, whereas they would not be covered in fee-for-service insurance reimbursement.

PSYCHOLOGY AND HEALTH ECONOMICS

Having surmounted the psychological (attitudinal) barriers to a successful future practice, the psychotherapist must now acquire business and management skills. For those psychologists who are like the present author, this is the most formidable barrier of all. It is as if we gravitated to psychology because we espouse statistics, but eschew anything that smacks of business or economics. We no longer have the luxury of our splendid isolation. What follows is our own "reality check."

How Did Managed Care Happen?

All goods and services follow the laws of supply and demand: increased demand over the available supply causes prices to escalate, while a glut of supply over demand results in prices falling. The glaring exception has been healthcare. An overproduction of practitioners should cause fees to drop; instead, the greater the number of healthcare practitioners the higher have been the fees. This is because the practitioner controls both the supply *and* the demand sides. It is the doctor who decides what is to be done, and how and when it will be done, and in the case of psychotherapy, how long it will take. All this is rapidly changing, because those who pay the bills (principally the employers) are taking the economic supply–demand control away from the doctor. As intrusive and arbitrary as managed care can be, when we had the control there was no incentive within our ranks to reduce costs by increasing our efficiency and effectiveness. Healthcare escalated to 2½ times the inflation rate of the general economy, with mental health and chemical dependency treatment driving the costs at a rate disproportionate to their perceived importance by society.

The Industrialization of Healthcare

After 200 years as a cottage industry, healthcare is industrializing. The supply–demand control of healthcare's goods and services has shifted from the practitioner to industrial interests. As in all industrial revolutions that preceded this one, there are six characteristics that constitute insights as to what lies ahead. (1) Those who make the goods and provide the services (in our case, psychotherapy) lose control of the production of their own goods and services. The control passes to business interests. (2) Since industrialization thrives on cheap labor, the master's level issue that psychology failed to resolve may well result in our demise. In addition, many practitioners have already experienced a reduction in income resulting from the lower fees "negotiated" as part of belonging to a MCO network. (3) Efficiency and effectiveness increase under industrialization, with a consequent reduction of the numbers of practitioners required. For example, 38 HMOs the size and efficiency of Kaiser-Permanente can treat 250 million Americans with only 290,000 physicians, half the present number, and with only 5% of the Gross National Product (GNP) instead of the current 14% (Kissick,1994). (4) Quality at first suffers, then reaches a new higher level as the industry grows out of its infancy. Practitioners are seeing this wide disparity in quality, and will also soon begin to see a stabilization. (5) The increased efficiency of industrialization makes possible distribution to the masses. As an illustration, no one would insist that Levitz furniture is of the quality of Chippendale, but the general population would not have adequate furniture without industrialization. Hence, "managed competition" is the centerpiece of every major health reform proposal under current study. To put it simply, everyone will have shoes, but there will be no more Gucci loafers. (6) Finally, there is a consolidation where the successful companies are buying the unsuccessful ones. This prediction, made years ago (Cummings, 1986), is exceeding all expectations in both intensity and timing. As predicted, the majority of healthcare in America may be in the hands of 12 to 18 "mega-meds" by the year 2000.

The Less Expensive Practitioner

Psychology's failure to find a place for the master's level practitioner has resulted in the formation of a subdoctoral psychotherapy profession that now has statutory recognition in almost all of the 50 states. The APA has continued to approve over 500 terminal master's programs in psychology, which are producing 6000 master's level counselors per year. There are now approximately 130,000 licensed or certified counselors, more than all the licensed psychologists and psychiatrists combined!

This historical shutting-out of the master's level counselors while encouraging their training, coupled with our failure to demonstrate that doctoral-level psychotherapists are more effective, is leading the managed care companies to look at the master's level counselor as a less expensive alternative. The public and the media have already adopted the generic word *therapist* which cuts across the various professions, whether these be doctoral psychologists, clinical social workers, or master's level counselors. The generic word is applied even to psychiatrists doing psychotherapy, but usually not to those performing medication therapy inasmuch as this is the one unique activity that excludes nonmedical therapists. Inevitably most of the psychotherapy of the future will be conducted by master's level "technicians" which will further reduce the demand for doctoral-level psychotherapists and redefine the role of the successful doctoral psychologist as will be described below.

THE PSYCHOTHERAPY OF THE FUTURE

The most powerful economic arguments for mental health benefits is the evidence that they reduce inappropriate medical care utilization (Cummings, 1991, 1994; Cummings & Follette, 1968, 1976; Follette & Cummings, 1967; Goldman and Feldman, 1993). In the 130 million Americans now covered by managed behavioral healthcare, most of the economic "fat" has been effectively wrung from the mental health system. There remains the far greater economic drain in the medical–surgical sectors resulting from the millions of physician visits by somaticizing patients (Cummings, 1994). Thirty years of research has demonstrated the medical cost offset effect in organized settings: the reduction of inappropriate medical–surgical care by the use of psychological interventions. The current rediscovery of the medical cost offset phenomenon indicates that the future of the doctoral level psychologist will be found in health psychology.

The doctorally trained psychologist is in a unique position to plan, research, and implement intervention programs for both the somaticizers and the noncompliant chronically physically ill (Cummings, Dörken, Pallak, & Henke, 1993; Pallak, Cummings, Dörken, & Henke, 1993), as well as behavioral programs for the millions who demonstrate faulty living habits. But the fact that the interventions of the future will be derived from empirical outcomes research, resulting in treatment protocols, there is an even broader role for the doctoral-level psychologist.

As previously stated, most of the hands-on behavioral treatment will be conducted by master's-level therapists working with empirically derived treatment protocols of targeted, focused interventions. Research, experience, and the nature of human diversity have shown that protocols serve only about 30 to 35% of the persons suffering from each condition being addressed. The master's-level therapists will need the clinical acumen of the doctorally trained therapist for the remaining 65 to 70% of patients.

Outcomes research is beginning to demonstrate that many psychological conditions respond more effectively to group therapy than individual therapy. In addition, there is a growing body of evidence that indicates preventive services in the form of psychoeducational groups reduce the demand for both psychotherapy and inappropriate medical–surgical utilization. These psychoeducational groups range from stress management, parenting programs, and smoking cessation to programs designed to improve compliance with medical regimens in hypertensives, diabetics, and other chronic diseases where noncompliance is rampant. Outcomes research has identified well over 100 potentially useful psychoeducational approaches.

It is very likely, as a result of empirical findings, that only 25% of the psychotherapy of the future will be individual. It is anticipated that another 25% will be group therapy, while half the psychological interventions will be preventive services in the form of structured psychoeducational programs involving small-group participation. The doctoral psychologist will be conducting the empirical research upon which the eventual design and implementation of these therapies will rest. It must be reiterated that the 25:25:50 ratio, or something resembling it, will be the result of tested effectiveness and not primarily a drive for further cost-containment.

Making Costs Predictable

The most important single characteristic that will define the successful psychologist of the future will be the ability to predict one's costs. This makes the psychologist (i.e., group of psychologists) eligible for capitation and able to assume risk. Without the ability to predict costs there can be no determination of the capitation rate for which the practitioners will assume the risk to perform all of the services. It also follows that the ability to control (reduce) one's costs makes possible a capitation rate that will be more attractive than that of one's competitors. Only the predictability of costs, therefore, will make the practitioner a participant in the future healthcare system.

Finally, the successful psychologist will have to market the group's products and services once these have been developed. Unfortunately, space does not permit an extensive discussion of marketing skills. Suffice it to say that most practitioner groups will need to purchase this imperative service.

It would follow from the foregoing that our doctoral programs in professional psychology, including the professional schools, are training excellent practitioners for the 1980s. The skills that future challenges require are not taught in the present curricula. In 1994 the California School of Professional Psychology's Los Angeles Campus launched the first managed care track, a historic event that is a harbinger to the doctoral programs that are lagging behind society's demands for the *new* professional psychologist.

SUMMARY AND CONCLUSIONS

The prediction that by the year 2000 more than 50% of current psychotherapists will be out of business (Cummings, 1988) is rapidly moving to fulfillment. The losers will be those psychologists who do not, or cannot, master the foregoing attitudes and skills.

The future professional psychologist will be primarily a health psychologist who will require retraining to acquire an enabling attitude for success, and a knowledge in the growing body of efficient–effective therapies. The most likely role will be that of a supervisor to master's-level therapists who are performing from empirically derived protocols of focused, targeted interventions, from which there will be as much as 70% exceptions requiring doctoral-level skills.

Furthermore, the future doctoral-level psychologist is in an excellent position to conduct outcomes research, and to plan and implement effective and efficient delivery systems in an expanded clinical management role.

In summary, the future doctoral practitioner will be an innovative clinician, a creative researcher, an inspired supervisor, a knowledgeable health psychologist, a caring skilled manager, and an astute businessperson.

3.

Behavioral Health after Managed Care: The Next Golden Opportunity for Mental Health Practitioners

Nicholas A. Cummings, Ph.D., Sc.D.

> *I believe we are entering an era in which the claims and aspirations of psychotherapy will become more circumscribed and focused. It may also spell a return to greater modesty, from which we should never have departed.*
> Hans Strupp

In predicting the rise and consequent course of managed care, and particularly managed behavioral healthcare, it was anticipated it would be only a transition in the new industrialization of healthcare itself (Bevan, 1982; Cummings, 1986, 1988; Cummings & Fernandez, 1985). As in all of the industrial revolutions preceding it, the industrialization of healthcare would necessarily evolve through a series of steps, albeit in an accelerated manner. Managed care as we know it today is merely the first of these steps.

The American Psychological Association (APA), in its eagerness to deny the important and enduring events which were rapidly

This chapter is reprinted with permission from the *Register Report* (January, 1995) published by the Council for the National Register of Health Service Providers in Psychology.

27

unfolding, misinterpreted the nature of these events, and characterized managed care as a "passing fad" (Wright, 1991, 1992). The American Psychiatric Association (ApA), even though it entered the new era in a disadvantageous position in relation to psychology, quickly worked through its own denial, and rapidly reached an accommodation with managed care.

By 1994 it was increasingly clear even to the APA that psychology had allowed an unprecedented opportunity to slip through its fingers. As will be indicated below, psychology found itself on the inside track when healthcare began to industrialize. Within a short time, however, organized psychiatry overtook and coopted psychology's advantageous position. Observing this turn of events, and with its denial still strongly in place, the APA leadership implied that psychiatry had been taken over by managed care, a response suggestive of "sour grapes." The fact is no one took over anyone. Sensing the intransigent opposition of psychology's leadership, and welcoming organized psychiatry's eagerness to reach an accommodation, the managed behavioral healthcare industry came to regard organized psychology as irrelevant. Whereas in 1985 professional psychology could have owned managed behavioral healthcare, by 1994 it was all but locked out. While many psychologists held important posts in managed care, including senior vice presidencies and CEO positions, these were due more to the individuals' own abilities and entrepreneurship than to any help from the APA.

Rather than lament what might have been, it would be more productive to anticipate future developments in the industrialization of healthcare, and focus particularly on the next opportunity that will be accorded professional psychology. Our predictions had to await the conclusion of political events on Capitol Hill, where the APA effort was asynchronic and predictably ineffective. The defeat of Clinton-style health reform now makes certain predictions possible, for even though the American people made it clear they did not want a government health bureaucracy, they have also overwhelmingly indicated they do want health reform. Therefore, until there is a single-payer system in the United States, an unlikely event in the foreseeable future, health reform will seek market-oriented solutions. Already events have provided us with a harbinger of what these will be, and although psychology regrettably missed the last opportunity, there will soon be another one if only we will seize it. But in order to comprehend what the next decade will bring and the opportunities that will be accorded psychology, it is important to understand the events of the preceding 10 years and the miscalculations that were made. Crying over spilled milk is not the subject of this paper; benefitting from past mistakes is.

A BRIEF HISTORICAL PERSPECTIVE

When, literally at the eleventh hour before adjournment several years ago, the Congress approved the concept of Diagnosis Related Groups (DRGs) for Medicare and Medicaid, it inadvertently ushered in the era of managed care and the subsequent industrialization of healthcare. With the limiting of reimbursement by diagnoses, hospitals were hit with adverse financial realities that caused many to become bankrupt. For the first time, armed with support from industry, labor, and consumers, the government took a decisive step in slowing down the inflationary spiral in health costs. Accustomed to a "cost-plus" reimbursement, hospitals and particularly charity hospitals could no longer compete and most became proprietary as a way of surviving. Many hospitals experienced 50% empty beds. The new proprietary interests, observing the government's inability to promulgate DRGs in psychiatry, quickly converted the empty beds to psychiatric and chemical dependency treatment. In addition, they launched an unprecedented television campaign to sell these new services, and seemingly overnight many Americans concluded the solution to all emotional and chemical problems was hospitalization at the expense of the insurance carrier. Within a short period, the inflationary cost to the nation for mental hospitalization and chemical dependency rehabilitation soared into the double and triple digits. Adolescent hospitalization, which had been a relatively minor inpatient cost, rapidly became a major cost. Wall Street declared psychiatric and chemical dependency hospitals to be a growth industry, and expanded national chains flourished. Paradoxically, while physicians and surgeons began to feel the loss of income and autonomy, brought on by the early years of managed care, psychologists and psychiatrists were prospering. No wonder denial was rampant when warnings were issued that the same fate that had befallen their medical and surgical colleagues was just around the corner.

The emphasis on economics is purposeful, for it alone explains what next occurred. The acceleration of the inflationary curve would have been slowed dramatically were it not for mental health and chemical dependency costs which were out of control and now driving the inflationary spiral. Having failed to tether psychiatry and chemical dependency costs, the federal government turned private industry loose to do the job by giving emerging managed behavioral healthcare companies encouragement, enabling legislation, and a de facto erosion of the laws governing the corporate practice of medicine. Overnight the managed behavioral healthcare industry was launched.

In forming the first psychology driven managed care company, Cummings (1985, 1986) offered the blueprint to psychology. He stated that he would cap American Biodyne at one-half million enrollees so as to serve as a demonstration that psychology could have its own delivery system, and he declared that there was room in the United States for 50 such psychology driven systems. He encouraged psychologists to found the other 49, an offer that was accepted by only a handful of psychologists who subsequently prospered. The majority of psychologists regarded the idea as fanciful, if not grandiose. Organized psychology staunchly opposed and berated the idea. Despairing, Cummings eventually removed the self-imposed cap in enrollment and American Biodyne (now owned by MedCo, a wholly owned subsidiary of Merck since Cummings' retirement) soared to 14 million enrollees in 49 states. This could have been psychology's own house.

THE INDUSTRIALIZATION OF HEALTH CARE

The course of the industrialization of healthcare was not difficult to predict inasmuch as it has followed the same sequence that occurred in every industrialization that preceded it. The only difference is that the steps evolved much more rapidly, not surprising in an age of accelerated technology and communication. These events have been documented elsewhere (Cummings, 1992) and will only be noted briefly.

1. As in all industrialization, control of the product or services (in our case psychotherapy) passes from those who make the product to business interests.
2. Industrialization thrives on cheap labor, and the incomes of practitioners are depressed. The proliferation of licensed master's-level counselors provides an attractive pool of practitioners who will be doing most of the routine therapy of the future.
3. The product is standardized and delivery is streamlined. In our case we are seeing a rapid integration in psychotherapy (Saunders & Ludwigsen, 1992) with more efficient and effective treatment modalities.
4. With healthcare emerging from a cottage industry to industrialization, the remaining cottage industry can no longer compete. The new industrialized system grows at a 20% annual rate for several years, swamping the old system.
5. These resulting economic changes enable the product to be delivered to the masses. Healthcare is gearing for universal delivery.
6. As market opportunities emerge, there is a sudden proliferation of managed mental healthcare companies, not all of which could succeed. There is now a period of consolidation where the successful companies are acquiring smaller and less successful companies, while larger companies are merging so eventually there will be a small number of giants delivering the services.

BEYOND MANAGED CARE

The transition from managed care to the next phase in the industrialization of healthcare has already begun, although it is still in the initial stages. As in all evolutionary development, the transition into the next phase will be uneven and with much overlap. It will be the dominant health economic force by the beginning of the next century. In the meantime, managed behavioral healthcare can be expected to continue to grow, but its current rate of 20% will begin to decelerate as the new modes of delivery steadily supplant it. So for those practitioners who will survive the present system, they would do well to heed the survival cogent offered by Shueman, Troy, and Mayhugh (1994), learn to become a prime provider rather then a preferred provider (Cummings, 1995b), and make the attitudinal changes necessary to succeed (Friedman & Fanger, 1991). For those who wish to be ahead of the curve, predictions as to the directions healthcare is moving are proferred.

There are a number of reasons why the current era of managed behavioral health is about to be supplanted. Although there is no doubt that managed behavioral healthcare brought mental health and chemical dependency costs under control, most buyers believe that future cost savings will be minimal. Some managed behavioral healthcare companies do not even pass on the savings to their client, believing that having curtailed the inflationary spiral is enough.

Few, if any, behavioral healthcare companies as presently structured will be able to conduct convincing outcomes research that will differentiate their effectiveness from each other in a highly competitive market. Most of the fat has been rung out of the delivery systems, excepting, of course, the bloat of the behavioral healthcare companies themselves. Demonstrated future health cost savings by behavioral health will be in medicine and surgery through medical cost offset research, showing the impact of psychological intervention on overutilization of physical healthcare providers (Cummings, 1994). This will necessitate the integration of current behavioral health carve-outs into the totality of healthcare delivery. Consequently, the managed behavioral healthcare companies as presently structured, as well as their networks, have a limited life expectancy. This leads us to the first of a series of predictions.

Prediction 1: Behavioral Health Carve-Outs Will Disappear

The primary reason specialized behavioral healthcare companies emerged in the first place is that the health insurers did not know how to control these costs. Now that the technology is available to everyone, carving out behavioral healthcare is unnecessary. The success of managed care has shown that employers-buyers no longer need to be baffled by the practitioner's psychobabble, or be awed by the so-called sanctity of the client–therapist relationship. The guru has been defrocked because current buyers know a great deal about our own profession with its frailties along with its real and potential contributions.

The trend in which large healthcare systems buy the behavioral care carve-outs is well under way. It is also part of the consolidation as a necessary step in industrialization.

Prediction 2: Medical Cost Offset Will Become the Most Regarded Outcomes Research

A recent survey has shown that employers overwhelmingly believe that psychological intervention can significantly impact on medical and surgical costs by effectively addressing the large group of patients who somaticize stress and emotional problems (Oss, 1993). Thirty years of medical cost offset research has demonstrated that the more integrated behavioral care is to the entire health delivery system, the greater the cost offset. (The reader is referred to Cummings [1993] for a more detailed discussion of the medical cost offset phenomenon than space permits in this paper.)

Prediction 3: The Future of Doctoral-Level Psychology Lies in Behavioral Health

With master's-level technicians doing the routine psychotherapy in the future, doctoral-level professional psychologists will become managers, researchers, and supervisors of therapy in the integrated behavioral care systems that will dominate our field by the end of the century. Empirically derived treatment protocols will enable master's-trained therapists to provide routine care. But as in all protocols, even the best, they are applicable to only about one-third of the patient category they are intended to address. The remaining two-thirds will require the skill and supervision of a doctorally trained psychologist.

At the present time psychology is the preeminent behavioral health profession, but psychiatry is making every attempt to usurp this status. It remains to be seen whether psychology allows yet another opportunity to slip through its fingers. But this need not be mired in another battle over turf. Ideally psychology and psychiatry will work in concert, along with nonpsychiatric physicians, in the behavioral health system of the future.

Prediction 4: Community Consortia Will Emerge and Dictate the Market

These groups will be dominated by the buyers who will insist not only on cost savings, but will monitor the extent and quality of services provided. The consortia will resemble the purchasing alliances proposed in the Clinton health reform proposal, but they will not have the force of law along with controversial government sanctions. Rather, they will constitute a market-oriented response with the power of economic force. The negative financial consequences will be severe for those providers who oppose these consortia (Neer, 1994).

Prediction 5: The Delivery Systems of the Future Will Be the Community Accountable Healthcare Networks (CAHNS)

The term used is the one proferred by Neer (1994), but it should be expected that other names may emerge as the concept is implemented over the next several years. These networks will be comprehensive and provide *all* health services: outpatient, inpatient, and partial care. They will receive prospective reimbursement (capitation) and, as their name implies, they will be accountable to the community consortium which selected them.

Such accountability is not new. When the Kaiser-Permanente Health Plan, the precursor to the modern health maintenance organization (HMO), was founded nearly 50 years ago it had strong labor union participation. As the primary buyers, these labor unions met regularly with the health providers and made their expectations known. This phenomenon was often characterized as an unofficial partnership between the doctors and the purchasers of healthcare. A similar participation is anticipated between the community consortium and the accountable network.

The primary examples over the years have been the various regional Permanente Medical Groups (PMGs) which serviced and were accountable to the Kaiser Foundation Health Plan (Cummings & VandenBos, 1981). Many differences exist between the PMGs and what is being envisaged in the future, and a more accurate example may be the Mullikin Group on the West Coast which has been extensively described (DeLafuente, 1993). Of importance is that these CAHNs will restore practitioner autonomy and self-respect, and will eliminate the managed care company as middle man.

These networks are not easily formed and managed, for a business as well as a caring attitude must prevail. But the astute psychologist will begin talking with like-minded medical and allied health practitioners with the goal of forming such delivery systems so as to be on the ground floor as equal partners with physicians. It is with this goal in mind that the anatomy of the CAHN of the future is described.

The Community Accountable Healthcare Network

The CAHN will be an exclusive provider group, serving a population or a geographical region. This trend is already discernible, as Exclusive Provider Organizations (EPOs) are the newest and fastest growing entities in the current managed care scene. Most follow the network model in delivering services, but there is an increasing interest in the staff–network model, and even the staff model, itself. It is apparent that the network model is not as efficient as the staff model, and as the American people become more accustomed to being managed, there will be a resurgence of the staff model. The group will still bear the name *network*, as it will be such in the broadest sense of the term, bringing together not only outpatient clinics, but also hospitals and partial care centers.

Two systems of healthcare will prevail at the turn of the century: the accountable healthcare network and the HMO, which is really an extensive group of health providers. The driving force of these systems will be the "physician equity model," a form of participant ownership that should include psychologists in the definition of physician. Forrester (1994) refers to the physician equity model as "the dark horse contender to dominate healthcare delivery in the future." For-profit practitioner groups can "forge an entrepreneurial trail with a zeal and speed" not possible in nonequity systems (Forrester, 1994, p. 1). It is important that psychologists begin now to assure equity in these systems of the future. Those psychologists who succeed will very likely be those who are involved in the initial formations of CAHNs.

The community oversight for these groups has yet to evolve, but current dissatisfactions among employer-buyers will make these inevitable. Distilling out all of the onerous features of the Clinton proposed purchasing alliances, advisers to industry are strongly recommending that the buyers take control of the market. With the failure of health reform initiatives in Washington, the way is now open for market-oriented solutions to move rapidly. The next several years will see even greater changes in healthcare than were produced by the last 10 years. The CAHNs will have on the boards or oversight committees community, employer, and provider representation.

As of this writing the initiative to form exclusive provider organizations has come essentially from physicians who also possess business foresight and acumen. Psychologists have been important participants, and it is hoped in the near future professional psychologists will demonstrate leadership in this regard.

The format for these exclusive provider organizations was enunciated almost 40 years ago by Sidney Garfield, the founder of the Kaiser-Permanente health systems and the architect of what was to become the modern HMO: "What makes a cutting-edge health system work is dedicated doctors who believe in the concept and are participant owners" (personal communication, May 1959). At the present time not all of the emerging exclusive provider organizations have participant ownership, but it is very likely that the ones which succeed in the future will manifest this format.

Ownership by the providers does not mean that the community accountable healthcare network will be a democracy. The landscape was cluttered in the 1980s with the failures of physician owned managed care. These physicians structured their organizations so that everyone had a voice, overlooking the propensity of providers to obsess any issue to oblivion. Participant ownership requires strong management, with a strict limitation on the providers' ability to meddle in administration.

Prospective reimbursement (capitation) will be the only method of payment, and skill in pricing the capitated rate is one of the keys to success—priced too low, the delivery will fail. On the other hand, pricing it too high makes the delivery system non-competitive. This will be a new era in pricing, eliminating "low-balling" practices prevalent at the present time. ("Low-balling" is underpricing one's competitors with the intent of making up the loss by skimping on the delivery of contracted services.) The community oversight will closely monitor the extent and quality of what is actually delivered.

Historically the acute care hospitals and their medical staffs have played a pivotal role in the American healthcare delivery system. In the future this will change dramatically with the acute care hospitals becoming equal partners in the accountable healthcare networks. Already we are witnessing the largest proprietary hospital corporation in the country developing all-purpose healthcare networks.

There is an oversupply of specialists, and psychologists must realistically regard themselves as part of that oversupply. Market forces will operate so that the accountable networks will be able to deeply discount the disproportionately high incomes of specialists. Professional psychologists have not been among the ranks of high-income specialists, but they can expect an erosion of present incomes. As noted in earlier chapters, there are just too many master's-level therapists available at much lower costs. The exceptions will be those psychologists who are supervisors and principal researchers, as well, of course, as those gifted psychologists who attain senior management positions.

The primary value of the doctoral-level psychologist will not be in routine psychotherapy. Supervising subdoctoral therapists will be important, but even more important will be the role professional psychologists can play in the behavioral health system, in that the buyers will insist they be a part of every community accountable healthcare network. This role will also include the ability to design and execute outcomes research, the pivotal investigations of which will involve medical cost offset. These will be integral to the success of the accountable network, but the number of doctoral-level professional psychologists in existence today will far exceed the future demand.

The health systems at the turn of the century must be able to demonstrate efficiency, effectiveness, and quality above that offered by their competitors. At the present time there seems to be an inability on the part of managed care companies to do this convincingly.

SUMMARY AND CONCLUSIONS

The industrialization of healthcare, which was initiated in the 1980s with the rapid expansion of managed care, will continue to evolve beyond the types of managed care as it is functioning today. Organized psychology, by seriously misreading the meaning of the events of the past 10 years, caused professional psychology to be of minor influence in the developments that occurred. The next series of events between now and the turn of the century present psychology with still one more opportunity to be a major participant.

Health maintenance organizations, which are essentially exclusive provider networks, and exclusive provider organizations will comprise what has been called the future, community accountable healthcare networks (CAHNs). These will be the predominant managed care companies at the turn of the century (Neer, 1994). The CAHNs will, as a necessity, have a cross section of the community leadership governing the network. The purchasers of healthcare will define the market.

Community accountable healthcare networks will be comprehensive and will offer all healthcare services. Hospitals and other healthcare facilities will be equal partners with the practitioners in these endeavors. It is predicted that the most effective and successful of the CAHNs will have participating ownership, termed *physician equity*, so it is imperative that professional psychologists become active with entrepreneurial physicians and allied health professionals in forming such exclusive provider organizations.

The future of doctoral-level professional psychology lies in behavioral health, that is, conceptualizing and implementing programs in behavioral medicine. They will serve as supervisors of the master's-level therapists who will be performing the routine psychotherapy, and they will be the leadership in the new wave of outcomes research. Many will be managers, and some will even be senior managers. There will be a serious impact on the oversupply of psychologists, and many will not survive the transition. It is anticipated that this time, for the sake of an already embattled profession, the leadership of organized psychology will read the signs correctly and promote professional psychology's participation.

EPILOGUE

Predictably, only about 15 to 20% of practicing psychologists will have the foresight, energy, and adaptability to become equity participants in the HMOs and CAHNs which will dominate the healthcare landscape in the next century. The fate of the majority of psychologists will depend on whether psychology succeeds in becoming a primary care profession as Cummings and VandenBos (1979) advocated a decade and a half ago. Two forces are important in this struggle: prescription privileges and the leadership of the *National Register*.

If psychology obtains the ability to prescribe psychotropic drugs, status in primary care will be enhanced. Furthermore, the prediction that the profession is destined to lose 50% of its doctoral-level practitioners will be cut to 25%. The other 25% attrition will be made up by losses in psychiatry, for with psychologists able to prescribe, the demand for more costly psychiatrists will diminish.

With the APA essentially regarded as irrelevant by the industry, the role of the *National Register* becomes very significant. Unfortunately, after years of short-sighted and needless polemics, the APA has locked itself out of the decision making process in the market oriented healthcare arena. Having bet on the losing horses in the national healthcare debate, it is now turning its resources toward promulgating restrictive, regulatory legislation in the states. This will only hasten the industry's contracting with the accountable healthcare networks as a way around such restrictions. The *National Register* has risen to the need and assumed the leadership in educating its registrants in a balanced approach to the realities, advantages, and disadvantages of the new healthcare climate. As the oldest meaningful credentialling organization in psychology, the *National Register* is poised to help the managed care companies in their search for qualified, competent practitioners. It is respected by the industry, as well as its members because it has taken the high ground. Failing in its attempts to open a dialogue with the APA, the industry will welcome the *National Register* which it regards not only as a sane voice, but also as a strong advocate in promoting professional psychology.

4.

Behavioral Practice: Notes and Observations from a Managed Behavioral Health Executive

Bruce Gorman

> *There will be more psychologists than people in this country.*
>
> Edwin G. Boring

I am not a behavioral health professional! However, in my various network development, program start-up, management and professional relations, and product development positions in managed care and managed behavioral care, I have enjoyed the opportunity to meet with clinicians throughout the country to learn about, present, discuss, and formulate policies and procedures which have a profound impact on delivery of care, professional practice, and behavioral health care delivery and financing. Additionally, I have had the opportunity to work in a close professional relationship with many behavioral health professionals including the editor of this book and several of its key contributors. One of the supreme unofficial honors of my career was being bestowed the mantle of an "honorary clinician" by Dr. Cummings.

I have learned much from these interactions with behavioral health professionals. Given my background and my many years of experience in managed care, I hope to bring a unique perspective to the business of professional practice which is of value to the reader. Clearly, the manner in which clinicians practice their profession is, and will continue to be, profoundly impacted by managed care principles and practices. According to Oss (1995), "of an estimated 185.7 million Americans with health insurance approximately 59.8% (approximately 111 million) are enrolled in some type of specialty managed behavioral health program" (p. 1). Many other individuals are enrolled in a medical managed care program with a behavioral health component. Except for a few clinicians who have and will develop a "carriage trade" niche of private pay patients, others are and to a greater extent will be, impacted by the changing healthcare market as exemplified by managed care.

Unfortunately, many behavioral health professionals, and, in some important ways, the professions themselves are ill prepared to address and manage these changes. This lack of preparedness has been evidenced to me and other behavioral health executives on many occasions during business meetings with behavioral health professionals, as well as during the process of network development and recruiting clinicians to serve on networks. Compounding this is, at best, inconsistency in leadership on the national level to appropriately address these changes, and, at worst, following a course of action which is counterproductive and often transparently self-serving.

The good news is that there is much that is good about behavioral health practice that can be built on to positively address and manage this change. In this chapter, I will summarize my experience in working with behavioral health professionals through several positive points to build on along with challenges which I shall address. Finally, I will make some suggestions and recommendations regarding how to address this change through courses of action which can be followed by individual clinicians, groups, and the professions in general.

Some of the key advantages and positive attributes of behavioral health professionals and their professions which I have observed and which can be built on to address the profound change affecting and increasing include:

1. Highly Qualified Professionals: The depth and breadth of experience and qualifications I have found in my interactions with and review of behavioral health professionals credentials indicates a strong group of dedicated professionals prepared to assist patients in meeting their needs. The amount of time and intellectual resources devoted to this healing profession speaks well for those who choose to make it their life's work.

2. Broad Base of Experience: Generally, the broad base of experience and interests available from most clinicians is extensive and comprehensive. In most suburban and well-served urban areas (more on geographic distribution later), most areas of interests and special needs of patients are adequately addressed. An exception to this is the often inadequate coverage for children and adolescents.

3. Deeply Oriented to Patient Care: Among other reasons it does appear that behavioral health professionals have chosen their profession based upon a profound commitment to patient care. The orientation to interacting and addressing patient needs and concerns is readily evident. This commitment must be maintained in the face of significant social, economic, and financial pressures.

4. Several Behavioral Health Professionals have Worked in a Group or Hospital Based Setting: Most of the clinicians I have met with and reviewed have experience in a group, or facility based setting, including time in a community mental health setting. The ability and willingness to work in these types of environments are crucial to future growth, success, and even survival as marketplace factors will continually demand choice, accessibility, comprehensiveness, and efficiencies in the delivery of care.

5. Low-Overhead Operations: Generally, the behavioral health professionals I have worked with can operate a very low-overhead operation. There is little in the way of equipment and large systems required to operate. These professionals are able to focus a significant portion of their activities on patient care and related activities. There will be even greater pressures to operate "lean and mean" as marketplace/cost-effectiveness measures continue and are augmented.

6. Orientation to Outpatient and Community Based Care: With the exception of the group of psychiatrists who are oriented to an inpatient practice, most behavioral health professionals are

generally interested in and trained toward providing services in an outpatient or community based environment when possible. This orientation could be augmented by significantly increased involvement in services provided in intermediate based settings such as partial hospitalization, day treatment, and intensive outpatient settings.

However, behavioral health professionals are presented with significant challenges in the face of managed care, changes in how behavioral healthcare is being financed and delivered, and changes in how their services are accessed and reimbursed. Based upon personal–business observations, some of the key areas that these professionals need to address include:

1. An Entitlement Mentality: For a variety of reasons (e.g., third-party reimbursement, licensure restrictions, and lack of monitoring), many professionals, and some would maintain, its professional societies, have developed the belief that they should be free to practice their profession with a relative lack of encumbrances and scrutiny from purchasers, managers, and in many cases, their patients themselves. This has been combined with the belief, up until recently, that they should be reimbursed their "usual and customary fee" (which in truth is neither) by a third-party purchaser with little attention to what the purchaser receives in return. This pervasive attitude is possibly the primary barrier facing behavioral health professionals in their ability to adapt to rapidly changing market conditions.

2. Inappropriate Reliance on Political and Legislative Solutions: In response to market factors that many professionals feel threatened by, their professional societies' response is often to sponsor legislation and in some cases legal action to resolve the issue. Examples include advocating for mandated service levels and promoting "any willing provider legislation." Oftentimes these actions only address immediate symptoms and are counterproductive to more lasting solutions that address market issues. While many of these actions are couched in terms of patient protection and advocacy, few observers, including the patients themselves, are fooled by what may be the true motivation, which is often to protect the status and status quo for the sponsors.

3. Lack of Focus on Outcomes and Values: As a result of the nature of the services provided by behavioral health professionals and the lack of an organized behavioral healthcare delivery system, and agreement on the precise nature of desirable outcomes, the purchasers of mental health and substance abuse benefits do not have a good handle on what they are receiving in exchange for their healthcare resources. Behavioral healthcare expenditures are coming under intense scrutiny by employers, managed care companies, governments, and society at large; services delivered by clinical psychologists are extremely vulnerable, because there is a widespread perception that the value in exchange for resources expended for these services is undefined, particularly in comparison to the return for physical medicine. Stated succinctly, purchasers want "bang for their buck," and don't feel that they have been receiving it from behavioral healthcare.

4. Imbalance of Supply and Demand: Most urban and suburban areas are characterized as possessing a significant oversupply of most behavioral health professionals (with the exception of psychiatrists). This is one of the reasons why clinicians who are selected to be providers in a network often receive a limited number of referrals (another key factor is the presence of "any willing provider" laws). In contrast, there is a significant undersupply of qualified professionals in many rural areas and inner-city urban areas. Most managed behavioral care companies are required to provide access to services within certain time or distance parameters. Behavioral health professions interested in fulfilling a market need, increasing or maintaining their level of practice, and assisting their customers (i.e., employers, managed behavioral care companies, managed care companies, and employee assistance programs) should explore means of providing care in these underserved areas.

5. Relative Inattention to Systems and Populations: The industry movement toward managed care, services oriented to outcomes, increased emphasis on value, and demands for cost-effectiveness require the approach for providing services for populations of individuals not just for the individuals themselves. This is particularly important in the delivery of services for Medicaid, Medicare, and other public sector consumers. With the exception of community psychiatrists, licensed clinical social workers, and certified

addictions counselors, many behavioral health professions are perceived to deal primarily with the individual and possibly the family in their orientation and in the development of treatment plans and solutions. Increasingly, managed care companies are required to deliver services to a group of complex populations and communities which can be greatly assisted by clinicians addressing these wide-scale community issues through the development of creative psychosocial, prevention, and community support programs.

6. Perceived Lack of Interest in Providing Services for the Seriously Mentally Ill: With some clear, notable exceptions at community mental health centers, hospitals and other facilities, and clinic based programs, many clinicians, particularly those involved in individual practice and working in small groups carry the perception that they are not interested in providing services for the seriously mentally ill. To a large degree, services to these individuals have become the purview of community mental health organizations, psychosocial support programs, and hospitals. Many private practice professionals have earned the reputation of wishing to deal with high functioning individuals who have support systems built in. A perception of possessing comprehensive services and systems to deal with these more difficult cases would serve many professionals and enhance ability to address key fundamental needs.

7. Variability in Documentation: Many behavioral healthcare companies have experienced a significant variability in documentation of treatment plans, goals, progress notes, and diagnoses among behavioral health professionals. In order to illustrate value, clinical improvement, utilization, and outcomes, it will be necessary to have consistent documentation to communicate to care managers, purchasers, and consultants.

8. Relative Lack of Business Systems: While behavioral health professionals have been reasonably efficient in keeping overhead costs down, there are ever increasing demands and requirements to increase efficiencies, provide documentation, and operate effective business practices. This will be particularly important as managed care practices progress from a case-by-case management relation to one of managing by quality and outcomes. While this movement holds significant promise for reducing administrative time spent with care managers, freeing up more time for delivery

of services, and reducing administrative costs, the provision of information which can only come from increased business practice sophistication will be required.

9. Lack of Product/Service Differentiation: Related to the oversupply issue of behavioral health professionals in many areas is the concern that individual professionals, particularly those who require a higher reimbursement (e.g., clinical psychologists), are increasingly unable to differentiate among their services. Certainly, this puts licensed clinicians who require less reimbursement (e.g., licensed clinical social workers, master's-level counselors, and marriage and family counselors) at a relative advantage. However, in the absence of the ability to illustrate the outcome/value of their services so that purchasers can ascertain their "return on investment," some behavioral health providers run the risk of having their services viewed as commodities with insignificant perceived differences.

These are clearly challenging times for behavioral health professionals. Nothing that the professional was prepared for in graduate/professional school or in internships prepared them for these challenges. For the most part, the previous generation of behavioral health professionals did not face this, as there was limited challenge to professional judgment and less scrutiny of benefits based upon growing resources and economic growth built up after the post-World War II era. While it may appear to be far removed from the day-to-day practice of behavioral health, the impact of the global economy and the need to be competitive has created a ripple effect where American business is carefully scrutinizing the cost of health care benefits and the impact that it has on their competitive ability and profit levels. It has become clear to American business that the cost of healthcare benefits cuts significantly into their ability to be competitive. One of the first areas to be cut or scrutinized is behavioral healthcare benefits, because of the inability of the behavioral health professions to prove that there is an adequate return on the investment for their services in the face of increasing competition for the use of benefit and profit resources. Specifically, when the need for behavioral health benefits is compared to the need for physical healthcare benefits, behavioral health benefits will always receive secondary consideration. When considering the reimbursement for behavioral healthcare services from government sources, such as those for employees and dependents of governments, Medicaid, Medicare, Champus; the reader needs only to look at the shrinking tax resources, the limiting of needed social and human services, and the pressures to balance public sector budgets, to realize that any significant growth in these resources is unlikely.

I have encountered many clinicians who consider managed care to be a threat to their independence, their professional standing, their clinical acumen, and their livelihood. Managed care is an easy target because it is the most present and pervasive force that impacts behavioral health professionals. Managed care has become the known stand-in and metaphor for economic, social, and market forces that have had a negative impact on many professionals, but which are considerably more difficult to understand. In fact, managed care is a far more positive and hopeful response to these economic, social, and market forces which are dramatically impacting the clinician. A far more draconian alternative is the significant reduction or outright elimination of behavioral health benefits and services driven solely by financial and economic factors. One need simply observe the number of medically indigent (i.e., those without health coverage of any type) estimated at 25 million, to realize that many individuals only receive behavioral health services in an acute, emergency situation, if they receive services at all. Managed care, when done well (and certainly not all of it is done well), employs clinical systems, outcomes, criteria, and guidelines to maximize the use of scarce and diminishing resources to provide appropriate and necessary care to populations and individuals who require services.

The astute behavioral health professional and their professional societies would be doing themselves, their patients, and their colleagues a service by working within the context of managed care principles and practices to constantly strive for the simultaneous and complex needs to deliver high quality, accessible, appropriate, and cost-effective care in the face of diminishing resources for this care. No responsible healthcare observer could reasonably contend that managed care is perfect, a panacea, or a comprehensive response to the changing behavioral healthcare delivery and financing system. However, clinicians and their professional societies can provide a valuable service by working with managed care systems, providing input for positive change and improvement, and constructively critique and facilitate improvement in these systems.

The good news is that there are activities and opportunities for professionals to respond positively to the challenges facing them as individuals, their profession, their patients, and the care delivery system. Some of these include:

1. Development of Integrated Delivery Systems: While still in its initial stages, the creation of these systems that integrate physical health care and behavioral healthcare, as well as creating a continuum of care for behavioral health, can increase access, effectiveness, and clinical and administrative efficiencies. These systems can significantly serve to reduce the need for case-by-case clinical management by managed care companies and provide more autonomy for behavioral health professionals.

2. Development of Behavioral and Multidisciplinary Group Practices: In some senses, a streamlined version of a larger delivery system, group practices can improve quality, increase efficiency, and reduce administrative costs for delivery of behavioral health services.

3. Flexibility in Location and Accessibility: Several professionals are locating portions of their practice in underserved locations where sorely needed services are required. This is being accomplished by subletting space for specific hours in physician and other health provider offices, working in combination with community mental health centers and developing satellite clinics and offices as part of larger group practices and systems.

4. Developing Working Relationships with Managed Care Companies: Through group practices, by serving on committees, by interactions through professional organizations, by serving on quality management and similar committees, clinical psychologists can have a positive impact on and interact with managed care companies and serve as more than a casual network provider.

5. Developing a Special Referral/Reimbursement Relationship with Managed Care Companies: Managed care companies

often have both formal and informal arrangements with professionals who have indicated that they can provide quality services within the context of a managed care environment. Included among these arrangements are retainers, subcapitations, preferred provider arrangements, subcontracting clinical management services such as intake and crisis intervention, and regional anchor groups. Managed care companies usually welcome assistance with network development, particularly in underserved areas.

6. Performing and Sponsoring Outcome Studies/Quality Management Technologies: Either through integrated systems, group practices, professional associations, or in combination with managed care companies, clinicians can contribute significantly to improving the delivery of services, clinical effectiveness, and treatment successes, by engaging in these activities. Additionally, this provides the opportunity for a positive critique of, and recommendations for managed care companies and systems.

7. Creatively Deliver Services for the Underserved and Medically Indigent: Either through working with community mental health centers, supervising interns, allocating some percentage of resources for providing care for the underserved, or performing occasional pro bono work, independent professionals can and do assume some level of social responsibility which illustrates their commitment to addressing socioeconomic issues.

8. Address Documentation and Communications Issues: Either through professional societies or working with purchasers and managed care companies, create common and comprehensive documentation which will serve to reduce the case-by-case management requirements or managed care relationships and therefore reduce administrative costs for providers and companies.

9. Spend Political and Government Relations Resources Positively: Activities which are mutually beneficial to professionals, patients, and society at large include those that create access, those that reduce barriers to care, those that relate to illustrating positive outcomes of behavioral services and interventions, and those that contribute to the objective of creating healthy communities in the face of scarce resources.

I have considered it to be an honor and a privilege to work, meet and do business with, and observe the important work of behavioral health professionals for a significant portion of my career. However, behavioral health professionals and their societies and institutions must continually strive to positively address and manage market forces and socioeconomic change. Only by assuming this proactive position can behavioral health professionals maximize the value of their services and the care of their patients.

PART II

The Practitioner
as Trainer and Supervisor

5.

Program Redesign for Graduate Training in Professional Psychology: The Road to Accountability in a Changing Professional World

Warwick G. Troy, Ph.D., M.P.H.
Sharon A. Shueman, Ph.D.

> *I have examined myself thoroughly and come to the conclusion that I don't have to change much.*
> *Sigmund Freud*

Periodically within organized psychology there are pressures for the development of enhanced models of education and training, which are mounted in response to perceived inconsistencies between emerging needs and prevailing practices associated with the preparation of psychologists, whether as scientists or practitioners or amalgams of both. Thus, we have the American Psychological Association (APA) sponsoring a series of national training conferences since the end of World War II and, more recently, conferences sponsored by the National Council of Schools and Programs in Professional Psychology (NCSPP).

The terms of reference, processes, and recommendations of this succession of training conferences reflect changing views of the discipline and profession of psychology. Changes relate both to what defines a psychologist and what the professional roles are in which a psychologist might engage. Predictably, given the variation in the normative stances of organizations represented in these conferences, significant contention characterized many of them. And yet, in the approximately 50-year history of such initiatives, the kind of world in which psychologists made their contribution was characterized by only one signal change: the emergence of the role of the professional psychologist as an independent provider whose services were reimbursed as healthcare by third-party payers on a fee-for-service basis. The era of the independent provider began in the 1970s and, by the end of the next decade, it had, for the most part, ended.

Such, however, is the essential conservatism of psychological education and training programs that the conferences held during this golden age of independent practice dealt only tangentially with the significant challenges associated with the professional preparation of the psychological provider, whether in independent practice or in organized care settings. The prime and urgent focus for organized psychology for the entire 1950s was the advancement of the guild interests of the independent provider community. And the energy, creativity, sense of strategic purpose, and tangible accomplishments associated with this period of advocacy were, without question, remarkable. At the same time, this kind of focus was generally not a hallmark of education and training initiatives. Rather, training programs lagged far behind both the needs of these venturesome psychological providers and the needs of consumers themselves.

Yet for most of the 1980s, the decade owned by the independent provider of health services, the signs of impending change were present in the exponential rise in the costs to employers for health services purchased for their employees. For a complex set of reasons organized psychology chose a path of absolute and active resistance to the development of the new arrangements in healthcare financing, organization, and delivery, currently called "managed care" arrangements, which was designed to slow down the rate of healthcare cost escalation.

It should be noted that, although we tend to view these managed care arrangements as new, they are not. Care has for all of recent memory been to some extent "managed," whether through traditional HMO mechanisms dating back to the 1920s, benefit designs typical of indemnity insurance (copayments, exclusions, session limits), or more recently via utilization review, peer review, selective contracting, and other regulatory or entrepreneurial strategies.

APA's construing of its political imperatives in terms of resisting managed care inroads on the incomes of a powerful constituency, independent practitioners, caused the Association to wink at the profession's obligation to develop a clearly articulated stance on accountability. Similarly, there was no particular call to the education and training community to improve the appropriateness of professional education and training for the new world of accountability and engagement in healthcare systems. Indeed, what perturbations there were in the education and training community were largely directed at the burgeoning schools of professional psychology (and particularly the free-standing ones) whose large number of trainees were seen to radically increase competition among licensed providers.

The animosity of the scientist–practitioner programs, however, was couched not in terms of competition. Rather, it invoked the threats to the profession posed by the (presumed) severely suspect quality of the trainees produced in such large numbers by professional schools. The scientist–practitioner training community, in its assumption of the role of guardian of training quality, devoted significant energy to efforts to use the specialty accreditation and degree designation processes to clip the wings of what it regarded as the professional school degree "mills." In this protracted internecine strife little attention was paid to the increasing irrelevance of training programs of *all* types to the imperatives, not only of the changing world of practice, but also of the needs of consumers. Interestingly, when such imperatives were addressed, efforts were more likely to derive from NCSPP initiatives than from those of the APA.

For the past 15 years, then, the education and training community has devoted a significant proportion of its energies to trenchant criticisms of both professional schools and clinical practitioners deemed to lack the kind of empirically derived skills appropriate to effective interventions. Such attacks have understandably failed to improve the competencies of professional psychologists to practice effectively in a world increasingly characterized by diversity and structural inequality. Furthermore, the implacable hostility of the increasingly guild-oriented APA toward all successive iterations of managed care precluded the development of a forum conducive to reasoned debate on the appropriateness of graduate professional education and training in psychology, and particularly how the profession develops and advances its obligations to its multiple stakeholders and sanctioners. In other words, organized psychology, in frittering away scarce resources and creative energies in internecine strife within the training community, and in insisting on fighting an unwinnable war against the evolution of health systems, has left its graduate students, entry level practitioners, and experienced professionals all less prepared than ever to play contributing (let alone renewal and leadership) roles in an increasingly complex professional world characterized by abrupt change and entrepreneurial corporatization.

In this chapter we attempt to draw a rather large-scale map designed at least to get us out of the woods, if not on the right road. We also hope to be able to describe this right road in such a way that lost travelers may recognize it if, perchance, they stumble across it: The Road to Accountability.

THESIS

The imperatives of integrated health systems operating under a variety of managed care arrangements, rapidly changing service structures, and gradual health reform, clearly require significant enhancements of professional psychology's training programs. More importantly, however, the key point of what has been erroneously called the managed care "revolution" for the education and training community, is that the particular set of imperatives with which this revolution is associated starkly points up significant and prevailing inadequacies in professional training that long antedate the mid-1980s when the signs of managed care were everywhere apparent.

Argument

Nothing less than wholesale redesign of doctoral training programs in professional psychology will suffice to meet the current and future imperatives of managed care and evolutionary health reform. There exists across the disciplines of behavioral health an extremely serious shortfall in provider competencies. This short-fall is not confined to skills-based competencies, but extends to knowledge- and values-based areas.

For the first time in living professional memory for mental health research and training, three paramount stakeholder insti-tutions—the federal government, professional associations, and academic as well as professional training programs—have ceased to be either unambiguous advocates or viable agents for the sweep-ing changes which confront our field. The intensity and pace of the changes now confronting behavioral healthcare are, and will continue to be, such as to raise serious doubts as to whether the various training communities in behavioral healthcare can do much to reduce the provider competency shortfall.

Managed care imperatives, with the emphasis on providers working appropriately as interdependent elements of integrated systems, moved to a place far beyond the capacity of academia to educate and train clinicians who can both effectively participate in and contribute leadership to these emerging services systems. Accordingly, immediate and wholesale system redesign of the pro-grams that educate and train professional providers is essential.

The Need for Accountability in Professional Education and Training

Formal accountability mechanisms include a wide range of structures and activities, such as accreditation of professional training programs, accreditation of institutions and programs providing services; profes-sional ethical codes; practice standards or guidelines; federal and state regulations; and licensing and credentialing. Such mechanisms are associated with provider accountability and professional compe-tence in only the most indirect way. Nowhere is there compelling evidence that they have any causal connection with professional behavior in the public interest. Instead, the entire panoply of these processes provides consumers with only minimal assurance of professional competency in those who practice. The essential self-regulatory nature of professions acting in their guild capacity vir-tually guarantees this lack of connection, with such bodies finding it much easier to stick with aspirational criteria for self-regulation.

Given the increasingly complex health system, these always ineffective mechanisms are even less useful to the consumer. The structure and processes of program redesign proposed for education and training in professional psychology must be constructed with the attitudes-values, knowledge, and skills associated with professional responsibility at the very heart of such redesign. The increasing empowerment of purchasers and their demands for outcomes management will drive formal system accountability in the behavioral healthcare industry and the delivery systems associated with them. The traditional external mechanisms noted above are becoming increasingly irrelevant.

Accountability cannot usefully be imposed from without. It must derive from the values and behaviors of the appropriately trained provider. The challenge to education and training in professional psychology—to develop providers who can work effectively as key elements of service systems characterized by interdependence of function and roles—will require not only a significant change in the way the technology of accountability is treated, but also a significant commitment to the development of an appropriate values stance by all trainees.

It is long past time for us to begin to do things very differently. Urgent managed care and health reform imperatives now make this responsibility inescapable. The task, once undertaken, can release the potential for appropriately trained and accountable psychologists—as scientists, practitioners, and advocates—to effectively serve the needs of consumers and society in multiple ways, ways which also recognize the contributions of our colleagues from other behavioral health disciplines.

This refocusing of professional education and training in the interest of the consumer and treatment outcomes will require collaborative partnerships between training programs and the industry. The development of operational linkages of the kind needed pose significant challenges to both parties, unused as they are to interdependent or even collaborative roles. It is a process that will be entered into cautiously, will be characterized by diversity of arrangements, and will take time. It is, however, a process that must be confronted.

This chapter has three main themes: (1) the identification of a minimal set of core competencies essential to the proper functioning of professional psychologists in the current and future world of corporatized healthcare and health reform; (2) a proposal for a normative framework for effective and truly accountable professional psychology training programs; (3) a treatment of obstacles confronting such efforts, together with specific recommendations on structure, mechanisms, and strategies for program redesign.

CONTENDING WITH THE NEW IMPERATIVES

For professional psychology and psychologists, the most urgent of the new imperatives comes from the forces that shape healthcare and of the reactions of the field to those forces. Indeed, it is difficult to take issue with the view expressed by Cummings (1995a) that, for the majority of entry-level practitioners, health systems will be the prime arena for the application of their professional skills. This is true despite the continuing chaos of healthcare and notwithstanding the significant reductions in income for psychological providers associated with the spread of managed arrangements. While appreciable numbers of longer established providers may survive until retirement using creative strategies to market themselves as fee-for-service (FFS) providers outside of managed care, this same option will not be available to the vast bulk of new or younger providers.

There is little doubt that the days of defining healthcare providers in psychology as psychologically trained therapists eligible to receive third-party reimbursement will soon be over. Open-ended reimbursement for generic therapy provided by psychologists has essentially ended. Cummings (1995a, 1995b) is surely correct in his prediction that for those doctoral-level psychologists committed to direct service provision, the professional future is in the specialist field of behavioral health services.

Let us briefly examine some of the key imperatives that will shape the roles professional psychologists will play in healthcare.

Involvement in Integrated Healthcare Systems

Most assuredly, the days of the solo, FFS provider are numbered. Furthermore, the prevailing trend toward consolidation of practitioners into integrated behavioral health group practices is but a transition stage to the formation of very large, multidisciplinary networks operating as truly integrated systems of care. Such systems will offer comprehensive healthcare, with behavioral health services being only a part of an entire smorgasbord of healthcare. Whether or not these new entities are called *community accountable healthcare networks* (CAHNS) (Cummings, 1995b), they, along with the large, traditional prepaid health plans (HMOs such as Kaiser-Permanente, Group Health of Puget Sound, or Harvard Community Health Plan) depend upon their structure as large integrated systems to enable them to accept financial risk.

For most psychologists these frameworks introduce a new world, a world redolent with such terms as *capitation, disease management, continuity of care, outcomes research, medical cost offset, adverse events,* and so on. It is a world which lives or dies by its use of population-based planning tools, clinical, administrative, and financial data management systems, health status indicators; clinical treatment protocols; interdisciplinary and multidisciplinary collaboration; quality assessment and management tools; and, above all, its capacity to predict utilization of services. This is the world of interdependent health services systems in which the capacity to deliver preventive services involving, for example, outreach to an at-risk population group is as critical as the system's readiness to provide highly specialized medical–surgical care. For the psychologist prepared to negotiate in and contribute to this world, professionally gratifying opportunities abound. It is manifestly *not* a home for the generic therapist, psychologically trained or not.

The Centrality of Human Diversity

The world of the large, integrated, comprehensive health system, committed, as it must be, to population-based planning, reckons with the reality of the diversity of beneficiaries who receive covered services through various plans. In both the FFS world and the early stages of managed care, persons with serious mental illness and other disabling conditions, many members of racial or ethnic minority groups, and other traditionally underserved populations, obtained services through shockingly fragmented public sector entitlement programs. Such vulnerable groups tended to lie very much outside the world of services for the privately insured. State health authorities are, however, negotiating risk contracts with managed care companies in state after state. Increasingly, public and private sectors are merging; quality of care questions remain as yet unanswered.

A key imperative bearing on future roles for psychologists is for these large care systems to factor in what we know about the interface between human diversity and health services. At this interface, issues surrounding help-seeking behavior, life-styles, professional communication patterns, clinical decisions based upon clinical tests normed on other populations, and so on, become critical. The drive toward maintaining quality of care through good outcomes under conditions of cost containment will ensure significantly increased attention by health system to the challenges of a diverse America.

In Pursuit of Healthcare Quality

Accepting risk through payment mechanisms such as capitation carries with it the significant risk of underservicing. Denial and delay of needed care are associated with poorer outcomes. In a capitated model, underservicing can come to haunt a system of care, since patients subsequently present sicker and require expenditures which greatly exceed any shorter term reduction in service costs the withholding system may enjoy. For the psychologist who appreciates the complex balancing act integrated health systems must perform in manipulating care planning, delivery, and health status of beneficiaries, a variety of professional challenges present themselves.

Quality issues—those which relate to access, appropriateness, effectiveness, and cost effectiveness—and the formal systems associated with their operation, depend upon a technology. Devices as diverse as patient satisfaction surveys, clinical record audits, client and provider focus groups, process and outcome research, clinical trials, use of empirically derived treatment protocols, and program evaluation, are representative of the technology of quality assessment and management. As the power of consumers grows, as regulatory responses to the healthcare industry develop, and as purchasers of healthcare increasingly discriminate care systems on quality management issues, the "assurance" of quality becomes both a burgeoning imperative and an expanding set of options for professional psychologists.

Traditional, New, and Emerging Roles for Professional Psychologists

Accountability precepts, integrated health systems as a prime vocational focus, human diversity, and quality assessment and management, have been identified as four key imperatives for the professional psychologist. These broad imperatives derive from an emerging world, and therefore are rather distant signposts for the road ahead. In this regard, depicting a number of the roles professional psychologists may play in this new world serves as a clearer signal. It is toward these roles that our ultimate focus of training program redesign must be directed.

Traditional Roles

The changes sweeping the world of healthcare only appear revolutionary. In fact, such changes occur on a gradation which minimizes hiatuses and underscores evolutionary development. This emerging world continues to provide many opportunities for what we call traditional roles.

Assessment: A renewed emphasis upon behavioral and functional assessment is critical. And, most importantly, assessment services are to be seen as part of the treatment planning process as they have not in the past. Group modalities such as in vivo assessment of family or social groups will remain. Knowledge of the inherent biases vis-à-vis racial–ethnic minority groups of many standardized instruments is critical, as is sensitivity to and knowledge of racial–ethnic minority issues, concerns, and needs, particularly in an assessment context. There will remain a clear role for neuropsychological assessment as part of interdisciplinary treatment. The initial interview will hold far more challenges: it will be a highly strategic and complex process serving at once assessment and treatment purposes. Increasingly, it may constitute the sole episode of formal healthcare. Treatment monitoring skills will be increasingly valued.

Proficiencies: Proficiencies such as health psychology and behavioral medicine will obviously be more critical than ever. Specialist behavioral health services, in their multidisciplinary collaborative form, will constitute a central focus for the doctoral-level provider. A challenge will be for such proficiencies to thrive in a new functional world devoid of departmental structures and organized operationally around teams. The capacity to demonstrate needed competencies in the discharge of required proficiencies and to achieve positive treatment outcomes will determine the penetration of psychological practitioners within emerging health systems.

Treatment: Psychoeducational approaches will be more prominent, as will be knowledge and strategic use of collateral (including community) resources external to the treatment team. Cross-disciplinary collaboration and effective communication will be more critical than ever, as will patient education and the development and implementation of prevention programs. The treatment needs of persons with serious mental disorders, as well as those with developmental disabilities and other potentially handicapping conditions, will figure prominently. Accordingly, forceful and strategic patient advocacy will be emphasized. The supervisory role of the specialist health psychologist in these developing systems will come to subsume master's-level practitioners of all disciplines.

New Roles

These are a heterogeneous set, some involving extensions of "traditional" roles. What may be called a "suprarole" unifies and incorporates this otherwise disparate set, namely, the evolution of the health-oriented psychologist as an expert in systems monitoring, development, and evaluation. Increasingly, the doctoral-level psychologist will operate in the macroworld of system *design*. From this, the following new foci suggest themselves.

Critical here is the role of the psychologist in translating empirical findings into clinical protocols targeted at specific presenting conditions such as depression, stress, and their myriad somatic correlates. This developing role has the psychologist involved as both a technical expert and an organizational facilitator in the search for increased *precision*.

The development and strategic use of information in the patient's interest is a new role for most psychologists. The development of manuals for patient self-management, self-assessment instruments, and materials for the delivery of psychoeducational treatment interventions are examples.

Provider profiling, a critical quality monitoring process for provider networks, is currently an underdeveloped mechanism, but one which shows significant promise. The need for profiling strategies affords opportunities for contributions from industrial–organizational psychologist and specialist clinicians alike.

New program development in health systems never ceases. Central to this ongoing endeavor is the need for a variety of prevention programs, the prime thrust of which is likely to be secondary prevention. In the effective discharge of this role, psychologists must be aware of the need for intersectoral linkages (e.g., with schools, housing, income support programs), a developed educational technology, and the need for collaborative and nonpatronizing relationships with community groups and grass-roots organizations.

Emerging Roles

Emerging roles are fewer and, for the most part, derive from the systems focus in health care. These roles are mainly technical, and have to do with the essential servomechanisms inherent in true systems. A particular example is the development and formative evaluation of quality monitoring and management strategies. Another involves the elements associated with the development of a management information system: needs and resource analysis, strategic plan development, organizational buy-in, and the like.

Finally, we would mention the very recently emerging challenge of *disease management.* This term is used to denote a whole complex of approaches designed to reduce both the incidence and prevalence of disease states (or disorders). Prevention in all its manifestations is a central component of the process; but so is patient self-monitoring and management, and the analysis of life-style behaviors antithetical to health. Patient monitoring devices and systems also figure prominently. Integrated approaches are essential, with system effectiveness depending on the extent and quality of system collaboration. It is a distinct advantage if, for a particular disease or disorder (e.g., adult onset diabetes or depression) a turnkey approach can be developed, tried on a trial basis, implemented, and monitored.

For the professional psychologist, the exercise of this single-role opportunity requires competencies that transcend both traditional specialty training in psychology, and psychology training itself; it calls for multispecialty and multidisciplinary skills. Increasingly, continuing change in health systems, driven by policy issues, market forces, applied science, and opportunism, both generates new and recycles traditional roles. More and more in this context, the disciplinary-based *practice* framework of a single field, such as psychology, proves inadequate to the challenge of effective role preparation for professionals.

New training models and structures as well as innovations in instructional design are urgently needed. The competency short-fall between new role opportunities and the professional preparation of practitioners is dismayingly large and increasing rapidly. The development of training systems for the acquisition and evaluation of *generic* competencies at least offers the possibility, not of bridging the gap, but of preventing it from widening in an ever-changing world. We turn to this issue next.

GENERIC COMPETENCIES FOR PROFESSIONAL PSYCHOLOGISTS

The thread we are following in this chapter has taken us from a consideration of the new and emerging world of health systems, to the key imperatives of this world with which psychology and psychologists will have to contend, to a review of the kinds of roles psychologists will need to embrace to contribute to and provide leadership in the world of healthcare and its systems of organization.

Generic Competencies

The capacity of professional training to retain its currency and relevance is vested in the extent to which a particular framing model and technology can be crafted to provide a schematic base which, in turn, supports changing role functions as they unfold. Effective training for the professions involves the acquisition of strategies appropriate to a variety of challenges associated with professional decision making. Effective training also provides the basis for the discriminating pursuit of lifelong professional learning. We return to this latter issue toward the conclusion of this chapter.

For professional training, then, the paramount issue is the development of a set of organizing schema that flexibly permit development into the myriad roles and challenges of a contributing professional life. For the purpose of this chapter, however, we limit the consideration to the role generic competencies play as an organizing apparatus for multiple roles: a base for induction and heuristic thinking about professional problems.

An Irreducible Set of Generic Competencies

In this regard the NCSPP has performed valuable work by identifying a set of professional competencies (Bourg, Bent, Callan, Jones, McHolland, & Stricker, 1987). The emerging world of healthcare and healthcare reform requires, however, that these contributions be revisited. We propose the following elements of a core set of generic competencies. For each area one should imagine a cluster of discrete competencies: some knowledge-based, some skills-based, and some based on the acquisition of appropriate attitudes and values.

1. Historical/Contextual/Policy Issues in Health
2. Normative Framework for Professional Services
3. Clinical Services Planning, Provision, and Management
4. Quality Assessment and Management
5. Applied Research and Program Evaluation
6. Business Administration and Management

Each of these areas is a large separate field of knowledge containing clusters of competencies. Nonetheless, it is difficult to imagine a doctoral-level professional being able to contribute effectively without some degree of exposure to each of these areas. In due course we will "unfold" these areas one by one into a larger set of competency clusters. Before attempting this, however, there needs to be a word about level and type of competency.

Competencies: Levels and Types

At all levels of curriculum development one faces significant selection challenges. Heated debates centering on what is to be included and what cannot be removed abound within training programs. And for professional programs, specialty accreditation criteria have figured prominently in such debates. It is important to appreciate, however, that the above list of six fields of inquiry and application is intended to define the kind of curricular target we are aiming at. Indeed, the operational issue was hinted at above. The word *exposure* was used in connection with the list.

We have earlier argued that the acquisition of a general schema (the elements of a broad conceptual framework) is essential for organizing learning at the individual level. This is all about knowing *how* as distinct from knowing *what*, though professionals need to know both. Thus, what we term *knowledge-based* competencies are designed to handle the knowing what tasks, and the skills-based competencies the knowing how tasks. One of the hazards of curriculum development is that it constantly forces us to choose among levels and types of competencies. Confronted, then, by the above list of very large areas, a challenge is to define "exposure." It probably does not involve skill-based competencies but presumably does involve the acquisition of some knowledge-based competencies. At the doctoral-level we simply cannot, nor should we, attempt to teach everything. We do need to provide for a mix of knowledge, attitudes-values, and skills, and we need to provide the requisite conceptual framework for them to assume meaning and to permit applications when appropriate.

TABLE 5.1
Competency Development Clusters

Contextual Issues	Technical/Quantitative
Public Health Concepts	Quality Assessment
Health Systems Organization	Quality Management
Healthcare Financing	Provider Profiling
Normative Issues	Applied Research
Consumer Focus	Health Services Research
Human Diversity	Program Evaluation
Clinical Services Delivery	Utilization Review
Functional/Behavioral Assessment	Outcomes Research
Risk Appraisal/Management	
Primary Behavioral Health Services	
Specialist Clinical Services	
Services Planning/Management	
Services Documentation	

So what our list says is that at the doctoral level students require some limited exposure (knowledge) about key elements within each of the six broad areas. The issue of mastery (high level) does not arise. The list further indicates that the world of work is large and it will ultimately pose problems for students who are not provided exposure to key concepts within each area. Curriculum development proceeds by keeping the list generally in sight while making selections among a pool of particular learning activities that would best illuminate the generic competencies at the desired level.

Let us return to the task of digging into a list to get a glimpse of what could serve as generic competencies for professional psychologists in a changing world.

Competency Development Clusters

Table 5.1 provides a breakdown of suggested competencies by area from the list on p. 69; area 6 is not broken down. Table 5.2 further illuminates area 3 on the list: the planning and provision of clinical services.

A Cautionary Note: This section on generic competencies is not designed as an exercise in curriculum development or instruc-

TABLE 5.2
Planning and Provision of Clinical Services

Redesigned Foci for Clinical Interventions
    Behavioral Health Services in the Cause of Wellness
    Population Health Focus
    Short-term Strategic, Targeted
    Focus on Health Education
    Patient Self Management Skills
    Multi-modal Formats
Areas for Competency Development
    Specialist Health Psychology, Behavioral Medicine
    Links with Primary Care
    Empirically Validated, Short-term Focused Treatments

tional design. It is intended solely as a means of portraying the general scope of the competencies around which programs could conceivably design learning experiences. If the list is large, it is because the new professional world is large and getting larger. The challenge, of course, for the curriculum designer is in handling the selection decisions, by type and by level. In this section we merely attempt a snapshot of the myriad of possibilities. Finally, the same list holds for postlicensure training. At this latter level, however, the need for organizing frameworks is less, and the generic competencies figure much less centrally since, by and large, core curriculum imperatives are less relevant.

THE SELF-MANAGEMENT OF PROFESSIONAL DEVELOPMENT

The ability of the professional psychologist to commit to and strategically plan for his or her own professional development—always important for optimizing personal satisfaction—is now a critical gateway to professional survival. The chaos and flux of the world of healthcare require as never before particularly finely tuned skills in monitoring the evolution of the healthcare system. To discriminate effectively among events, and to discern and interpret trends, requires a well-developed sense of policy issues associated with healthcare financing, organization, and provision. It requires also an understanding of the motive forces of entrepreneurial corporate activity as played out within federal and state governments and the industry.

If one of the goals of preservice education and training is to enable the professional psychologist to *become* a player, then providing the entry-level professional with strategies for vocational self-management clearly assists the same person to *remain* a player in a world in which the prediction of developments is a clear challenge. Therefore, such strategies, together with a general framework for planning and integration, become an essential part of the preservice training experience.

Suggested Strategies

Strategies may usefully be classified according to focus: those bearing on the need to manage key resource people in the professional's life; those affecting the professional's management of information; and strategies associated with incorporating the outcomes of the first two approaches within a lifelong plan for professional development.

Resource Contacts: The exploitation of mentors, whether opportunistic or strategic, has long been a means available to the entry-level professional seeking advancement. The role of mentors will extend well beyond the journeyperson's first appointment. Professional mentors will assume more importance than their academic counterparts and a regular succession of mentors will be the rule rather than the exception. Maintaining contact with peers will become a real priority, particularly since job changes will be more frequent. Peer-to-peer information exchange will flourish, and contact among peers will assume a strategic importance well beyond that which it has traditionally held. Lastly, the role of the "visible player" will become central. Contact with opinion leaders in government, the corporate world, and academic policy analysts will be prized and put to strategic use by the professional psychologist committed to maximizing control in a changing world through more effective management of people and information.

Acquiring and Using Information: The entry-level professional's routine reading must extend beyond the discipline of psychology, to include journals dealing with health policy, health services administration, medical information, health economics, and the health services industry. Systematic perusal of national newspapers will become a professional obligation rather than a personal indulgence. Industry developments at the macrolevel create ripples which may deeply affect job creation and disposition. Multimedia electronic communication and developments in instructional technology will be used routinely as vehicles for monitoring developments in the field and for professional self-improvement.

A Plan for Professional Self-Development: The message of this section is that in a professional world characterized by flux and change, reliance on traditional approaches may well be hazardous. Traditional academic mentors are no longer in the center of the knowledge stream; industry and policy contacts are essential. Accordingly, attendance at particular conventions will come to be driven more by the perceived need to meet certain people, to be exposed to industry gossip, and to hear about changes in, for example, service development, health systems, or disease management strategies. The conduct of business meetings at professional and industry meetings will become as routine as it is essential. One's strategic professional self-management plan should include provision for acquiring the requisite continuing education requirements. Finally, increasing numbers of doctoral-level psychologists will seriously approach the personal challenge of obtaining a postdoctoral credential in fields outside psychology; for example, in law, public health, or health or business administration. For the entry-level professional, therefore, lifelong learning will have changed its traditional focus from aspirational to obligatory.

ISSUES IN TRAINING PROGRAM REDESIGN

In this section we shall examine a complex set of issues bearing on planning for and restructuring training programs in professional psychology. We take up, in turn, the following issues: general assumptions and imperatives associated with program redesign, obstacles to be confronted, the structure and mechanisms (processes) of enhanced programs, and implementation strategies for redesigned programs.

General Assumptions and Imperatives

In the second section of this chapter we identified and discussed a set of imperatives of a very global kind, those deriving from the new world of health systems. We used these to signal the kind of roles professional psychologists could usefully play in a changing world. In this section, however, we enumerate a normative framework for training redesign. The "imperatives" for training we identify here derive from a set of what we hold to be nonnegotiable assumptions which speak to how training is to be configured or organized if the professional psychologist is to acquire those competencies we earlier identified as essential to a changing context of practice.

Let us begin by setting out these assumptions—the values base for program redesign. The appropriate and accountable doctoral-level program should:

1. Reflect the essential continuity of training across levels: that is, it should provide a strong base upon which subsequent postdoctoral learnings depend and derive their substance.
2. Be able to assume that its entering student body is appropriately informed as to the realities of the world of professional practice they will subsequently enter; that is, that they have indeed made an informed choice in selecting professional psychology as a life's work.
3. Strongly and consistently drive home the multiform nature of the professional psychologist as applied scientist, program developer and evaluator, wide-ranging consultant, health specialist, facilitator, trainer, supervisor, and system developer.
4. Reflect in its curriculum and role-modeling arrangements a direct service focus centering on the acquisition of specialist health services competencies informed by clinical services as part of a comprehensive technology of health systems practice.
5. Explicitly prepare students for life-long professional development.

6. Have at its core a health service system in which students are actively involved in ways reflecting the multiform roles of psychologist.
7. Deliver and constantly improve services appropriate to the needs of at-risk, vulnerable, and traditionally underserviced populations as an integral and consistent part of the program.
8. Display a mix of faculty who collectively provide energetic, consistent, and effective modeling for students across the entire spectrum of roles students will ultimately embrace.
9. In its organization and curriculum, formally and systematically provide for professional competency acquisition and evaluation.
10. In its curriculum and role modeling, depict a treatment and management model conceived of in terms of the general health as well as stated interests and concerns of the patient.
11. In its curriculum and role modeling, systematically reflect an explicit valuing of and sensitivity to human diversity in all its manifestations.
12. In its curriculum and role modeling, incorporate a "guided practice" model in which a sequential process of preparation-induction, rehearsal and operational commitment, monitoring, supervision-feedback, analysis-reflection-incorporation is used as the framework for competency acquisition.

Obstacles to Program Redesign

Innovation inevitably confronts obstacles. External barriers include the deadening effect of specialist accreditation criteria; significant reduction in federal support of demonstration programs; the increasing irrelevance of professional associations as effective resources for program redesign; and the continuing domination of training by academicians. Among internal obstacles one may note the essential stasis and inflexibility of faculty-owned curricula which particularly resist innovative proposals for instructional design; criteria for faculty promotion and tenure; faculty ignorance of the changing imperatives of the world of work; competency and resources shortfall within programs; and the inappropriate expectations of new trainees.

Structural Mechanisms of Program Redesign

What few innovative proposals for program redesign have emerged have invariably focused on curricular reform. Too infrequently, however, do we hear calls for significant structural and operational change. We have already noted one, an imperative to the effect that professional training should be on a continuum, a gradation; vertical integration by level. Currently, doctoral-level training is said to be structured by a typology of training models. This is nonsense, of course. Intramodel variation is great and there is minimal formal structure. At the in-service level, postdoctoral skill development is dominated by ad hoc, vendor-driven arrangements.

A detached observer might well conclude after having been exposed to a number of training programs that the connection between curricular activities and student competency acquisition is at best poorly developed. Essentially, programs are not truly *about* anything: they simply *are*. The rhetoric about what they stand for is rarely matched by what they actually do. It is all very loose. Faculty teach classes, but they are not held responsible for student competency development. In any event, they are there for the most part to produce publishable research, not to act as multifaceted professional exemplars. What passes for mechanisms for professional competency development involves shipping students off into external "field training" sites. Faculty only rarely supervise. Operational links between service delivery and research are rarely drawn.

The main problem is that, by most standards, training programs are not cohesive operational entities in which inputs are formally linked to outcomes. In short, they are not *managed*. Until programs depart from the academic model and yield to procedural–operational arrangements characterized by collective accountability, this linkage can never be wrought. Training programs will remain unable to ensure the acquisition of needed competencies while they continue as entities whose operations are devoid of active management, and whose personnel are not formally held responsible for the defined characteristics of its products.

We list below a few of the structural changes we believe are essential to an accountable professional training program.

1. Seamless functional integration of the training program and a service delivery system.
2. Care planning and clinical management form the hub of professional roles and activities.
3. The clinical and financial data base becomes the focal point with professional training for the functional integration of services and outcomes management.
4. The bulk of the faculty are actively involved in policy issues, treatment planning, services delivery, and process and outcome evaluation.
5. Students and faculty work interdependently as part of service teams, as consultants, as evaluators, and as consumer advocates.
6. Faculty have joint appointments with care systems and, in turn, professional staff serve as clinical faculty. Performance criteria for faculty reflect these roles. This arrangement reasonably presupposes the development of formal collaborative partnerships between the program and private and public organized care systems.
7. Faculty research includes, for example, the development of criteria for the measurement and credentialing of professional competencies and health services research.
8. Programs have a formal advisory council which includes representatives from the healthcare industry, consumer–carers groups, state and local governments, students, and the community at large.

Strategies for Implementation of Program Redesign

As we have earlier noted, resistance to innovation abounds. In the end, however, there are probably only two likely approaches to program change. One is driven from the top by a credible, forceful leader who, while involving constituencies, assigns tasks and manages the time frame. The other is characterized by a kind of diffusion model. In this model, change does ultimately come, but slowly, and its end products may not reflect the original goals. The prevailing contingencies of academic programs make the diffusion approach more likely if, indeed, there is a commitment to change.

Finally, it should be said that one cannot be particularly sanguine about the likelihood of self-initiated and self-directed change on the part of training programs. The necessary contingencies are simply not there in the traditional academic world. One might hope that certain obvious moral imperatives might become a motive force powerful enough to energize programs into confronting the challenges of redesign. This remains to be seen, however.

SUMMARY OF KEY RECOMMENDATIONS FOR TRAINING PROGRAM REDESIGN

This chapter concludes with a highly selected summary of "recommendations," whether explicitly or implicitly advanced in the chapter.

1. Articulation of what it is to be a health services provider serving primary care and specialist roles.
2. Knowledge of principles of healthcare financing, organization, and provision.
3. Knowledge of public health concepts in guiding service development and organization.
4. Capacity to work knowledgeably and effectively with diverse populations, particularly those traditionally underserved and at risk.
5. Developed competencies in health psychology/behavioral medicine; prevention; functional assessment; strategic focused psychotherapy; patient education and resources assessment; patient services development and advocacy.
6. Developed competencies in integrated care monitoring.
7. Management and documentation within interdisciplinary frameworks.
8. Developed competence in quality assessment and management, outcomes research, development and management of clinical information systems.
9. Knowledge of business and technology of systems development, services contracting.
10. Organization appraisal, organizational development, and change management.

11. Exploitation of developing technology which can support changes in instructional design.
12. Establishment of base for lifelong professional development, a process involving investment by trainees in their own professional growth through a process of strategic, self-directed inquiry.
13. Functional integration of training programs and services, academic faculty and services staff, faculty research and applied research needs of services systems.

FINAL COMMENT

It is hoped that this chapter serves the purpose of beginning the signposting of our road to accountability. While some of the signs are in place, the road is a long one and no reliable road map is yet available.

6.

The New Undergraduate Education Required of the Future Prescribing Behavioral Healthcare Practitioner

Janet L. Cummings, Psy.D.

If you can't do, teach; and if you can't teach, credential.

Nick Cummings

In 1988, this author entered the School of Professional Psychology (SOPP) at Wright State University, which had recently begun an experimental curriculum sponsored by the American Psychological Association (APA) designed to prepare Psy.D. graduates to qualify for proposed prescription privileges. In addition to the usual graduate psychology courses, the experimental curriculum included a two-year series on physiological psychology, neurology and neuroanatomy, psychopharmacology, and health psychology.

The students in this program were expected to gain the same working knowledge of this material that medical students would. In fact, several of the courses given to these Psy.D. candidates were identical to those taught in the Wright State University School of Medicine, and in fact an instructor from the medical school was recruited to present the same material and administer the same examinations.

Most students in this experimental program were unprepared to understand the material presented. Although most managed to memorize enough facts to achieve passing (often barely passing) examination scores, their understanding of the concepts presented was insufficient to give them the working knowledge necessary to qualify for prescription privileges. Furthermore, by the time they completed this course sequence, most of these students felt so frustrated and intimidated by the physical and biological sciences that they indicated they would not pursue prescription privileges for themselves when they would be able to do so. It is also unlikely, based on this experience, that these students will ever provide an advocacy voice in favor of prescription privileges for psychologists.

On the other hand, the small percentage of students who came into the experimental program with a strong undergraduate background in the biological sciences did quite well with the new curriculum. These students not only had an easier time memorizing the facts and achieving high test scores, but were able to gain a working knowledge of the material sufficient to prepare them for proposed prescription privileges. These same few students also gained the confidence necessary to pursue these privileges, both for themselves when available and as an advocacy voice toward gaining these privileges for psychologists.

The majority of the students in the experimental curriculum were unsuccessful in mastering the material, not because they lacked intelligence or motivation, but because they lacked the background and knowledge base necessary. Students entering medical school have a strong undergraduate background in the physical and biological sciences because medical school admission requirements demand extensive knowledge of chemistry, physics, and biology. Therefore, the courses offered both in the School of Medicine and the School of Professional Psychology were at a level appropriate for the medical students. On the other hand, most of the Psy.D. students had little or no prerequisite knowledge. One can clearly see why they were unsuccessful with the experimental curriculum. It was like placing a child with second grade reading skills in a high school literature course.

This author was fortunate to have been one of the few students in the experimental curriculum with the ample training in the physical and biological sciences necessary to succeed in the program. It is this author's intention in this chapter to discuss changing trends in the roles of psychologists which necessitate the new graduate curriculum, then to propose changes in undergraduate education necessary to prepare students for the new graduate programs.

CHANGING TRENDS IN THE ROLES OF PSYCHOLOGISTS

The Psychologist as Medication Manager

Many proponents of prescription privileges for psychologists believe it is likely that psychologists will, within the next decade or two, be eligible to prescribe. Nonphysician professions such as dentistry, optometry, podiatry, and nursing (nurse practitioners) have already gained prescription privileges, and psychology may not be far behind. The APA's Council of Representatives, at its August 10, 1995 meeting, voted in favor of developing new curricula to prepare psychologists to prescribe. The Council also voted to draft legislation which, once enacted by individual states or by Congress, would give prescription privileges to psychologists (Martin, 1995). A recent survey of physicians indicates that 50% of the most recently trained family physicians support prescription privileges for psychologists (Rosofsky, 1995), and their support may aid psychology in obtaining this privilege in a timely manner. Furthermore, the Department of Defense is currently sponsoring the Psychopharmacology Demonstration Project (PDP), a pilot training program for military psychologists to gain the credentials necessary to prescribe psychotropic medications. Congress continues to support this program despite psychiatrists' lobbying against it (*Practitioner*, 1995).

Should psychologists become eligible to prescribe, only those psychologists with an adequate knowledge base will be able to undergo the education and supervised experience necessary for certification. It will be these psychologists who make themselves marketable (and perhaps indispensable) in an era when other once-thriving practices will have disappeared.

In the meantime, while awaiting prescription privileges, psychologists (as well as other behavioral healthcare practitioners who may never be eligible to prescribe) can fill a very crucial role in medication management of patients. According to a recent article in the APA Monitor (Cavaliere, 1995), "More practicing psychologists are seeing the value of being well-versed in psychopharmacology" to serve as "medication advisers" to physicians. These advisers assist in the establishment of psychological diagnoses for patients, decide which patients are likely to benefit from psychotropic medications, and advise physicians on the benefits and side effects of medications appropriate for particular diagnoses. Because few family physicians have a thorough knowledge of psychological diagnoses and psychotropic medications, more and more of these physicians are depending on psychologists to advise them in their management of patients with psychological disorders. Many family physician group practices now include a psychologist as a vital member of the practice and provide that psychologist with a steady caseload of patients about whom the physicians wish to receive advice and coordinate care.

Case Illustration: Arlene and Her Arthritis: Arlene was a homemaker in her midfifties who suffered from osteoarthritis. For several years, Arlene's primary care physician (PCP) had treated her with various steroidal and nonsteroidal pain relievers, anti-inflammatory medications, and topical preparations. The PCP also recommended an exercise program designed to alleviate arthritis symptoms. However, the patient did not comply with this recommendation. She gave the exercise program only minimal effort for a very brief period of time, saying that any exercise made her pain more intense.

Arlene continued to complain that her pain was gradually worsening instead of getting better, and one day told her PCP that she felt very depressed due to her limited ability to perform tasks she enjoyed (such as knitting and playing with her toddler grandson). She went on to tell her PCP that she sometimes felt as though her life were no longer worth living.

The PCP referred Arlene to a psychologist with whom she had a working relationship. After evaluating the patient, the psychologist suggested a trial of Elavil to target symptoms of both depression and chronic pain.

After six weeks on Elavil, Arlene reported significant decrease in depression, as well as some reduction of her pain. Although her pain had not been completely alleviated, she felt good enough to begin compliance with the prescribed exercise program.

In many managed care settings, psychologists serve as case managers for patients who receive a variety of services. (For example, a patient may be seeing a psychiatrist for medication while participating in a group therapy program, all under the coordination of a case manager.) The most cost-effective managed care companies have learned to utilize psychologists and other behavioral healthcare practitioners to establish psychological diagnoses and make treatment recommendations before patients are given access to expensive time with a psychiatrist. The behavioral healthcare practitioners then monitor each patient's progress in both psychological and psychiatric treatment modalities, continue to make recommendations to the psychiatrist for on-going medication management, and help patients comply with their prescribed medication regimens. This type of case management position requires a thorough working knowledge of psychotropic medications, as well as good diagnostic skills. As the healthcare system in America continues to be increasingly oriented toward managed care, behavioral healthcare practitioners who can offer this type of comprehensive case management service will find their services in demand.

Case Illustration: Case Management of an Agoraphobic: Jean, a 35-year-old female, presented for treatment in a managed care setting several months after the onset of panic disorder with agoraphobia. Following the initial intake with the therapist who would serve as her case manager, the patient was referred to the managed care center's six-month group treatment program for agoraphobia which was led by another therapist. The patient specifically requested a referral to a psychiatrist for medication to relieve her frequent, severe panic attacks.

The psychiatrist prescribed Xanax and instructed Jean to use it as needed for panic attacks. The case manager objected to this as-needed use of Xanax because of the drug's potential for physical dependence and because the drug is less effective in alleviating existing panic than in preventing panic attacks. The psychologist discussed these concerns with the psychiatrist, who then agreed to place the patient on an appropriate dosage schedule.

The case manager monitored the patient's progress in the group treatment program by studying the group therapist's case notes and through monthly or bimonthly face-to-face contact with the patient. As the patient attended the group program and learned skills to manage her panic attacks and phobias, the case manager suggested to the psychiatrist that her Xanax dosage be decreased by small increments. As the patient's skills increased, her need for and use of the medication decreased, so that the patient was able to discontinue Xanax use altogether shortly after graduation from the agoraphobia group program, and without experiencing withdrawal symptoms.

Case Illustration: Martin Almost Goes Manic: Martin, a 20-year-old male college student, entered treatment at a managed care center because of a depressive episode of recent onset. Because of the patient's report of prior cyclical bouts of depression (less severe than the current episode), his report of a family history of endogenous depression (manic-depression) and apparent vegetative signs of depression, Martin's case manager referred him to a psychiatrist in the center for medication. The case manager suspected that the patient was experiencing the onset of manic-depression.

The psychiatrist placed Martin on Prozac, which provided relief from most of his depressive symptoms within a few weeks. The case manager, aware that Prozac can precipitate mania in predisposed individuals, monitored the patient very carefully. He observed the early signs of a manic episode in Martin during a routine therapy session and scheduled an appointment for the patient to see the psychiatrist the next day, several weeks prior to the regularly scheduled monthly medication appointment.

Before Martin arrived for this psychiatric appointment, the case manager discussed his observations with the psychiatrist and suggested that Prozac be discontinued. The psychiatrist accepted this recommendation, discontinued the Prozac, and placed the patient on lithium. Thus, Martin was spared what could have been a full-blown manic episode, followed by the usual plunge into depression, because his case manager recognized the need for a medication change.

The Psychologist as Manager
of Medical Conditions

For the profession [of psychology] to continue to grow and matu-
rate, we must train the next generation of psychologists to function in non-traditional settings such as hospitals, consultation/
liaison, second opinion, primary psychological care, psychopharmacology and nursing homes. At the same time, we must protect and nurture our primary identification as the preeminent
provider of psychological assessment and outpatient psychotherapy. To continue to train psychologists to provide only a
narrow band of services increases the probability . . . that psychology (and not necessarily psychological services) . . . could be
viewed by policy makers as a high-priced and "optional" discipline (Resnick, 1995).

As the profession of psychology continues to expand into
these nontraditional settings, psychologists have the opportunity
to bridge the gap between psychology and medicine by providing
behavioral management of many medical conditions. Some medical conditions can be successfully managed behaviorally, with little
or no medical intervention, whereas other conditions are best
treated with a combination of aggressive medical treatment and
behavioral management. Whether behavioral management is the
primary component of treatment or an adjunct to medical intervention, behavioral healthcare practitioners can play a crucial role
in the treatment of many medical conditions.

Psychologists have traditionally been called upon in hospital
and managed care settings to help noncompliant patients achieve
compliance with physicians' prescribed treatments and to help
patients cope with acute health crises and adjust to chronic illness
or disability. However, behavioral healthcare practitioners can go
beyond these traditional roles by providing behavioral interventions which directly impact medical conditions.

A large number and wide variety of medical conditions can
be treated wholly or partly through behavioral intervention. However, the following few examples are offered to demonstrate the
manner in which behavioral healthcare practitioners can provide
behavioral management of medical problems:

Hypertension: Some cases of hypertension, or high blood pressure, require medication, whereas other cases can be treated by behavioral intervention alone. Many high blood pressure cases in which medication is absolutely necessary can benefit from behavioral intervention as an adjunct to medical treatment. Behavioral healthcare practitioners can help high blood pressure patients stop smoking, lose weight, and maintain healthy weight, and alter their diets to reduce sodium intake. They can teach stress management and anger management skills to reduce the impact of psychological problems on the physical disease.

Asthma: Although most asthmatics require medication, at least intermittently, psychological intervention can serve to reduce the frequency and severity of asthma attacks, and thereby reduce the need for medication (Mrazek, 1993). Because stress can trigger and exacerbate asthma attacks, relaxation training can have marked impact on reducing symptoms. Furthermore, psychotherapy can help patients learn to manage their emotions, thus alleviating some asthma symptoms. Family therapy aimed at reducing family stress can reduce the frequency and severity of attacks in asthmatic children.

Mitral Valve Prolapse: Even the most severe cases of this congenital heart valve defect can benefit from behavioral management, and the majority of cases can be managed without cardiac medications or surgery (Frederickson, 1988). Behavioral healthcare practitioners can help mitral valve prolapse (MVP) patients decrease their sugar and caffeine consumption, increase their water intake, regulate their sodium intake, and adopt heart-healthy, low-fat diets. The practitioners can help patients develop balanced exercise programs which provide adequate cardiac workouts without exacerbating symptoms by overworking the heart. Biofeedback and other relaxation techniques are often indispensable in the management of MVP, as these patients are particularly prone to the development of panic attacks and phobias.

Behavioral healthcare practitioners who can provide behavioral management of medical conditions need a background in physiology, health, and nutrition sufficient to understand the nature of their patients' medical problems and to be able to explain the problems in ways their patients can understand. They need a working knowledge of medical terminology that will allow them to glean information from medical literature when they are confronted with a medical condition outside their knowledge base. Perhaps most importantly, these practitioners need to be able to understand the mechanisms by which medical and behavioral interventions influence physiology, and to be able to explain these mechanisms to their patients. Therefore, the behavioral healthcare practitioner who can effectively provide behavioral management of medical conditions is one with a working knowledge of anatomy, physiology, nutrition, and pharmacology.

PROPOSED UNDERGRADUATE CURRICULUM

Although the APA Education Directorate is currently looking at graduate education in psychology in order to propose necessary changes in the graduate curriculum, it may be many years thereafter before the undergraduate psychology curriculum catches up with those changes and begins to adequately prepare students for the new graduate curriculum. Meanwhile, undergraduate psychology students who plan to attend graduate school in psychology and enter the arenas of medication management and behavioral management of medical conditions can tailor their own educations in such a way as to be equipped for the new graduate education and for jobs in these arenas.

This author studied a sampling of university catalogs for both state and private schools throughout the United States and discovered considerable variation in course requirements for a psychology major beyond the core undergraduate psychology courses. Only one of the universities sampled offered an optional biology emphasis within the psychology major. However, the universities were similar in that their undergraduate psychology programs included a number of courses (generally half the requirement or more) from outside the field of psychology. The universities were also similar in that all allowed the student to select these nonpsychology courses from a wide range of possibilities, whether they called these electives General Education, General Institute Requirements, University Requirements, College Requirements, Restricted Electives, Unrestricted Electives, or whatever else.

An undergraduate student could easily become prepared for the new graduate curriculum in any of the universities sampled simply by making wise choices from lists of electives. When confronted with a list of possible courses under the heading of General Education, College Requirements, etc., the student can gravitate toward courses in the areas of biology, chemistry, nutrition, and physiology.

It is strongly recommended that the psychology student anticipating the new graduate curriculum and working in the area of behavioral management of medical conditions take as many of the following courses, or their equivalents, as possible:

Biology: General introduction to the main features and principles of biology, with emphasis on heredity and the bearing of biology on human life.

Chemistry: Periodic table, chemical equations, theory of gases, thermodynamics, chemical equilibria, acids and bases, and solubility.

Exercise Science/Metabolism: Introduction to energy metabolic pathways and fuel use during various modes of exercise, with emphasis on effects of exercise on metabolism.

Exercise Science/Psychology: Examination of the effects of exercise on the quality of human life, with emphasis on individual differences, special populations, and mental health changes.

Genetics: Introduction to nucleic acid structure and function, gene expression, and transmission genetics.

Nutrition Science: Introduction to the principles of nutrition, with emphasis on properties of nutrients in foods and metabolism of protein, fat, and carbohydrate.

Physical Anthropology/Human Variation: Introduction to genetic differences among human populations, with emphasis on blood groups, plasma proteins, physiology, and morphology.

Physics: Introduction to general principles and analytical methods of physics, with emphasis on applications in biological sciences.

Physiology: Introduction to human anatomy and functioning of major organ systems.

In many cases, some of these courses or their equivalents are offered as two-semester or three-trimester sequences rather than as single courses. In such instances, it is recommended that the student take enough of the sequence to cover the material described above. Furthermore, students who develop a particular interest in one of these areas may wish to take more advanced courses in that area. For example, a student who hopes to specialize in the treatment of obesity may wish to take further courses in the areas of nutrition and exercise science. A student who wants to work with physicians to help manage cardiac patients may choose to take further courses in physiology.

In addition to these courses, it is recommended that undergraduate psychology students anticipating a career involving medication management of patients (with or without prescription privileges) also take the following courses:

Biochemistry/Metabolism: Fundamentals of cell metabolism and biosynthesis of amino acids, nucleic acids, and proteins.

Biochemistry/Molecules: Introduction to macromolecules with emphasis on proteins, enzymes, membranes, cell motility, and cell division.

Biology/Cell Function: Membrane receptors and signal transduction, cell cycle, cell growth and division, extracellular matrix and cell-to-cell junctions, cell development, and immune system.

Organic Chemistry: Introduction to the nomenclature, structure, chemistry, and reaction mechanisms of organic compounds.

Students planning to someday gain prescription privileges may wish to do further study in these areas. However, these courses should be more than sufficient to prepare students who plan to work as nonprescribing medication managers for the new graduate curriculum.

Even though it is unlikely that universities will alter their undergraduate psychology requirements in the near future to adapt to the new graduate requirements, undergraduate students may easily tailor their own educations to prepare themselves for the future. They can begin to decide what new arena may be of interest to them and to prepare themselves academically for eventual success in their chosen arena.

7.

Conducting Psychotherapy Supervision in the Managed Care Era

Thomas D. Kalous, Ph.D.

> *First take the log out of your own eye, and then you will see clearly to take the speck out of your brother's eye.*
> Gospel According to Matthew,
> Chapter 7, Verse 5

With the evolving healthcare system, there is growing emphasis on cost effectiveness. As a result, the amount of direct care provided by doctoral level mental health practitioners will probably decrease. At the same time, clinical supervision opportunities are likely to expand for doctoral level practitioners (who will be referred to as "psychologists") in a variety of settings. Until recently, most clinical supervision occurred within university training programs and internships. However, the need for well-trained supervisors in nonacademic environments is increasing as the marketplace changes.

A number of factors are working together to increase demand for qualified clinical supervisors. First, there are increasing regulations requiring postgraduate supervised experiences for licensure/certification. Second, while it is less expensive for managed care companies to utilize master's- and bachelor's-level therapists, closer supervision of their services may reduce risks and increase quality of care. Psychologists will be in a unique position to oversee the care provided by these less trained clinicians. Third, as members of multidisciplinary group practices, psychologists may also be asked to provide quality assurance through consultation, peer review, and direct clinical supervision. Fourth, a large number of practicing psychotherapists will need to retrain themselves in more efficient and effective therapy methods if they are to compete in the new marketplace. Supervision can and should play a large role in this retraining process.

While it is true that the demand for supervisors is likely to grow, not all psychologists are prepared to take on this responsibility. Very few have received formal training in supervision and many suffered through poor supervision themselves. In fact, less than 25% of the clinicians who attend this author's supervision seminars across the country report that they received training in supervision in their graduate programs. In order to be an effective clinical supervisor, one must be well versed in the catalytic paradigm as described by Cummings (1995b) and be adequately trained in supervisory processes and theory. Successful supervisors will possess a unique combination of skills, abilities, and knowledge that are not necessarily inherent in the traditional roles of psychotherapist, counselor, and psychometrist. Effective supervision requires the application of clinical knowledge and interpersonal skills and a broad understanding of legal and ethical issues. In addition, supervisors must be able to monitor, teach, motivate, and support others in their clinical work. Clinical supervisors can be instrumental in moving the profession forward by guiding their supervisees through the paradigm shifts that are the essence of this book.

This chapter will provide an overview of the requisite theory and skills needed to be an effective clinical supervisor. Specifically, the implications of the catalytic paradigm for clinical supervision practices will be examined. In addition, some legal and ethical issues will be outlined. Finally, risk management strategies for supervisors will be reviewed as the steps to effective clinical supervision are detailed. Case vignettes will be used to highlight a "catalytic" approach to supervision.

DEFINING CLINICAL SUPERVISION

Supervision can be defined legally as a professional relationship between a more experienced or highly trained mental health professional, the supervisor, and a junior mental health professional, the supervisee. The supervisor is called upon to *direct and evaluate* the clinical practice of the supervisee and is charged with helping the supervisee become a more effective practitioner. It is the responsibility of the supervisor to ensure the welfare of the supervisee's clientele. Also, supervisors have the responsibility and authority to remove supervisees from the therapist role if they are not able to perform up to clinical and operational standards.

Consultation differs in that the consultant does not direct the clinical work of the consultee. Instead, consultants provide information and suggestions on an as needed basis. Consultants' suggestions are not binding and therefore they are not responsible for the actions of the consultee.

Despite the differences in supervision and consultation from a legal standpoint, the processes can look much the same. The supervisor-consultant gathers information about specific cases and psychotherapeutic processes and provides guidance or suggestions to the supervisee-consultee. Supervision–consultation interventions are intended to move therapy forward and help the supervisee-consultee to grow as a therapist. While reference is made only to supervision throughout the rest of this chapter, many of the concepts apply to consultation, as well.

In order to increase the likelihood that supervision will be effective and satisfying for all parties (i.e., supervisor, therapist, payer, and client), some basic conditions need to be met. While research on clinical supervision is sparse, a few factors have been identified as key elements in assuring effective supervision. The first and most powerful factor appears to be that of congruence between the supervisor's and supervisee's theoretical approach to psychotherapy (Putney, Worthington, & McCullough, 1992). Given the emphasis on briefer modes of therapy, effective supervision in a managed care setting will most likely occur when the supervisor and the supervisee both believe in the efficacy of efficient therapy approaches. If one or the other has not accepted the paradigm shifts detailed by Cummings (1995b), supervision can become adversarial in nature and ultimately clients will suffer.

Second, effective supervisors seem to have personality traits that enhance their ability to help supervisees grow (Powell, 1993). Primarily, they welcome mistakes as learning opportunities and are supportive of the work their supervisees do. Additionally, they possess a good sense of humor that puts supervisees at ease. By reducing tension within the supervisory dyad, less time is spent on political power struggles and more time can be spent helping the supervisee develop. This is especially important given that time is also of the essence in supervision.

Third, it goes without saying that supervisors must also be astute clinicians themselves. Generally, the more clinical experience the supervisor has, the more she has to offer her junior colleagues. In a managed care system, good supervisors will possess a number of years of brief, intermittent therapy practice themselves and will be skilled at facilitating the work of others.

Fourth, as mentioned above, effective supervisors are also risk managers. They need to be intimately aware of laws and ethics that apply to the practice of psychology and related fields as outlined by Disney and Stephens (1994). Each state has laws specific to the practice of clinical supervision. Before practicing as a clinical supervisor, it is a good idea to review and understand the laws that govern these practices in a particular jurisdiction. The legal and ethical issues that arise in the clinical work of supervisees is likely to surprise novice supervisors. Often, supervisees are so focused on the clinical aspects of their work that they miss important legal and ethical issues. Because supervisors and managers can be held legally responsible for the work of supervisees, it is vital that supervisors be on constant lookout for such issues to arise.

In addition to legal risks, larger numbers of clients are being afforded access to behavioral health care systems through managed care. As a result, the number of high-risk cases being referred to practitioners is on the rise. Clinical supervisors will need to be actively involved in the treatment planning and decision making with regard to high-risk cases. Therefore, it is wise to develop protocols to help supervisees identify high-risk cases and to encourage them to discuss these cases in detail during supervision.

A GENERIC MODEL OF SUPERVISION

Before going into more detail about risk management strategies for supervisors, a discussion of a transtheoretical model of supervision may be helpful. This model can be applied to a variety of supervision contexts and works well with many different approaches to psychotherapy. However, due to the focus of this book, this discussion will be limited to the model's application in a managed care setting.

Bernard (1979) developed a model of supervisory training that can help supervisors create appropriate, focused learning environments. She argued that there were three main content areas that constituted focused supervision: overt therapy skills, conceptualization skills, and supervisee personal issues. Bernard defined overt therapy skills as the actions and interventions of the therapist within a psychotherapy session. For example, solution focused therapists often utilize presuppositional language in order to instill hope and actively search for solutions that the clients already have available to them. Interventions designed to elicit such information would constitute examples of therapy skills.

Conceptualization skills, on the other hand, were defined as the covert therapy skills that drive overt therapy skills (Bernard, 1979). In other words, diagnosis, client dynamics, and theoretical stance of the therapist constitute conceptualization issues that might be discussed by the participants in the supervision. Brief therapists tend to conceptualize client problems much differently than their longer term oriented counterparts. Helping therapists make theoretical shifts is part of the conceptual work that supervisors and supervisees are likely to work on together.

Bernard also believed that the personal issues of the supervisee might be appropriate fodder for supervision. For instance, attitudinal resistance to solution focused models may play itself out in supervisees' work. Clinical supervisors need to be aware of how such dynamics may affect therapeutic and supervisory relationships. Supervisees who have been trained in dyadic therapy modes may spend much of their time searching for pathology, and as a result their psychotherapy may lack focus. In supervision, they may try to convince supervisors of the inadequacy of the catalytic model.

Supervisors must also look out for supervisees who allow their own personal issues to drive their interventions. Space does not allow for a discussion of how to deal with impaired professionals in training. However, supervisors may want to familiarize themselves with the works of Bradley and Post (1991) and Olkin and Gaughen (1991) who provide guidelines and suggestions for dealing with impaired students in clinical programs.

According to Bernard's model, if the supervisory dyad is discussing or working on any of these areas, then supervision is likely to be focused appropriately. In addition to these content areas, ethical and legal concerns should also be considered appropriate content areas for supervision. Supervisors are increasingly being sued for not providing adequate training and supervision. Therefore, time spent discussing and reviewing legal and ethical issues is an essential part of quality supervision.

The second dimension included in Bernard's model is that of the style of intervention being utilized by the supervisor. She stated that supervisors could take on the following roles within supervision: teacher, therapist, or consultant. In a teacher role, the supervisor could provide information directly to the supervisee, assign readings, or act as a role model for the supervisee. Teaching is an important aspect of supervision in the catalytic model. Providing skeptical trainees with research data and encouraging them to read some of the many available books on brief therapy and its development can reinforce the appropriateness of the model. Also, teaching therapists how to intervene with certain clients in certain situations can be invaluable. This is particularly true for less experienced therapists. As therapy becomes more and more protocol driven, supervision will focus more on teaching methods and less on esoteric matters.

No less important is the role of the supervisor as therapist. As mentioned above, therapists' personal issues often color their work. Supervisors may need to act as therapists from time to time in order to help supervisees understand these dynamics. Taking on the therapist role also allows for significant role-modeling to occur. Whenever possible, supervisors should utilize "therapy" techniques that parallel those the supervisee is honing. A good rule of thumb is to take on the role of therapist only to deal directly with issues affecting the therapy provided by the supervisee. In general, supervisors should provide direct feedback to supervisees and leave personal issues for supervisees to work out with their own therapists.

Again, it could be argued that other appropriate roles are available to supervisors. For example, supervisors need to be evaluators and risk managers. Nonetheless, it is up to the supervisor to create a supervisory environment that allows for the proper focus and promotes client welfare and supervisee growth. The supervisory environment is defined by the role the supervisor chooses to play in combination with the content of the supervision session at any given moment (Bernard, 1979). For example, when teaching supervisees how to prescribe the symptom when clients are "resistant" to change, the supervisor has created a teacher–psychotherapy skills environment.

IMPLICATIONS OF PARADIGM SHIFTS FOR SUPERVISORS

Bernard's model provides an overview of what should happen in supervision. However, the supervision provided in managed care environments is likely to be impacted by the paradigm shifts espoused by Cummings (1995b). Each of the paradigm shifts has unique implications for the practice of clinical supervision. This section will provide a brief overview of the implications of these paradigm shifts.

Paradigm 1: Therapists Will See More Clients for Briefer Episodes of Treatment

This shift will likely have the greatest impact on supervision as it will require supervisors to spend more time managing risk. With increased numbers of clients, it becomes almost impossible to discuss every client your supervisee sees on a weekly basis. Therefore, it is important to develop ways to track larger numbers of clients and identify those that are at risk for harming themselves or others or that have special circumstances that make them more likely to be involved in legal action. One way to do this is to have supervisees keep a weekly log that provides summary data for each client contact. This log might include information on diagnosis, risk level, and type of contact (i.e., individual therapy, group therapy, telephone contact, etc.). Reviewing this log prior to supervisory sessions allows supervisors to prioritize which clients to discuss.

Paradigm 2: Brief, Intermittent Therapy Episodes

This paradigm requires the supervisory dyad to change its focus in supervision. Brief therapy may require therapists to utilize therapy skills and interventions with clients that are not as familiar to them. Therefore, discussions about interventions to be utilized by the supervisee will be driven by therapy intervention that is consistent with the catalytic model. For example, solution-focused dyads will spend much of their time focusing on overt counseling skills and discussing ways for the supervisee to elicit solutions and strengths that clients bring to therapy. Regardless of the specific approach, many of the skills needed to be an effective brief therapist involve setting the stage for change in the first session. As a result, the first session may become a main focus of clinical supervision, especially for supervisees who are less experienced with this mode of therapy.

Paradigm 3: Moving Away From "Curing" Clients to Acting as a Catalyst for Inevitable Change

The second paradigm speaks more to the overt counseling skills involved in brief therapy while paradigm 3 has more to do with covert therapy or conceptualization skills. In other words, the catalytic model will encourage the supervisory dyad to focus on reconceptualizing client issues and therapy processes. The dyadic model encourages therapists and supervisors to conceptualize client issues in terms of characterological deficits that require intensive, long-term therapy. Discussions in supervision often involve in-depth analysis of clients' presenting pathology and define problems in such a way as to justify lengthy treatment. However, research has not supported the relative efficacy of interventions based on the dyadic model. Supervisors who operate well within the new paradigm will help supervisees conceptualize client problems in such a way that problems are solvable and represent barriers to normal development. For example, supervisory dyads are likely to spend time examining two questions. First, why did the client choose to come to therapy now? Second, what are the client's implicit contracts (i.e., unspoken expectations) with regard to therapy? Exploring these conceptualization issues is likely to help therapists be more effective and efficient in their work. Also, supervisors will help supervisees understand the limits of psychotherapy in terms of effecting personality change while reinforcing its effectiveness in helping clients function better as a result of increased coping skills and increased empowerment. Therapists will also need to find ways to encourage clients to maintain those changes with little on-going intervention.

Paradigm 4: More Change Occurs Outside the Therapist's Office than Within It

The implications for supervision under this paradigm are quite similar to those for paradigm 3. Effective supervisors will help supervisees understand that good therapy occurs when clients feel in control of the change process and perceive that they have worked hard in and out of therapy in order to improve their lives. Because many therapists are attracted to the field, because of a drive to help others, they are susceptible to creating client dependency. Cummings and Sayama (1995) describe this phenomenon as a need on the part of many therapists to feed their own narcissistic needs. Supervisors may need to help supervisees identify such needs and work toward empowering clients while decreasing dependency on therapy. This may require that the supervisor take on the role of therapist within supervision from time to time.

Paradigm 5: Therapy is the "Yeast for Growth" and Is Available as Needed Throughout the Lifespan

To effectively work within this paradigm, supervisees should be socialized to all of the catalytic paradigm shifts prior to beginning to work with clients. Time spent teaching supervisees about brief, intermittent therapy approaches and the rationale and research supporting their use, is very helpful.

Paradigm 6: Therapy Includes the Use of Every Healing Resource in the Community

Supervisors will need to be aware of community resources and encourage supervisees to make appropriate referrals as part of effective therapy.

Paradigm 7: Reimbursement for Services Will Move Away from Fee for Service to Case Rate or Capitation Systems

At the same time reimbursement for providing services is changing, so are laws regarding how supervision should be financed. In California, it is now illegal for supervisees to pay supervisors directly for providing supervision. Instead, the state laws encourage supervisees to be employed by supervisors or both to be employed by a third party. With the advent of capitated rates, this type of employment arrangement can be easier to implement. One barrier to this arrangement is that most managed care companies require that practitioners be licensed in order to provide contracted services. Unfortunately, this requirement could limit postgraduate opportunities for new therapists and lead to a limited pool of adequately trained therapists. In order to ensure that new practitioners are trained in the catalytic paradigm, more supervised postgraduate experiences in the managed care milieu will need to be developed.

SETTING THE STAGE FOR EFFECTIVE CLINICAL SUPERVISION

In accord with the paradigm shifts just reviewed, it is helpful to make several assumptions regarding the nature of supervision and psychotherapy. As with traditional modes of psychotherapy, traditional approaches to supervision often include assumptions that actually impede progress rather than promote it. These attitudes were not based on malicious intent, they were simply misguided. Therefore, this author has developed six assumptions that are somewhat analogous to Cummings' paradigm shifts that should help supervisors maintain an appropriate perspective while allowing for maximum growth of supervisees. Initially, an example of how not to approach supervision might be helpful.

During a recent consultation to an APA approved predoctoral internship site, this author was asked to help resolve a dispute between a supervisor and an intern. The intern had been reprimanded for refusing to work with a known perpetrator of domestic violence. Her reason was that she preferred to work with domestic violence survivors and felt that she would not provide the perpetrator with good services given her personal feelings. Her supervisor believed she was being insubordinate and needed to "work through" her underlying psychological difficulties if she were ever going to be an effective therapist. In fact, the supervisor went so far as to describe the therapist as suffering from "borderline personality disorder" and as being "stuck in her anger." Therefore, the supervisor decided that the therapist should provide services to this perpetrator in order to help the therapist "work through" her issues.

This example highlights some of the difficulties that arise in the dyadic paradigm of clinical supervision. First, the supervisory dyad had come to an impasse, and as the situation had been defined by the supervisor, there would be a winner and at least one loser. If the supervisor were to win, the supervisee would lose, and most likely, so would the client. Supervision requires the supervisor to look for ways for all parties to win, especially the client. Second, by diagnosing the supervisee, the supervisor had taken the stance of a therapist who had not made the shift to the catalytic model.

After speaking with the supervisee in some detail, no signs of an axis II disorder were detected. Instead, the discussion revealed a reasonable woman who was trying to act ethically and responsibly. By pathologizing the supervisee, the supervisor created a power struggle that was not likely to help the supervisee grow nor was it in the best interest of the client.

The supervisor was reminded of his primary duty to protect the client and to ensure adequate services were being provided. In addition, it was suggested that the most appropriate course of action would be to refer this client to someone with an interest in the treatment of perpetrators of domestic violence. The supervisee and the supervisor were encouraged to explore other ways to "work through" the supervisee's issues while finding a win-win compromise.

Such power struggles can be avoided if clinical supervisors can adopt the following assumptions about the nature of supervision.

Assumption 1: Supervisees Are Well-Meaning and Try to Do the Best Work They Can

It is unlikely that a therapist intentionally tries to hurt his or her clients. Mistakes are made, but intentional harm is rare.

Assumption 2: Supervisees Will Not Benefit From Being Diagnosed

It is better to focus on the supervisee's changeable behaviors than on diagnostic labels. As with solution-focused therapy, focusing on strengths and identifying exceptions to problems can help build on competencies. If a supervisee is truly impaired, then referral for treatment and appropriate legal and ethical action should be taken.

Assumption 3: Supervisees Move through Fairly Predictable Stages of Professional Development with or without Quality Supervision

Understanding these developmental processes can help supervisors intervene more effectively. In general, the less experienced the supervisee the more will be the benefit from being taught specific skills. As supervisees develop, they are more open to exploring their own personal reasons for becoming therapists and they benefit more from therapeutic and consultative supervision approaches. As they become more confident in their skills, the more they tend to focus on conceptualization issues in supervision. Stoltenberg (1981) and Loganbill, Hardy, and Delworth (1982) have provided detailed discussions of psychotherapists' developmental stages.

Assumption 4: The Supervisory Relationship Is Very Important

Unfortunately, supervision is often treated as an inconvenience or as less important than therapy itself. Yet, good, consistent supervision will likely improve quality of care and should therefore positively impact client satisfaction.

Assumption 5: It Is Best to Assume that Supervisees Know What They Need

By negotiating goals up front and respecting supervisees' points of view, supervision can run more smoothly. It helps to remember that supervision is a catalyst for growth much the way psychotherapy is. Therapists grow more outside of supervisory sessions than in them. Therefore, supervision should provide an atmosphere that allows supervisors to challenge supervisees within a highly supportive atmosphere. Building on supervisees' strengths is more helpful than pointing out every flaw.

Assumption 6: Supervision Is a Collaborative Process where the Supervisee Provides the General Direction and the Supervisor Guides the Process

In other words, supervisees should decide on the initial goals of supervision and supervisors should create the appropriate learning environment. Of course, there are exceptions. Because client welfare is the most important goal of supervision, there are times when the supervisor will need to decide on the goals of each session, as well. However, if the ground rules for dealing with such exceptions are discussed early in the relationship and it is made clear that the client is the reason for therapy, these exceptions should not be problematic.

These six assumptions set the back drop for collaborative, supportive supervisory environments. Within this framework, supervisees are more likely to hear and accept challenges and criticism. Any such challenges should be focused on skills and attitudes that the supervisee can change. While it is difficult for supervisees to change personality traits, they can change their behaviors and cognitions.

SUPERVISION AS RISK MANAGEMENT

Along with joining your supervisees in their efforts to grow and learn, supervisors must also be on the lookout for legal and ethical issues that can arise not only within psychotherapy relationships but also within the supervisory dyad. Space does not allow for a thorough discussion of legal and ethical issues; however, a few common concerns will be highlighted. For more information on legal and ethical concerns in supervision, the reader may refer to Disney and Stephens (1994).

First, as with psychotherapy, it is best to avoid dual relationships within supervision. Because supervisors can be held legally responsible for the actions of their supervisees, objectivity is necessary in order to avoid potentially damaging situations for clients and supervisees. For example, by becoming too much of a friend to supervisees, supervisors may lose their willingness to challenge their supervisees. This, in turn, may limit supervisees' ability to provide the best possible treatment.

Dual relationships can be damaging to supervisees, as well. In a recent consultation, a supervisor had approached a number of his supervisees asking them to join him in a business proposition that was unrelated to the provision of mental health services. In order to become part of this business, the supervisees were required to invest fairly large sums of money with no guarantee of financial return. One of the supervisees asked for outside consultation when he began feeling a great deal of pressure from the supervisor to invest money. The supervisee did not want to invest but was afraid (and rightfully so) that not doing so could lead to negative outcomes for him. As it turned out, the supervisor was about to provide evaluations of the supervisees' performance as interns and those evaluations were to be sent to the supervisees' graduate schools. This kind of dual role is clearly unethical and in some states illegal.

Two rules of thumb apply to the ethical provision of supervision. First, assure that no harm is done to clients. Second, do no harm to supervisees. As one might surmise, sexual relationships between supervisor and supervisee are also unacceptable.

In terms of legal issues, clinical supervisors take on significant legal risk. By definition, supervisors can be held legally responsible for the actions of their supervisees. If a supervisee acts unethically or illegally, the supervisor can be held accountable. Recently, a psychologist was found liable in a civil suit because his supervisee had sex with a client. The court ruled that the acts of the supervisee were under his purview as a supervisor and the doctrine of *Respondeat Superior* was applied. In other words, his role as supervisor made him vicariously liable for the supervisee's actions. This was a rather extreme judgment on the court's part and is included to alert supervisors to some of the risks inherent in providing supervision. Not all courts would have found him liable depending on the details of the case.

In addition to the court's findings, the state board reprimanded the supervisor because it felt he had not provided adequate supervision. His supervisory practices consisted of meeting with this supervisee once a month over lunch, a level of supervision that was clearly below the standards of practice.

TEN STEPS TO EFFECTIVE CLINICAL SUPERVISION

In order to provide adequate clinical supervision, supervisors will need to devote sufficient time and effort to supervision. All too often clinical supervision is treated as an after thought, especially in agency settings. This is probably the case due to service delivery systems' focus on productivity and their lack of understanding of the risk involved in not devoting adequate resources to supervisory practices. However, adhering to the following steps to clinical supervision and documenting supervision processes carefully can help supervisors manage much of the risk inherent in this important role.

Step 1: Evaluate Your Ability to Supervise

Before deciding to take on the role of clinical supervisor, one should ask, "Am I truly prepared to be a clinical supervisor?" Someone who is prepared will have a strong background in providing the type of services their supervisees are providing. It is unethical to provide supervision for specialty areas that are outside one's competencies as a psychologist. For example, a psychologist trained and experienced only in the provision of services for adults should not supervise the work of a trainee providing services for children.

Also, before taking on the role of supervisor, one should have been trained in supervision theory and practice. Continuing education workshops are available for practitioners who would like to become supervisors and there are increasing opportunities for advanced training in clinical supervision through professional seminars, national associations, and training institutes across the country. The American Association of Marriage and Family Therapists (AAMFT) has a highly developed program for training and certifying its clinical supervisors. AAMFT's standards are the most rigorous of all standards for supervision training in the country.

Step 2: Evaluate a Potential Supervisee's Strengths and Needs

One way to reduce risk as a supervisor is to closely screen potential supervisees prior to agreeing to provide supervision. Asking for letters of recommendation and talking to persons familiar with their work can help supervisors identify quality supervisees.

It is also important to assess a supervisee's general level of experience and training. The less experienced the supervisee the more likely she will be to need structured, didactic interventions. As supervisees gain experience and confidence, they tend to benefit more from less directive interventions and more collegial approaches. Understanding their developmental level as therapists allows supervisors to tailor supervisory environments that can foster growth. Again, Stoltenberg (1981) and Loganbill et al. (1982) provide good overviews of such developmental processes and offer suggestions as to how to match supervision strategies to the needs of the supervisee.

It may also be wise to ask potential supervisees directly about their preferred theoretical orientation and their attitudes with regards to providing brief, effective therapy. Choosing supervisees with similar attitudes and theoretical stance is likely to improve the supervisory relationship.

Step 3: Conduct a Role Induction

Research by Bahrick, Russell, and Salmi (1991) indicated that satisfaction with clinical supervision can be improved if supervisees know what to expect from supervision. Taking the time to socialize supervisees to their roles and explaining the particular approach to supervision reduces the likelihood that they will be disappointed. Bahrick et al. (1991) simply introduced supervisees to Bernard's model of clinical supervision in a 15-minute introductory session. This brief introduction led to significant improvements in supervisor and supervisee satisfaction.

It may also be wise to describe the supervisor's approach to therapy in some detail. While the purpose of supervision should be to help supervisees develop their own style of psychotherapy, supervisors' theoretical stances will influence their supervisees. The more supervisees know about the supervisor's approach at the onset of supervision, the more likely they are to find ways to incorporate that influence in positive ways.

As mentioned earlier, some supervisees will come to supervision with negative attitudes regarding the catalytic paradigm of psychotherapy. Socializing these supervisees presents a unique challenge. Trying to change their attitudes too soon can have a negative effect.

This author recently supervised a therapist who had been trained in a nondirective, affective-oriented mode of therapy. She wanted to learn how to survive in private practice in a managed-care dominated metropolitan area. However, she was very angry that she would not be able to continue to practice in her preferred mode. Attempts to explain why third-party payers were no longer willing to pay for longer term approaches such as the one she had been using merely elicited arguments designed to convince the supervisor that insurance companies should pay for such therapy approaches. This approach had back-fired.

It became helpful to join this supervisee in her frustration. Allowing her to vent her frustration and grieve the loss of her expectations about what a career in psychology was going to be enabled her to eventually hear why the mental health delivery system was changing. By validating her emotions, she was helped to find a way to listen to this author's socialization attempt. Finally, she eagerly accepted the invitation to read a few books on brief approaches to psychotherapy. This was the first step in the retraining of a talented provider.

Step 4: Review Legal and Ethical Issues

Before starting actual clinical supervision, it is wise to review legal and ethical standards with supervisees.

About a year ago, this author was asked to consult on a lawsuit that was brought against a psychologist who had supervised a number of paraprofessionals providing phone coverage for a 24-hour crisis line. The supervisor had set aside time to go over legal and ethical issues with this group of supervisees at the time they were hired. However, one supervisee missed this group supervision session. Unfortunately, that particular paraprofessional later arranged for a meeting with a woman who had called the crisis line. A romance blossomed between the woman and the crisis worker and a sexual relationship ensued. It turned out that the woman was married to a lawyer and he sued the psychologist for causing him harm. The lawyer's argument was that the psychologist had not provided adequate training and supervision to the paraprofessional. While a verdict has not been reached, the moral of the story is to never assume that supervisees know how to act ethically. Always review legal and ethical standards before a supervisee provides any services under your supervision.

Step 5: Negotiate the Goals of Supervision

Before actually providing supervision, one more step is necessary. Henry Kissinger once said, "If you don't know where you're going, any road will get you there." Meeting with a supervisee for a goal-setting session can help improve the effectiveness of supervision.

As with therapy, the first session of supervision is very important. Negotiating goals of supervision is much the same as negotiating the complaint in solution-focused therapy. By using presuppositional language and focusing on behaviors, attainable goals can be negotiated. An effective question to ask supervisees is: "What will be different about you as a therapist due to our work together?" This question assumes supervisee growth and empowers them to define the goals of supervision. Supervisors can guide supervisees' responses by focusing on skill areas that are important to therapy processes (e.g., therapy skills and intervention, conceptualizing and understanding client issues, and supervisees' personal issues that might affect their work).

Step 6: Think and Act Like a Supervisor

After adhering to steps 1 through 5, the supervisor is finally ready to conduct supervision. However, supervisors are prone to making some common mistakes. First, because of their backgrounds as psychotherapists, supervisors often have difficulty switching mindsets from therapist to supervisor (Borders, 1992). Many supervisors try to get supervisees to become their surrogate therapists. Such supervisors spend much of their time telling supervisees what to do and how to do it. This didactic approach does not appear to be very effective (except with novice therapists) and supervisees often leave such supervision feeling very dissatisfied.

The second way in which supervisors fail to make the transition from therapist to supervisor is by focusing too much on the client in supervision. Much of the supervisory session can be spent on trying to conceptualize client dynamics with little attention being paid to how to help the supervisee be a more effective therapist. Focusing on the supervisee's behaviors and thought processes in the session is often more productive than pondering client issues ad infinitum. Also, focusing on dynamics present in therapy sessions can be very enlightening and lead to appropriate treatment interventions.

For example, a current supervisee came to a recent supervisory session prepared to discuss a high-risk client. He wanted help in this case because he was feeling stuck and was unable to help the client become less depressed.

The client was a 42-year-old woman who had recently separated from her husband. She had become quite depressed, even though it was her idea to separate and she was looking forward to the upcoming divorce. During the course of treatment (i.e., three sessions) her depression worsened and she became suicidal. This was in spite of the fact that the supervisee had done an excellent job helping the client define her goals and contracting the steps the client could take to alleviate the depression. Also, the client had been appropriately referred to a psychiatrist and was taking antidepressants.

The supervisee conceptualized the client's depression to be the result of the guilt she was feeling about having an ongoing affair with her best friend's husband. This was particularly troublesome for the client because of her religious beliefs. As a result, the supervisee had explored ways in which the client could terminate the affair or reconcile her belief system with her actions. This approach hit a dead end. The client refused and the supervisee asked, "What should I do?"

It turned out the right answer to the question was not to give the supervisee the answer directly. This would have been congruent with trying to get him to be the supervisor's surrogate therapist. It was also inappropriate to spend a great deal of time conceptualizing the client's problem in terms of cognitive distortions or resistance to treatment. Instead, it was helpful to explore the dynamics that were emerging between the therapist and the client.

The supervisee was asked how he felt working with the client and he confided he was quite frustrated and felt stuck. What was frustrating to him about the case? He responded that the client was resistant to all of his suggestions. On the one hand, she was asking for help in reducing her depression, yet she refused to do the things that would help her the most. This simple inquiry led the supervisee to identify the client's unsaid expectations about therapy. She wanted her depression to go away, but she did not want to make any changes herself. She wanted her therapist to magically fix her. In other words, she was not a customer for therapy. By understanding this, the supervisee decided to confront her directly and let her know what her choices were. She could decide to change her behaviors or modify her belief system or she could choose to be depressed. He also told her that he could not make things better for her without her joining him in the change process. This confrontation led to the client's saying, "My God, you're right. I was looking for you to save me. I guess I have to do that." She ended the affair and immediately got more involved in her church. Her depression lifted in less than 3 weeks.

By staying one step ahead of the supervisee in mind while remaining one step behind him in actions, the supervisor empowered the supervisee to find the answer he was looking for. As with clients in therapy, having supervisees generate answers in supervision is much more powerful than generating answers for them.

Step 7: Monitor and Document the Progress of Supervisees and Their Clients

There are many ways to monitor the work of supervisees. All too often, however, supervisors depend on supervisees' self-reports of what is happening with clients. This is not an advisable practice in that self-reports are not a reliable means of collecting information. If at all possible, actual samples of supervisees' work should be reviewed on a regular basis. These samples are best taken from live observation of therapy sessions through one-way mirrors or by viewing portions of videotaped sessions. Reviewing actual work samples allows for more in-depth supervision to occur and is a wise risk management strategy.

Live observation is valuable. However, the supervisees are not able to see themselves in action and immediate feedback interrupts the therapy session. At the same time, feedback provided after an observed session relies on the memories of the parties involved. Therefore, videotapes are probably the most valuable tool for supervisors to utilize. They allow the supervisor and supervisee to review sessions together and the quality of feedback afforded is unsurpassed. Audiotapes can be helpful, but a great deal of data are lost in terms of nonverbal interactions between client and therapist.

In addition to reviewing samples of live or taped sessions, it is also wise to review a supervisee's charts periodically. Almost all managed care companies review client charts as a way of assuring and improving quality. By reviewing charts, supervisors can provide feedback on quality of charting and can keep abreast of the treatment and discharge plans for larger numbers of clients.

It is not enough to simply monitor the work of supervisees. Supervisors who are interested in managing their own risk will also document their work with supervisees. Keeping progress notes of supervisory meetings provides evidence that supervision is being provided and that client welfare is being monitored. While no standards exist for how to document supervision, it may be helpful to develop forms that meet the needs of the organization in which the supervision is taking place. In particular, documentation of discussions regarding cases that are deemed high risk should be included in the clients' charts. As lawyers are quick to remind psychologists, "If it isn't documented, it didn't happen."

Step 8: Renegotiate Goals

As supervision unfolds, information about supervisees emerges that was not available at the time the relationship started. About two to three months into the relationship, it is a good practice to provide a midterm evaluation and renegotiate the goals for supervision. A good evaluation is one that holds no surprises for the supervisee. In other words, good supervision involves ongoing feedback and the midterm evaluation should simply be a summary of the feedback already provided. This evaluation naturally leads to a discussion of where to go next. Again, behavioral and attitudinal goals that are attainable should be identified. This time, supervisors may want to make suggestions based on their observations of the supervisee's needs and strengths.

Step 9: Evaluate Supervisee's Performance at End of Supervision

When the supervisory relationship comes to a close, a thorough evaluation of the supervisee's strengths and weaknesses as a therapist should be provided. This evaluation should also give feedback with regard to progress made toward the goals that were mutually agreed upon. Once again, this evaluation is not a time for surprises; it should simply summarize the feedback given during the supervisory process.

A number of evaluation tools have been developed and published that can help guide the evaluation process. Bradley (1989), Michaels (1982), and Powell (1993) provide overviews of these paper and pencil tasks.

Step 10: Elicit Feedback from Supervisee

In order for supervisors to become better at what they do it is essential that they allow supervisees a forum for candid feedback. A written evaluation of the supervisor at the end of the relationship allows the dyad to bring closure to the relationship and acts as a form of feedback as well as a ceremony marking the end of an important relationship. It is essential that supervisors openly accept this feedback and learn from it.

It should be noted that time-limited supervision is likely to be more useful than ongoing supervision. A period of 6 months to a year is probably about as long as one supervisee should work with one supervisor. After that amount of time the supervisor's suggestions begin to be redundant and little is passed along that is new to the supervisee. Changing supervisory dyads can help rejuvenate the supervisory experience.

CONCLUSIONS

By now it is probably apparent that supervision done correctly can be time consuming and yet very rewarding. In order to provide good learning opportunities while managing risk appropriately, supervisors will need to take supervision quite seriously. Adequate supervision probably requires a time commitment of about 2 hours of a supervisor's time for every 10 hours of clinical service each supervisee provides. A minimum of one hour of face-to-face, individual supervision should be provided on a weekly basis. Some states, including California, require graduate level trainees to receive a minimum of the equivalent of one hour of individual supervision for every 5 hours of direct service. Again, it is wise to be intimately familiar with the laws that govern supervisory practices in one's jurisdiction.

It may also be wise to provide group supervision opportunities to supervisees. Making formal case presentations can be valuable learning experiences and they allow supervisees to learn from each other. Also, group supervision can be a time-effective means for monitoring high-risk cases. Focused and well-structured groups permit discussion of difficult cases and supervisees can receive suggestions about how to manage those cases effectively. Peer consultation, along with good documentation, is an excellent combination for risk management.

Regardless of the context in which supervision or consultation occurs, the processes involved can be fun and exciting. While our profession is struggling with the challenges of providing mental health services in an ever changing environment, the need for quality clinical supervision is on the rise. Mental health professionals who prepare themselves adequately to be clinical supervisors are also likely to be well prepared to meet these challenges and thrive in the era of managed care.

PART III

The Practitioner as Manager and Astute Businessperson

8.

Can a Practitioner Manage a Comprehensive Health System?

Greg T. Greenwood, Ph.D., M.B.A.
Kristina L. Greenwood, Ph.D.

> *Just as it is impossible to be both high and low risk, we can't expect both autonomy and security.*
>
> *Morris R. Schechtman*

The experiences which we have encountered as traditionally trained psychologists who have made the transition to managers of comprehensive health systems have been remarkable in facilitating our professional and personal growth. While we were both initially introduced to managed care by joining American Biodyne at the same time in 1986, we have taken different career paths since then. As described within this chapter, Kris has maintained a strong emphasis on the clinical aspects of management, while Greg has ventured more into the business side of managed care operations.

KRISTINA L. GREENWOOD:
EXPERIENCES AS A CLINICAL MANAGER

During the 10 years of my professional career, I have been fortunate to have had a variety of experiences and to have achieved goals that I never could have imagined while a doctoral student in a traditional clinical psychology training program. I attribute a great deal of this to "being in the right place at the right time," as behavioral healthcare was beginning to change quite dramatically at the time of my graduation from Bowling Green State University in 1985. My first position as a newly licensed staff psychologist was at South Central Community Mental Health Centers in Bloomington, Indiana. This role was consistent with my traditional background, as I primarily provided assessment and therapy services in the adult outpatient and intensive outpatient programs. After a year, however, I had the opportunity to join American Biodyne's new staff model operations in Indianapolis, as one of a start-up group of seven psychologists hired to perform direct services for Biodyne's first fully at-risk contract.

After working as a staff psychologist for Biodyne for two years, I was offered the chance to move into a clinical management role. My various management experiences with Biodyne over the next four years included work as a center director of a staff model operation and regional clinical director of a four-state area that included HMO, PPO, and other service delivery arrangements. Subsequently, I was promoted to the position of corporate training and development director, which included oversight of all Biodyne training programs for staff, network providers, and clinical managers, as well as involvement in the development and implementation of a quality management program.

When my husband, Greg, and I relocated to Texas in 1992, I became director and later vice president of clinical operations with a large behavioral healthcare group practice in Dallas, which was owned by a psychiatrist and included a multidisciplinary staff. This group practice was one of the first in the Dallas/Fort Worth metropolitan area to provide a full continuum of services for a large capitated managed care contract at full risk. After 2½ years with that organization, I joined CORPHEALTH, Inc. in May 1995 as vice president of clinical development. CORPHEALTH is a managed behavioral healthcare company which specializes in the integration of healthcare systems and currently covers over 700,000 lives throughout the United States, with corporate offices located in Fort Worth.

Throughout these various experiences, I have discovered that there are significant parallels between becoming an effective manager in a comprehensive health system and the transition from being a traditional practitioner to a brief, solution-oriented therapist. This process of transition has been described by Nicholas Cummings as involving seven "paradigm shifts" (Cummings, 1995b). In particular, a catalytic therapist as well as a manager in a dynamic behavioral healthcare system must be active, focused, responsive, efficient, and creative in order to be effective in a rather fast-paced and constantly changing environment. I will now describe my experiences both as a traditionally trained psychologist and a practitioner and manager within the new managed care systems, as a means to illustrate some of these common paradigm shifts.

The Paradigm Shift to Brief Episodes of Care

The paradigm shift from seeing relatively few patients for lengthy courses of treatment to seeing patients for brief episodes of care is relatively consistent with the experiences that many practitioners have had in working with community mental health populations during their graduate or internship training, and often within postdoctoral work settings in the public sector. Within the current healthcare environment in private settings, there has been a marked shift in focus from individual based care to populations. This shift emphasizes the need for maximizing resources and making behavioral healthcare available to as many people as possible, and not just accessible for the "privileged" or those with comprehensive insurance coverage. This trend is especially encouraging to the future of behavioral healthcare service delivery, as it emphasizes the importance of mental health as an essential component of general health.

By necessity, when a fixed group of people within a service area has access to limited services and/or resources, there is a trend toward delivering treatment in a shorter term model. It is also the case that services in such settings tend to be delivered in response to a "crisis" that is being experienced by a patient, rather than a desire for personal growth or self-actualization. This reality is ideally compatible with the planned practice of brief episodes of treatment, as the patient will often choose to terminate treatment once the crisis or initial presenting problem is resolved. This is consistent with Kardner's crisis theory as described in "A Methodological Approach to Crisis Theory" (Kardner, 1975). Community mental health settings also frequently expose a practitioner to nontraditional forms of treatment, such as group modalities, day treatment and partial hospitalization programs, crisis triage services, and medication groups.

I gained some experience in working with patients in a brief time frame during my graduate and internship training, as well as my first postdoctoral position at a community mental health center. However, the first time that such short-term practice patterns were presented within a model that was planned, rather than occurring by default, was through my training and initial experiences with American Biodyne in 1986.

I was fortunate to have had such an experience early in my professional career, although it felt so "right" and consistent with my intuitive sense of what treatment could and should be, that I suppose I would have embraced such concepts even if the exposure had been later in my career. It helped that the psychodynamic theoretical base that I had acquired during graduate and particularly internship experiences was consistent with the manner in which Nicholas Cummings conducted training for Biodyne clinicians. The things that changed most dramatically were the pace of the therapy (i.e., "hit the ground running"), the integration of techniques from various schools of therapy that may actually be employed by the therapist, and especially the activity level of both the therapist and the patient.

As I practiced as a staff psychologist for the first two years of my career with Biodyne, I became much more comfortable and proficient with the diverse techniques of therapy. I believe that this is the case for many practitioners, who may acquire the intellectual "big picture" of theoretical ideas, but need to develop their own sense of what actually works and doesn't work when it comes to dealing with actual patients.

Within my roles as a manager of a comprehensive health system, I have trained numerous clinicians who deliver direct treatment services (as a therapist in a staff model clinic or network provider for a managed care company), as well as clinical case managers who conduct utilization review with providers. It is essential that clinicians recognize and take into account that the transition from a traditional practice pattern to a managed care role cannot be "forced." It has been my experience that a number of people say and may actually believe that they can work as a brief, solution-oriented therapist, but their actual practices are inconsistent with this. It is not an easy transition, as many therapists may shorten the actual length of an episode of care, but really believe in their hearts that they could have done more, or the patient might have benefited from a longer term treatment. It takes an honest search of one's beliefs and practices to stay focused and continually ask, "In what ways is the patient ready to change?"; "What are realistic and observable treatment goals?" and other challenging questions that do not give the therapist much time to lay back and "assess" a great deal. Truly brief therapy is active, not passive, and requires continual consideration of changes if an approach or technique is not working well, for the benefit of the patient's progress.

In addition to training practitioners and the case managers who interact with them, my roles in management have also included a focus on identifying what is required to be a "preferred" provider or how to define and establish a "smart network." This addresses issues of provider profiling and "report cards," such that therapists must be not only *efficient* in terms of using brief therapy approaches, but must also demonstrate *effectiveness* with such techniques. Depending upon the types of patients and disorders that a therapist works with, these questions cannot be simply addressed by an examination of how many sessions a provider utilizes, or the average length of stay per episode of care. The more complex, but ideal definition of efficiency takes into account the outcomes that the therapist achieves with patients, who may encompass a rather select group for a specialist provider, or a diverse group for a generalist. The issue of outcomes has been extremely challenging to define, measure, and analyze in a meaningful way for both the provider community and clinical managers within managed care companies.

In this regard, it is an advantage that psychologists' traditional training has focused heavily on research (i.e., the scientist–practitioner model). Thus, the research on treatment outcomes that has been supportive of managed care practices (e.g., outpatient chemical dependency treatment is just as effective as inpatient;

group modalities are more effective than individual therapy for many disorders) can be more easily considered with an open mind. Psychologists' training in scientific methodologies also helps to prepare them for scrutinizing the more traditional theories and practice patterns which have been challenged in the research literature.

The Paradigm Shift to Intermittent Therapy Throughout the Life Cycle

The paradigm shift from viewing treatment as continuous and occurring weekly or more often to treatment as brief and intermittent throughout the life cycle is sometimes easier for practitioners to accept because it generally reflects the reality in practice. Clinicians who have practiced in many settings have come to realize that most people do not want long-term (and sometimes never-ending) therapy. Some of this reflects the social stigma that is still attached to "mental illness," but it is also the case that people in pain want relief, or a "fix" as soon as possible. Many therapists seem to experience relief themselves that the expectation is no longer that they must foster the patient's dependency and "keep" someone in treatment longer than the patient desires or really needs. It is rewarding to the patient and the therapist to mutually agree to discontinue treatment at appropriate times, with the understanding that the patient may return as needed in the future.

Practitioners who successfully make this paradigm shift also tend to be practical, and relatively familiar with the various techniques and models of therapy. An emphasis during graduate training or experiences with classical psychoanalytic theoretical concepts may seem contradictory with the catalyst model, but there are many articles, books, and continuing education opportunities which describe ways in which these traditional concepts may be incorporated into briefer models of treatment (e.g., Bloom, 1992; Budman & Gurman, 1988; Cummings & Sayama, 1995; Mann, 1973; Sifneos, 1987; Strupp & Binder, 1984). This idea may also be integrated with the research on psychotherapy which a psychologist in training has usually encountered, such that no particular model or technique has been demonstrated to be "superior," but the therapeutic relationship between the practitioner and patient is central to perceived success (Frank, 1984).

With respect to my own experiences, although I chose to concentrate on psychodynamic principles during my internship training, I came to the conclusion that there were marked similarities among the different theories, regardless of the differences in terminology. Even though I still tend to conceptualize cases in terms of psychodynamic principles, the techniques which I have used have varied greatly, depending upon the patient's presentation and what seems to be best tailored to the individual's capabilities and strengths. What has been helpful in my own work as a therapist or in consulting with providers is to determine what therapeutic approaches seem best suited for the patient, and to be very active in switching to a different strategy sooner rather than later if something is not working effectively. Furthermore, if an approach or technique has not worked previously, there is no need to repeat it over and over. Too often, the patient has been "blamed" as being "resistant," and the therapist will rigidly keep trying to accomplish something that is doomed to failure at a particular time and juncture within the therapeutic process. Dr. Michael Bennett's work on the phases of focal psychotherapy is especially relevant in determining the patient's "readiness" for change (Bennett, 1984, 1989).

An emphasis on this catalytic model of treatment has been particularly useful to me in training and selecting providers who will work well within a managed care system. It is very important that therapists establish at the outset the expectation that treatment will be as brief as possible, as well as intermittent throughout the patient's life, particularly if the individual has experienced or believes that therapy is "supposed to be" continuous and longer term in nature. While some patients, especially those with dependency needs, will resist or reject the idea that therapy is ideally brief and intermittent, many will actually be relieved that they can be helped and then be free to live their lives without the constant "crutch" of therapy. It has often been helpful to borrow an analogy from the medical model in these circumstances, such that the initial "dose" of therapy will assist the patient with understanding and making changes in attitudes, behaviors, and life situations that will lead them toward better functioning and satisfaction.

However, this "dose" of therapy is not a "cure" and the patient may occasionally require a "booster shot." Furthermore, an educational approach may be utilized to advise the patient of some warning signs and descriptions of symptoms which may indicate that a return to treatment is warranted.

In working with providers and case managers in a managed care setting, the concept of brief intermittent therapy throughout the life cycle also becomes central to the focus on "maximizing the patient's benefits." Most patients with insurance benefits have limitations on the number of inpatient days and outpatient sessions that are covered during a year, so that limiting the number of sessions per episode of care or spacing out sessions as quickly as possible becomes appropriate, to ensure that the benefits are not used up more quickly than necessary. This reality provides yet another incentive for the therapist to work as rapidly as possible, and to encourage nontraditional forms of treatment (e.g., self-help groups, community resources, etc.) that the patient may utilize to facilitate and reinforce his or her progress.

The Paradigm Shift to Therapy as a Catalyst for Growth

Another paradigm shift which is closely related to the transition to intermittent therapy involves the traditional concept that the therapist is the vehicle for change, with an emphasis on treating psychopathology. This is a carryover from the medical model, which promotes the "doctor" as the "healer" who can "cure" an "illness." This idea is often attractive to both the patient and the therapist, as the patient wants to depend on someone for relief from emotional pain and suffering, and the therapist's ego is inevitably gratified. Most therapists discover rather quickly, however, that the catalyst model, which proposes that the therapist is merely a catalyst for the patient to change and return to a natural homeostasis, is the reality, because the patient will not be changed unless he or she is open and ready for it.

Most traditional training programs for psychologists have tended not to explore the fallibility of the medical model "cure" concept, although this may be changing in more recent years. It becomes clouded by a number of factors, including the emphasis and research on biological influences which play a significant role in many disorders such as depression, schizophrenia, and perhaps even addictive disorders. It becomes tempting at times to oversimplify this and be attracted by the concept of "cure," when many patients will respond quite favorably to psychotropic medication. However, most practitioners have had early experiences with patients who clearly demonstrate the complexities of a biopsychosocial model of psychiatric disorders, where the concept of "cure" is not as easily incorporated. For example, even patients who benefit from medications still need intermittent therapy to ensure that changes in beliefs, behaviors, and life-styles will reinforce their progress. It becomes more apparent that the notion of "cure" is overly simplistic and even misguided, when characterological (DSM-IV, Axis II) disorders are considered (APA, 1994). For such problems, most practitioners have discovered that they may play the role as "guide" in the therapy process, but lasting change is unequivocally the responsibility of the patient.

The paradigm shift to the belief that therapy is an artificial situation has also not been well addressed in traditional graduate training programs, but seems to be realized through the experience base of the psychologist. This is in direct contrast to classical psychoanalytic training, where therapy is perceived as the most important event in the patient's life. Most therapists have gained an appreciation of the power and natural impact that the patient's real life experiences have in affecting his or her mental status and progress, whether positive or negative, regardless of what was happening during therapy. However, the therapist learns that this challenge can be successfully addressed by encouraging the patient to examine the patterns of emotions, attitudes, and reactions, in order to develop a greater awareness of his or her role in a developmental context and thus set the stage for genuine behavior change.

It is also of interest to consider that patients who react as if therapy (and the therapist) are the most important things in life may actually be dealing with dependency and transference issues. Thus, it is not the therapist who is most important, but events or relationships in the patient's life that are being recreated within the therapeutic relationship. The fact that significant changes occur and keep occurring long after therapy has been discontinued is also reassuring to most therapists, who may see the positive impact of the therapy long after the patient has terminated a course of treatment.

The manner in which this principle has been illustrated most powerfully to me is with patients who have actually returned to therapy, after a previous course of "intermittent therapy throughout the life cycle." Through these experiences, I have seen first hand how this process has unfolded. Some patients have changed significantly since I had first seen them, and yet become "stuck" in a somewhat familiar place that could have been predicted based on what they were working on previously. It has been my experience that the "booster shot" concept works very well, in that patients are able to build quickly upon their previous gains, and may even be ready to tackle something that they were not ready for during the prior course.

The paradigm shift to the belief that therapy is yeast for growth outside therapy, which also reinforces that formal treatment is often interrupted and intermittent, is another fundamental expectation for the therapist to establish with a patient. While problems may be resolved and situations or symptoms may improve, the issues of the patient's life cannot be "cured" or "eradicated" like an infection or virus. The patient's past experiences will always be a part of life, and the treatment focus should concentrate more appropriately on adaptation and adjustment, so that growth may proceed. Even more biologically based disorders such as schizophrenia and depression have been manifested and understood in the context of a person's life experiences. The catalytic therapist will work with a patient to clearly understand this, and get away from the notion of "cure" or total happiness as an expected outcome of therapy. There is no "magic," but the patient can accept the fact that he or she has the ability and the responsibility to overcome obstacles, and work toward realistic treatment goals.

One way in which these paradigm shifts have been considered and approached by managed care companies is through efforts to measure outcome and determine what factors may play a role in recidivism. While the traditional notion of "cure" is not expected through any particular course of treatment, it is of great interest to determine what occurs or doesn't occur that impacts negatively on a patient's progress. Such investigations are helpful in establishing what is the ideal type of follow-up care for particular patients with particular disorders, especially as treatment tends to be intermittent rather than continuous, either by design or default. Issues of noncompliance, which tends to be very high among certain populations and disorders, also may be examined to determine what can be done to counteract this pattern. In addition, behavioral healthcare has been demonstrated to be a significant (and likely underestimated) factor in medical cost offset research (Cummings, 1993; Cummings, Dörken, Pallak, & Henke, 1993), which has far-reaching implications for what has yet to be accomplished with respect to preventative health care.

Another focus of many managed care systems is conducting follow-up surveys to determine the impact of a particular course of treatment. This approach to outcomes research is seen as essential to determining not only which providers are "successful," but also to explore what "practice patterns" are most efficient and effective. This is a very complex and difficult but vital area of investigation for managed care companies, and it is a fairly new area of emphasis within behavioral healthcare. Since managed care companies have become very similar in their approaches to pricing as a means of competition in the marketplace, the newer emphasis has been on what company can demonstrate the best results in terms of quality of care. This is even more complicated by the lack of common definition of what is meant by "outcomes," although some recent efforts have been initiated. For example, CORPHEALTH is one of 19 managed care companies throughout the nation which are members of the American Managed Behavioral Healthcare Association (AMBHA). This trade organization is in the process of implementing a joint venture project on a standardized "report card," which will assess the overall performance of the delivery systems of the participating member companies (AMBHA, 1995).

The Paradigm Shift to the Mobilization of Community Resources

The use of community resources to facilitate and support the mental health of a population, instead of relying solely on traditional modalities of individual and group therapy, is a more encompassing approach to treatment which emphasizes what many people seek from therapy with respect to positive, healthy relationships. Research clearly demonstrates that social supports are essential to mental health and are instrumental in the treatment of many disorders, including depression, chemical dependency, and even severe and persistent mental illness. The use of community resources also reinforces the notion that change can and will occur outside of the therapy situation, and these resources will not be necessarily transitory. Practitioners who have worked in community mental health settings have often developed a sense of how other resources may be mobilized to benefit the patient. As managed care has influenced practice patterns toward briefer, intermittent models, therapists in private settings have also been encouraged to consider other options, such as self-help groups and community resources, which can augment and sometimes replace more traditional forms and settings of therapy. One of the best examples is the use of Alcoholics Anonymous and other 12-step programs, which have demonstrated successful outcomes for many patients who have never been involved in any form of traditional psychotherapy.

In addition to the integration of community resources and a new emphasis on preventative health care, some relatively novel approaches have been developed by managed care companies in response to contracts with public sector populations, such as Medicaid and Medicare. This relatively "new frontier" has presented unique considerations and challenges with respect to issues such as social services, transportation, and government regulations. As one example, managed care companies have expanded the modalities by which care may be delivered to include home healthcare as a way to improve access to services, prevent costly inpatient care when possible, and improve treatment compliance.

The Paradigm Shift to Prospective Reimbursement Systems

With respect to the change from traditional fee-for-service economic models to prospective reimbursement or variations on capitation, many practitioners who have not been exposed to these different reimbursement systems are often fearful of the impact on their practices. Some of this is based on misconceptions, and some of it may be in reaction to a realistic change in economics for many therapists. Thus, the new emphasis on population based care has been viewed as more restrictive and potentially less lucrative. In addition, there are incentives, as well as competition, for practitioners to join various provider network panels, or associate with groups of clinicians rather than continue in a solo practice.

Some of the challenges that I have encountered as a manager toward achieving this paradigm shift have involved the education of providers who have been trained as traditional clinicians regarding some of the business and financial concepts that go hand in hand with managed care. These concepts and their implications for service delivery are frequently misunderstood and even practiced as involving "quotas" or other equally disconcerting notions. In reality, prospective reimbursement may be viewed as limiting to the therapist, or perceived as granting greater autonomy. It seems most important that the therapist has grasped the other concepts and paradigm shifts with respect to managed care practices (e.g., targeted, focused therapy which is intermittent throughout the life cycle) before the advantages of the prospective reimbursement model can be understood and practiced in an appropriate, ethical manner.

Therapists who have made this transition can be financially successful as they deliver services to a greater number of patients in an effective and efficient manner. Once this has been demonstrated to a managed care company, the therapist will also be more attractive because the company can invest its resources in fewer administrative controls (e.g., frequency of utilization review), and the provider network may be reduced to a more manageable size. The therapist benefits even further from this situation, as he or she will receive a greater number of referrals to support the practice.

As a manager, I have evaluated the provider's readiness for taking partial risk, subcapitation, or case rates, and availability for consultation during implementation. In addition, I have developed further knowledge through networking with the business managers of managed care organizations, as well as gaining from my experiences in implementing the clinical operations of programs based on various reimbursement models. One of the challenges as a clinical manager of such systems is to ensure that these financial arrangements do not inhibit the quality of services rendered to patients, so that neither over- nor underutilization occurs. Furthermore, there is typically less scrutiny and utilization review under such arrangements, yet it is still necessary to monitor how care is delivered, so that the autonomy given to providers does not result in a compromise of quality.

The Paradigm Shift to Developing New Expertise and Management Skills

As my experience with the paradigm shifts described above has been integrated with my roles as a manager, I have also been challenged by the need to develop knowledge and skills in other new areas which are relevant to today's managed care operations. I have especially enjoyed learning and developing expertise in the area of quality management. As healthcare and particularly managed care have been very carefully scrutinized, regulatory standards have been developed, such as the Utilization Review Accreditation Commission (URAC) and the National Committee on Quality Accreditation (NCQA). As a result, comprehensive quality management programs have been integrated within service delivery systems as a means to monitor and improve numerous aspects of quality, including utilization management, credentialing, medical records, member rights and services, and preventative care. As mentioned previously, managed care companies are also responding to the challenges of "proving" that they provide quality services and ensure successful outcomes of treatment.

My experiences in management have also involved frequent interaction with other multidisciplinary behavioral healthcare professionals, as well as professionals in medical–surgical healthcare, such as primary care physicians, medical directors, and healthcare administrators. With respect to personnel management, regardless of the individual's professional training or background, it is necessary to maximize one's abilities to adapt positively to change, reinforce flexibility, mobilize problem-solving skills and resources, and to create a spirit of entrepreneurial adventure.

Although I have maintained a strong emphasis on the clinical aspects of operations in my various management roles, it has frequently been necessary and quite valuable to learn more about the "business" of managed care, as I have often worked with individuals in various administrative, financial, and marketing roles. The joint projects which involve working directly with colleagues and other business-oriented partners are numerous, including the drafting of written responses to Requests for Proposals (RFPs) for new business contracts, implementation of start-up operations and transition to new delivery systems, development of innovative products and services, and the operationalization of clinical delivery systems into cost–resource projections as a means of budgeting. I see it as the primary objective of my role as the chief clinical manager within these interactions to balance considerations of cost with quality, in order to maintain and ensure the integrity of the clinical services which will be rendered to patients.

In conclusion, my roles as a manager in a dynamic behavioral healthcare system have required that I be active, focused, responsive, efficient, and creative in order to be effective in a fast-paced and constantly changing environment. Fortunately, I have had the opportunities to develop these skills over the years through my experiences and through learning from and working with some incredibly talented and visionary professionals, many of whom are also contributing to this book. The first 10 years of my professional career as a psychologist and manager have been extremely rewarding and challenging. I'm looking forward to the rest of the journey and feel that there are great opportunities ahead.

GREG T. GREENWOOD:
EXPERIENCES AS A BUSINESS MANAGER

In this section, I will not be directly addressing the paradigm shifts as described by Nicholas Cummings earlier in this book since they are primarily clinical fundamentals that practicing clinicians must master if they are to effect the changes necessary to survive. However, they are also relevant to the psychologist as manager in developing and directing a comprehensive behavioral health system, and were explored in this context earlier. I will be addressing the complexities of the business aspects relative to a traditional practitioner's transition to a managerial role. Suffice it to say that these paradigm shifts had to be taken into account in setting up a comprehensive care delivery system, as they impact significantly on the system's ability to function successfully.

During my 10 years of experience in managed behavioral healthcare, all but the initial four months have involved a role in some type of management, ranging from center director with American Biodyne in 1986 to my current position as vice president, behavioral health with Blue Cross and Blue Shield of Texas, Inc. My experience prior to managed care was as a practicing psychologist, first as an assistant professor at the Indiana University School of Medicine in the Department of Psychiatry, where I supervised clinical psychology interns and psychiatry residents and provided clinical services at a community mental health center. I subsequently worked as a staff psychologist at another community mental health center, prior to joining American Biodyne as a staff psychologist.

My preparation to assume a managerial role began in graduate school. My training as a psychologist prepared me in a unique way to understand the clinical aspects of the important role of behavioral health disorders and treatment. This traditional training also allowed me to enhance my "critical analysis" orientation and skills. Lastly, it provided me with other skills that I have found to be extremely useful in the business world. Key among these are the ability to critically evaluate a situation, the capacity to size up people and circumstances, and the ability to devise solutions that are supported by important stakeholders in order to accomplish the intended goals. Without question, I have found my training as a psychologist to be a major plus in preparing me for the roles I have played in management.

While my training as a psychologist was useful in a number of ways, it also biased me in some respects to thinking that *how*, and more importantly, *what* I was trained to practice were the best ways of doing things. It became necessary to recognize that maintaining an open mind about many things would be most productive. While I was trained in a psychodynamic tradition (in fact my mentor was a psychoanalyst), and taught the benefits, if not necessity, of longer term treatment to effect the kind of changes necessary in my patients for lasting results, I found this to be difficult in practical terms. Since most of the clinical services I provided had been in a community mental health center setting, the particular patients that were seen at these centers were middle class, fairly well educated, motivated, and highly verbal. Although my patients were good candidates for traditional psychodynamic therapy, money and time were pragmatic concerns for many of them, most of whom had full-time jobs and were raising families. Similar pragmatic concerns existed for the patients of the interns and residents I supervised, but for different reasons. As with most training programs, the interns and residents rotated through and could see a patient for a maximum of one year, and generally for a shorter period. It meant that progress needed to occur quickly, or the patient would have multiple therapists over time. I also found the use of hospitalization for many of the patients overly restrictive and an inefficient use of resources. To use an old cliché, it was like trying to kill a fly with a shotgun. Faced with the many pragmatic issues relative to my training and what these patients needed, I thought that there must be a better way to provide the treatment needed.

It was at this time that I was exposed to managed care, and the conceptualizations of Nicholas Cummings regarding "brief, intermittent psychotherapy throughout the life cycle." To me, this thinking was interesting and appeared that it could help overcome some of the pragmatic concerns I had encountered earlier. In addition, having kept up with the changes that were taking place at this time in healthcare, the managed aspects of the care as well as the novel reimbursement approaches were similar to what had been occurring in the medical and surgical area of healthcare on a substantial basis for a number of years, and made sense to me. As a result of my willingness to consider the possibility that what I had been taught may not be the best way to deliver behavioral healthcare, I took advantage of the opportunity to get into managed care. Such an openness to other ways of doing things has served me well throughout my career as a manager, because handling change successfully requires flexibility and the ability to adapt quickly.

Another important component of making the move into managed care was anticipating the future of behavioral healthcare.

My experiences during my relatively brief period of time out of graduate school had alerted me to concerns that existed with respect to providing behavioral health services, including their availability, cost, and perceived value by others. Recognizing these problems and the developing trends in behavioral healthcare, as well as my desire to be a part of what could develop, I felt a move into managed care was most appropriate. Part of what concerned me was the fact that there was an increasing possibility that behavioral health benefits would be substantially reduced by groups and insurance companies, unless behavioral healthcare costs could be controlled in another manner.

Accepting the Challenges of a Management Role

During my 6-year tenure at American Biodyne I held the positions of staff psychologist, center director, state director, and ultimately vice president and northern region general manager. As these opportunities presented themselves, I accepted the challenge of each, but not without apprehension and anxiety. My formal training for most of these roles was minimal, and the background experience I had was not much more significant. But I had a desire to become more knowledgeable about the business side of behavioral healthcare, and in fact sought out these opportunities.

As my training and experience had not prepared me specifically for these roles, I discovered that there were two very important aspects to meeting the challenge. One was hard work (including very long days) and the other involved asking a lot of questions. In addition, I read and watched others as much as possible, and paid attention to my own thoughts and gut feelings about things. While others may have had prior training and experiences in meeting the demands of a management role, it was necessary that I devote more time and attention in order not just to perform, but to excel in my roles. I also recognized the advantages of receiving more formal training and thus planned to obtain an MBA from Indiana University, where I had been accepted into their evening program. However, my schedule and the related necessity of business travel mitigated against this. I subsequently pursued an MBA at the University of Texas, Dallas immediately upon my move to Blue Cross and Blue Shield of Texas.

At the end of my tenure at Biodyne, I had progressed from being a psychologist delivering traditional clinical services to a senior manager who was responsible for profit and loss, finance, marketing, customer service, claims payment, network management, contracting, and many other aspects of the managed care business. Besides hard work, my active quest for knowledge and the motivation to develop the necessary skills to succeed, the most critical factor in the success I experienced was selecting the right people for the jobs that had to be filled as a part of my staff. Selection of these key individuals, I believe, played a significant role in my success. I surrounded myself with highly energetic and bright people who were uncompromising in getting the job done. They were not necessarily the most experienced, but they were the best in meeting the total demands of the job and situation, all things considered. My most critical piece of advice to aspiring managers is not to underestimate the importance of your staff in your own success. They truly can make or break you. If you are threatened by people on your staff who may exceed your competence, try being successful as a manager with staff who do not challenge you. It will be tough if not impossible!

I chose to pursue a managerial opportunity at Blue Cross and Blue Shield of Texas (BCBSTX) for a number of reasons. A key factor was my concern over the increasingly tumultuous nature of healthcare and the resulting impact on the industry. A shakedown was going to occur, and managed care was undergoing many changes. I also felt that the integration of behavioral health with medical and surgical services would become more important over time, and that increasing opportunities would exist in the insurance industry, a major purchaser of the carved-out behavioral health services. Thus, based on this perspective of the future, I believed that if I could find a situation where an insurer planned to develop its own managed behavioral health services system (or had its own and was looking for management talent to run the operation), it might afford more long-term opportunities for me, as well as the chance to work more intensively on the development of the behavioral health and medical–surgical interface—behavioral medicine—which I felt to be the next frontier for behavioral health.

The Transition to New Opportunities
at Blue Cross and Blue Shield of Texas, Inc.

When I joined Blue Cross and Blue Shield of Texas, in May 1992, it was as executive director of mental health. BCBSTX had recently initiated a major push into managed care and had quite astutely recognized the importance of giving special attention to mental health and chemical dependency. When I joined BCBSTX there were seven individuals working in behavioral health, four registered nurses and three technical staff. Today, our staff totals 78, including a full-time medical director and four other full-time psychologists.

The position at BCBSTX offered a unique opportunity in many ways, as well as many challenges in areas that I had not been exposed to previously, such as working within a large, complex organization and acquiring detailed knowledge of the operations of an insurance company. Other opportunities included the chance to develop a quality behavioral healthcare program, and to integrate it with medical and surgical services. As an organization, BCBSTX was undergoing a significant strategic redirection in response to the changes occurring in healthcare. Historically, as a traditional indemnity plan, BCBSTX was in the throes of a rapid transformation into a managed care organization. The implications of this change required BCBSTX to acquire managed care expertise, which was accomplished quite proficiently by hiring many key people with years of managed care experience. Furthermore, the structural requirements (both organizational and work processes) for a traditional indemnity company as compared with a managed care company required a complete overhaul of the existing structure, from the computer system to provider contracts. As a result, the tasks to be accomplished were enormous.

My first order of business was to develop an understanding of the current organization, its structure, and the patterns of interaction (e.g., alliances and conflicts) among key individuals in the organization. The importance of doing this cannot be understated. This task was even more difficult at the time because the organization was undergoing very fundamental changes. I had to learn both the workings of an insurance company (technically BCBSTX is not an insurance company but a "nonprofit hospital service corporation") as well as the "politics" of the organization. I pursued knowledge about the operations of an insurance company in two ways. First, I met with key individuals throughout the company who could describe the areas in which they worked and what they did. This was accomplished through meetings set up especially for this reason, as well as other meetings to address some specific issues. I asked a lot of questions, many of which I repeated until my knowledge was enhanced. I also read books which specifically described such operations, and gained a comprehensive knowledge base that supported my efforts.

As I developed an understanding of the politics of the organization, I found my training as a psychologist to be of significant value with respect to the structure and interpersonal dynamics. Still, however, it required dedicated attention to this task. Without recognizing the importance of how the organization operates, who related to whom and how as well as critical issues for key individuals, a strategic plan to enhance and integrate behavioral healthcare could have failed.

In coming to BCBSTX, it was important to develop specific goals for what I wanted, and needed, to accomplish. Certainly the ultimate goal was to develop the best behavioral health program in the marketplace, but this goal was inevitably long-term in nature. In order to be successful, I focused on the needs of BCBSTX in the near to medium term, while targeting a "best practices" goal for several years down the road. My near- and medium-term goals were to build a behavioral healthcare program that would support the sale of our health product and which was good enough so that groups would not be tempted to carve out their behavioral health benefits. A primary concern was also to achieve credibility within BCBSTX by achieving positive results with the behavioral health program and serving as a valuable resource-supplier to my internal BCBSTX colleagues within other departments. One of the most enjoyable and challenging opportunities at BCBSTX was building an operation essentially from scratch.

In order to accomplish this goal, not only was it necessary to develop the necessary infrastructure for a successful enterprise, but it was often necessary to envision the future so that the newly developed system took into account the changes in healthcare that were occurring. In this respect, consideration of the seven paradigm shifts that are described elsewhere in this book played a very important role. Ignoring these developments could have resulted in a program that would not meet my interim goals for the organization, much less my long-term goals.

In the early phase of development, BCBSTX had contracted with a company to help with setting up the infrastructure, rather than dedicate its own internal resources at a time when these resources were in short supply. This was a strategic decision that had been made by upper management prior to my coming on board, in addition to the decision to develop the capability internally rather than use a vendor on a long-term basis. Representatives of the contracted party provided assistance with respect to the needs of BCBSTX, but I also found it helpful to talk with friends of mine in the industry, as well as to tap into my own expertise. Over time, the components of the basic infrastructure (provider network, utilization management, and customer service components) were established and the operation was functioning quite well. The results, from a point early on to the present time, have been quite positive and very encouraging. The program was successful in meeting the goals I had established, and a degree of credibility was created that became invaluable in continuing with the process of enhancing the behavioral health program.

The Transition to Achieving Longer-Term Business Goals

With the basics in place, I was now faced with moving the program forward toward my stated goal of being recognized as a "best practices" behavioral health program. Very important in this effort was maintaining contact with experts in the industry, as I tried to sort out the questions and solutions that were necessary to move things forward. This was especially significant since I had experienced some degree of isolation while the operation was still in its infancy. Because I was the expert at BCBSTX in this area, I was the primary person that others looked to for anything relative to behavioral health. Due to the size of the operation at that time, other internal expertise was limited to one person with a background in the areas of customer service, claims, and utilization management, which thankfully complemented my own expertise. Thus, running ideas by others, or finding out how they viewed things, was exceedingly important. I was fortunate to be able to consult with a significant number of friends and colleagues whose opinions and resourcefulness I respected. Equally important was hiring additional expertise for internal positions. As additional management staff were hired, it allowed for an enhanced discussion and critique of the direction in which behavioral health might be headed, and how BCBSTX should respond. This also allowed more resources to research new areas that were developing and had to be addressed in our overall operations.

As this occurred, we were able to expand our areas of involvement and offer assistance to more people within BCBSTX, always maintaining the mindset that these people were also our customers. As BCBSTX explored getting involved in CHAMPUS, Medicare risk, and Medicaid projects, we proactively offered our assistance in researching and developing the model for delivering behavioral health services in these arenas. We decided to enhance our visibility as behavioral health experts by our willingness to handle all behavioral health matters for the company, while keeping up to date with new developments in the behavioral healthcare market.

Having accomplished the first two goals of establishing a behavioral health program that supported the sale of our health product and was strong enough that we were not a prime target for competitors with carved-out behavioral health programs, we were able to focus more actively on the goal of developing an industry "best practices" program and expanding our sphere of activity. While these two new goals were similar and complementary, they required attention to different things. For example, the time had come to enhance the visibility of the behavioral health program. My staff and I also wanted to offer our program as a carved-out product at the same time. In order to accomplish this, we decided that we needed a distinct identity.

This venture entailed getting into a totally new area for us, the development of a market identity and marketing materials which were specific to behavioral health. Fortunately, BCBSTX had excellent resources available to guide and assist us in the process. We also consulted with outside companies in selecting a name that could be registered (ultimately selecting INROADS^{SM} *Behavioral Health Services*), worked closely with copy writers to develop the marketing materials, and ultimately wrote a large portion of the copy ourselves. In the end, we developed first class marketing materials to use in enhancing our visibility and viability in the marketplace.

As we expanded our sphere of activity, we took on increasing roles in many areas including responding to requests for proposals (RFPs) for new business contracts. With the development of the carved-out product, it was also necessary to work more closely with the proposal writing section within BCBSTX, as well as the actuaries, in the pricing of this new product line. Development of the carved-out product line also necessitated involvement with the State of Texas Department of Insurance.

At the same time that we were expanding our basic program to include new products such as a statewide Employee Assistance Program (EAP), a natural extension of our current programs, we also worked on projects leading toward the development of an industry "best practices" program and new developments that were occurring in healthcare which we needed to incorporate into our behavioral health program. Many of these activities involved a major commitment of resources, and thus the skillful prioritization of tasks to be accomplished with finite resources.

Accreditation by the National Committee for Quality Assurance (NCQA) became a priority for BCBSTX as a whole. We continue to work with the quality management department of BCBSTX in order to ensure that we incorporate the NCQA standards into all aspects of our behavioral health program. Outcomes studies are also a key area and one that we are devoting increasing attention to for several reasons. First, the demonstration of positive outcomes for subscribers receiving care is becoming increasingly important in competing successfully in the healthcare market. Second, outcomes tie in directly with assuring quality care, and lastly, outcomes relate directly to cost effectiveness of the resources devoted to providing care. In my role, I oversee the determination of what should be looked at, how the study should be designed, and of course the costs. The actual day-to-day handling of our outcomes efforts are the responsibility of one of my staff, also a clinical psychologist, and such a role is well suited to psychologists.

Outcomes studies also may allow for the opportunity to work with academic institutions or other organizations in a collaborative manner.

Other major areas of development include provider profiling (report cards) and expansion into delivery services in government programs such as CHAMPUS, Medicaid and Medicare risk programs. Provider profiling entails the development of a means to identify the most effective and efficient providers within a large network. My clinical background as a psychologist is of great benefit in examining providers' practice patterns and overseeing the design and refinement of provider profiling. Entry into government programs entails the development of a good working knowledge of public health, and combining that with managed care knowledge in creating a delivery system that will meet the needs of these special populations.

In my role at BCBSTX, I have had to develop working knowledge and relationships with virtually every department in the company. Included, although not an exhaustive list are: actuarial, centralized training, claims/customer service, comptroller/finance, corporate communications, data processing, dental, facility services, federal employee program, government relations, group underwriting, health industry relations and development, healthcare benefits, human resources, internal audit, legal, life operations, marketing administration, medical, Medicare, membership, network management, and provider reimbursement. My role as a manager of a comprehensive behavioral health system is without a doubt challenging, and there is never a dull moment.

CONCLUSION

In conclusion, we believe that the answer to the question which is the title of this chapter, "Can a practitioner manage a comprehensive health system?" is *yes*, a traditionally trained practitioner can make the transition and prosper as a manager of a comprehensive healthcare system. While our paths in accomplishing this transition have been different, we have also benefitted from the unique situation of being partners in marriage as well as colleagues in the same profession. Many people have wondered how we have managed this successfully, as we had also worked together for many years at Biodyne. Our belief is that we have prospered due to a great deal of commitment to our personal and professional goals, and have always tried to support each other as well as benefitting from the support of our friends and colleagues in the healthcare field. We have often commented to each other that although our experiences over the past 10 years have been challenging and have required great flexibility and adaptation to change, we would not have wanted it any other way. We hope that this perspective is encouraging to the new generation of practitioners, as the behavioral healthcare field is undergoing massive changes and the need to adapt is imperative.

9.

Practice Survival Strategies: Business Basics for Effective Marketing to Managed Care

Charles H. Browning, Ph.D.

Denial is not a river in Egypt, but it still runs deep.

BUSINESS BASIC NUMBER I:
ADJUSTING ATTITUDES AND SHIFTING PARADIGMS:
BECOMING MANAGED CARE FRIENDLY

Grief as Denial

Because mental health professionals had it so good prior to the 1990s, many of them are having a difficult time today mourning the loss of what they regard as the good old days. But many clinicians are smart enough to understand the economic realities that have brought about the managed care phenomenon. They know that healthcare costs rose 193% between 1983 to 1993. They realize that mental healthcare costs are increasing twice as fast as other healthcare costs, and most clinicians accept the fact that some economic adjustments are inevitable. Most clinicians also know that logic, reason, statistical reports, and intellectual understanding

do not help much in working through the emotional pain of grieving the loss of a dream.

Grief is precisely what makes it so difficult for many therapists
to accept the impact managed care is having on their professional
lives. All the positive things described above, all the aspects of their
professional dream, have, in the past few years, been snatched away
from them. And although visionaries like Nicholas Cummings and
others warned them over a decade ago that this day would arrive,
many clinicians found themselves devastated when the reality of
the effect on their practices of managed care became apparent.

Like other grief processes, the loss of professional autonomy,
wounded identity, and financial insecurity threw many therapists
into shock. Rage followed, accompanied by deep denial with resistance that has a substantial segment of the professional mental
health community steadfastly in open defiance of the managed
care movement (Burlingame & Behrman, 1987).

The Many Anguished Faces of Denial:
Attitudes that Need Adjusting

We can almost predict which clinicians will still be clinical colleagues a few years from now in the next millennium, and which
will be doing other things. In their own words they portray attitudes that will give them "provider non grata" status with most, if
not all, managed care organizations. Observe carefully the attitudes and perspectives of these therapists and then head in the
opposite direction:

The Adversarial Attitude: "I call it 'mismanaged noncare' and I'll
have nothing to do with it in my practice!" A managed care company would have to be quite desperate to allow this clinician to
get past the first phone call to provider relations.

The Entitlement Attitude: "Hey, I've invested the better part of my
life preparing to be a good clinician; attended the best schools,
had the best internships and residencies, spent 20 years doing
quality work, and along comes managed care. They should come
begging to have me as a referral resource." Come begging they will

not. Any therapist, no matter how accomplished, who treats life these days with a betrayal-of-entitlement attitude will also be treating fewer and fewer patients.

The Guru Attitude: "Listen, I pride myself on the work I do. My patients stay in treatment with me for a long, long time because they know that I can give them insights that they can find nowhere else." This may be true, but before long most of this good doctor's patients will find their healthcare benefits managed by an HMO, PPO, MCO, or IPA and they will very likely have to bid farewell to their long-time professional friend.

The Freud-Was-Right Attitude: "I spent years of my life training and practicing in-depth psychotherapy and I'll be damned if I'll let some clerical gatekeeper dictate to me how to treat my patients!" Yes, dear doctor, we all agree that Sigmund was a genius. He opened our eyes to how the subconscious works. But if he were alive and in the grip of today's economic woes, he'd probably be focusing his genius on dynamic brief therapy. Those holding this attitude forget that Freud invented brief therapy and encouraged its use and development.

The Pandering Attitude: "Any clinician who talks about partnering with managed care is selling out and sleeping with the enemy. I won't stoop that low." Some seasoned realist has warned, "If you don't come down voluntarily, you'll be brought down the hard way." It's far easier to redefine our enemies and turn them into allies than to go down in flames saying, "I told you so." One therapist sees managed care organizations (MCOs) as dictatorial gatekeepers who try to block patient referrals from them. Another sees the same MCOs as distributional gatekeepers who funnel them new client referrals. Based on their attitudinal perspective, which clinician do you think actually gets the referrals?

The Good-Old-Days Attitude: "I've always been in solo practice and have run my office the way I see fit. I'm not taking on any partners now, not even managed care. I'll go it alone." The good old days were good, no question about it. We all miss them. But being cruise director of the *Titanic* will very soon find us scrambling for a lifeboat.

The Sanctuary Attitude: "I find all my identity and fulfillment in my work and my long-lasting relationships with my patients. They need me and I need them, and that's the way it's going to stay." As we all know, there are some in our profession who choose their role because it offers them the ego bolstering benefit of being needed. But if this therapist persists in this way, and doesn't think about rescuing his or her career, it may be necessary to find another endeavor.

The Hatred and Loathing Attitude: "I detest and despise everything managed care stands for and will do all I can to resist it!" Clinicians in independent practice have long enjoyed the privileges of all that the words *independent* or *private* imply. Anger, rage, hatred, and loathing are normal parts of this grief process. Do we encourage grief and rage ad infinitum? Or do we gently and compassionately tell colleagues to mourn their losses and move toward acceptance of new realities?

The Fight and Fury Attitude: "I will join together with a coalition of colleagues and we will fight to the death every effort managed care exerts trying to take over mental healthcare in our community." In one sense, these therapists are to be admired for their tenacity. But philosophical idealism in the late 20th century will not pay the bills.

The Unfairness Doctrine Attitude: "After all of my graduate education, internships, experience, continuing studies, research, the blood-sweat-and-tears I've poured into my profession, and all the people I've helped all these years, now managed care comes along and tells me whom to see, how long to see them, and how much I get paid for the privilege. It's just not fair!" How true. It isn't. But as we tell our teenagers when they complain about some unfairness in life, "L.I.F.E. really means: LIFE ISN'T FAIR EVER."

The Bitching Attitude: "As professionals we shouldn't have to put up with all these controls and conditions. Why should we cooperate with a system that is cold and money-driven? Is this what psychotherapy is all about?" For everything there is a season, a time for getting things off our chest, and a time for getting on with it. Our profession is being remodeled and resocialized.

The Superman Attitude: "I may be seeing fewer patients than before, but it's only temporary. My reputation in this community and with colleagues will keep referrals coming with full-fee patients, not managed care's K-Mart clients!" Some therapists think they're above such things and that they are and will always be impervious to managed care. Time will tell a different story.

On Adjusting Attitudes
and Shifting Paradigms

Success in private practice these days requires more than a mastery of wise business and marketing principles (although these are crucial, and we will present the strategic basics in the next two sections). Success requires converting adversarial, hostile, resistant attitudes so that the clinician projects a cooperative, team-player spirit when approaching and working with managed care organizations (Boland, 1991; Browning & Browning, 1994a; Cummings, 1992; Poynter, 1994).

Paradigm Paralysis and Paradigm Shift: To survive and thrive in a managed care marketplace, the mental health professional must undergo an attitude adjustment and a paradigm shift. The "Paradigm Paralysis" below represents attitudinal rigidity that can severely damage a clinician's reputation and the future growth potential of his or her private practice. Its antidote, the "Paradigm Shift," represents acceptance of an inevitable reality and an appropriate accommodation to it. It also represents the foundation for potential success and practice survival. What is the result of making this adjustment and shift? More client referrals from managed care.

BUSINESS BASIC NUMBER II:
STRATEGIES FOR APPROACHING MANAGED
CARE ORGANIZATIONS

As clinicians intent on survival in our own new, but sometimes scary world, we must also learn what managed care wants and doesn't

Paradigm Paralysis	Paradigm Shift
"No one has the right to tell me how to treat my clients!"	"Cooperative teamwork in treatment planning with case managers is a must."
"How dare they tell me when to terminate my client!"	"How can I help my client find rapid and lasting solutions since benefits are limited."
"I'll charge whatever I please at my standard and customary rate."	"I'm willing to accept reduced fees in order to help more clients, and to stimulate more referrals."
"There's no way I can survive with the reduced rates managed care pays."	"In a few short years managed care may be the only game in town, and $70 is better than $0 an hour."
"I absolutely refuse to put up with all their annoying paperwork."	"Every piece of paper I submit helps my clients get the services they need, and helps me to demonstrate my skill as a valued panel provider."
"Managed healthcare won't be around for long. Things will eventually return to the way it used to be back in the good old days."	"It's obvious that more patients are being covered by MCOs. To survive and succeed in the future, I'll provide the kind of quality brief therapy that will position myself and my practice as a valued panel provider."
"It's too late to get involved with managed care. All the panels are closed to my solo practice."	"To have a chance to get myself listed on those closed provider panels, I'll explore joining a well-established clinical group in my area."
"There's no way I can get involved with managed care because I'm told that they don't need anyone in my area."	"I'll find out from provider relations where they need more providers, and I'll open a satellite office in that location."
"I resent having to justify my diagnoses and treatment procedures to a bureaucrat."	"Case managers' input can help me make more precise diagnostic workups that are linked to brief therapy treatment plans."
"Managed care is set up to deny services to needy people."	"Managed care enables more clients to obtain cost-effective, quality services."
"Managed care is the enemy and obstacle to effective work with my patients."	"Case managers and utilization reviewers are, with me, part of the client's treatment team."
"Managed care is threatening the survival of my practice "	"My cooperative relationship with managed care can produce more new client referrals without doing other costly marketing."

Paradigm Paralysis	Paradigm Shift
"My training and clinical reputation will sustain practice growth without managed care."	"Managed care is here to stay. To sustain the growth and survival of my practice, I must become a cooperative, valued provider."
"I'll use whatever treatment modalities I choose. I don't do brief therapy."	"Time-sensitive, solution-focused strategies will best meet clients' needs within the scope of their limited benefits."
"Therapy itself is the primary source of patient change and symptom reduction."	"I place strong emphasis on adjunct resources and homework assignments to help the patient become less dependent."
"Therapy will take as long as necessary to help the patient improve functioning."	"Short-term, goal-focused treatment is not optional, it's mandatory."
"Therapy should focus on problems and underlying etiological pathology."	"To be effective and efficient, therapy must emphasize solutions, strengths, exceptions, wellness, and positive functioning."
"I must help patients attain insight, awareness, and causality."	"To be effective and efficient, I must help patients focus on achievable goals that are present and future oriented."
"Therapy must focus on feelings."	"Effective and efficient therapy must focus on cognitive functioning and behavioral patterns."
"Therapy must help the client focus on past traumas and early memories."	"To be effective and efficient, therapy must help the patient focus on current stressors, reframed cognitions, and functional behavior."
"The kind of so-called treatment managed care wants is unethical."	"Providing time-sensitive, solution-focused treatment is not only ethical, but it also gives clients the results they want."
"Managed care is more interested in cutting costs than helping people."	"Providing quality care and containing costs helps preserve future mental health benefits for more people."
"I'm not going to bother with managed care. It won't be around for long. Things will eventually return to the way it used to be back in the good old days."	"Every year managed healthcare becomes more influential and more patients are covered by MCOs. To survive and succeed in the future, I'll provide the kind of quality brief therapy that will position myself and my practice as a valued panel provider."

want. The expert on this subject is the person in charge of provider relations. To give you first-hand advice on what to do and how to do it, an interview with the director of provider relations for a large managed behavioral healthcare corporation based in Southern California is reported. Although MCOs vary in some of their policies, the advice offered here represents typical guidelines for a successful approach. To summarize the advice of this provider relations director, to become an active and busy member of a provider panel:

1. Overcome your fear of managed care by becoming educated about how it works. The best way to do this is to ask provider relations representatives about their needs and how you can be a part of meeting them.
2. Managed care seeks clinicians with LCSWs, MFCCs, Ph.D.s, Psy.D.s, and M.D.s. No licensure or degree is given more weight than another, unless a specific symptom demands a more specialized licensure.
3. Workers' compensation is a high-demand area for many managed care companies because so few therapists deal with it.
4. Forensic psychology is not a high-demand specialty and would not likely open too many panels to a provider or produce many referrals.
5. Some other high-demand specialty areas include chemical dependency, child and adolescent therapy, Adult Child of an Alcoholic (ACA) issues, and brief couples therapy.
6. Managed care expects brief, solution-focused therapy, getting quality results in less than 12 sessions. A therapist not comfortable or competent with these expectations might not be comfortable or successful working with managed care.
7. Some of the "red flags" provider relations look for in the application include items left blank, sloppy or illegible entries, misspelled words, and instructions not followed precisely.
8. Many MCOs frown on providers who try to bypass provider relations to market directly to case managers, especially in the early stages of the relationship.
9. Provider relations is not just a gatekeeper, but a marketing representative, a liaison, and even an advocate between the clinician and the case manager.

10. Clinicians need to think of provider relations as their advocate and an extension of their front office where new patients are screened and helped to become engaged in the treatment process.
11. Most MCOs do not prefer an IPA over a group practice, but this is changing rapidly.
12. Some MCOs still prefer to deal with individual providers, but group practices are becoming more desirable, focusing on specialty areas of the individual group members.
13. When told that "the panel is closed," find out what specialty areas and what locations are in most demand, then try to supply that need.
14. Ask many questions before submitting your application materials so you may avoid being among the 70% that are rejected.
15. Many MCOs "rate" providers for effectiveness. Clinicians who do their own outcomes research can become even more valued as providers.

Understanding and Working With Managed Care's Contracting Cycle

The behavioral healthcare environment is highly competitive and volatile. Many corporations and employee groups are turning to managed care plans to administer behavioral and chemical dependency benefits to workers. Bids are requested from many managed care organizations. The company that can show the best cost containment, quality of service, and service convenience for members receives the contract, usually for a 2- or 3-year period.

Prior to bidding on these contracts, many states require the MCOs to demonstrate an extensive provider network (panel) at a location convenient to all employee subscribers. Therefore, when an MCO contemplates "courting" new contracts in a given geographical area, it will solicit new providers to join its preferred provider panel. This provider recruitment phase offers to the clinician the most opportune and easiest access to the provider network, because a complete network must be demonstrated. During the recruitment phase the MCOs will oversubscribe the network, including on the panel far more therapists than could ever reasonably be utilized. This is to make its network appealing for marketing purposes.

Once the MCO has formed its provider network through an open provider recruitment phase, it then aggressively markets its contracts to employer groups in that area. Once those contracts are secured, only those therapists on the existing panel receive referrals, and eventually only a select few of those.

It is clear, therefore, that timing is of the essence in getting your practice listed on a provider panel during this open window of opportunity. The best way to do this is to carefully follow announcements of the moves and plans of MCOs in specialized professional publications. Subscribing to the following periodicals and newsletters will keep one's finger on the pulse of MCOs planning to recruit new members in an area, so that providers can take advantage of timely opportunities:

Psychotherapy Finances
Ridgewood Financial Institute, Inc.
13901 U.S. Highway 1
Juno Beach, FL 33408

Open Minds—The Behavioral Health
 Industry Analyst
1016 Clemons Street, Suite 407
Gettysburg, PA 17325

Mental Health Weekly
Manisses Communications Group, Inc.
P.O. Box 3357
Providence, RI 02906

Behavioral Healthcare Tomorrow Journal
Institute for Behavioral Healthcare
1110 Mar West Street, Suite E
Tiburon, CA 94920

AMCRA Monitor
American Managed Care
 & Review Association
1227 25th Street, N.W., Suite 610
Washington, DC 20037

Managed Care Week
Atlantic Information Service, Inc.
1050 17th Street, N.W., Suite 480
Washington, DC 20036

Managed Healthcare News
P.O. Box 10460
Eugene, OR 97440

Practice Strategies Newsletter
442½ E. Main Street, Suite 6
Clayton, NC 27520

In their search for skilled, solution-oriented providers, many MCOs will send open panel letters inviting membership in their networks. To receive these letters, it is important for a clinician to be listed as a clinical member in his or her professional association's referral directory. Psychologists should explore listings in the

National Registry of Providers in Psychology (202) 833-2377. Clinical Social Workers should seek inclusion in the American Board of Examiners Directory (304) 587-8783. Licensed Marriage and Family Therapists are pursued through their clinical membership in the American Association of Marriage and Family Therapy (202) 452-0109. Psychiatrists will find it most useful to affiliate with local IPAs, local psychiatric societies, the American Society of Addiction Medicine, and the National Association of Managed Care Physicians. The membership directory of the American Psychiatric Association is seldom used by MCOs for geographical contact because it is alphabetically organized.

Another excellent source of information on local managed care panel openings is through the marketing department at local mental health and chemical dependency hospitals. Most hospitals, regardless of size, invest substantial funds in marketing activities. In recent years hospitals aggressively researched MCOs in an effort to fill empty beds. The practitioner should contact hospitals where staff privileges are held for their knowledge of MCOs doing provider recruitment. Check with these hospitals, also, to see if they are forming their own provider hospital organizations (PHOs).

Attending professional conferences is an excellent way to (1) forecast MCO activities in your area by networking with the "insiders" face to face, and (2) introduce yourself to many provider relations and case management personnel (the decision makers) to establish your visibility. Local and national meetings are listed in the publications listed above.

When introducing yourself to MCO provider relations personnel, there is a wrong way, and a right way:

How to Get Rejected, Fast

When your application packet is opened, how can it quickly and effectively be distinguished from the other 29 received that day which are bidding for the one position on the panel? Most applications arrive with a generic form letter introducing the practitioner. They look something like the following ineffective generic practice introduction letter:

I am contacting you concerning my interest in becoming a provider with your network.

You will find enclosed my application, curriculum vitae, copy of my license, and professional liability insurance.

Please contact me at (714) 987-6543 at your convenience so we can discuss my becoming a provider with your company. I look forward to hearing from you soon.

> Sincerely,
>
> Seymour Rejections, Ph.D.

Even though this letter may seem logical and appropriate, it clearly illustrates how not to do it!

Strategic Elements of Effective Practice-Profile Introduction Letters

If you want the decision maker to be favorably impressed with your qualifications, it is necessary to present your practice as offering something that other applicants do not. To do this you need more than a generic cover letter per se; you need a succinct practice profile cover letter. In marketing strategy this is called "positioning" (Reis & Trout, 1986).

The following is one example of a practice profile letter that successfully connects with the needs of most managed care organizations as you determined them from initial telephone contact with provider relations:

> We appreciate this opportunity to offer our clinical services to (name of MCO) and clients in the north Orange County area. Here's a brief description of the Active Solutions Counseling Group.
>
> Active Solutions is a group practice with 10 clinical staff members. We are panel providers for several managed care companies and have provided quality, cost-effective, and time-efficient cognitive and behavioral healthcare services for over 20 years.

Location: Our primary offices are in north Orange County adjacent to Long Beach, convenient to the 405 and 605 freeways. Cities nearby include Lakewood, Cypress, Buena Park, Seal Beach, Huntington Beach and Anaheim.

Psychiatric Consultation: We have two psychiatrists who provide medication management as well as emergency and urgent care.

Orientation: We provide brief, solution-focused, cognitive-behavioral outpatient services. Our reputation in the community is one of providing quality and time-efficient services. In addition to traditional modalities, we also offer Christian Therapy by licensed, credentialed psychotherapists for patients who specifically request this service.

Services Menu: We specialize in symptom-reduction therapy for children, adolescents, adults and the elderly.

Tx Modalities:
Crisis Intervention	Individual Therapy
Group Therapy	Couples Therapy
Family Therapy	Aftercare Support Groups

Areas of Specialization:
Chemical Dependency	Bereavement & Child Loss
Anxiety Disorders	Obsessive Compulsive Disorders
Depression	Domestic Violence
Sexual Abuse Issues	Terminal Illness Issues

HIV & AIDS-Related Disorders (for patient & family)

Services Available: Three secretaries are available to personally assist patients, in addition to a 24-hour, 7-day-a-week answering service. Same-day or next-day appointments for managed care patients are typically available. Early, evening, and Saturday appointments are available to accommodate patients' work schedules. Some limited Sunday appointments are available.

Managed Care Experience: Since the mid-1970s the Active Solutions staff has worked closely with EAP managers with large aerospace companies and labor unions, providing short-term interventions. For the past 6 years we have become actively involved with many managed behavioral healthcare programs as preferred providers.

Our average course of treatment is 8 sessions. We are a group which rigorously reviews the clinical activity of staff to ensure that enough, but not too much, care is being provided.

Tx Reports: Clinical updates and treatment plans are done on time, succinctly, clearly linking brief interventions to symptoms, with estimated discharge dates defined early on.

Aftercare Support Groups: We offer no-cost, aftercare support groups for those patients who need continuing care beyond their plan benefits to maintain progress and prevent relapse.

Outcomes Research: We do outcomes questionnaires on all patients at intake, at discharge, and 6 months following discharge, and report statistical and patient assessments of symptom change and satisfaction.

Computerized Tracking & Billing: Patient treatment sessions, end-dates, copayments and billings are tracked electronically to assure timely terminations and accurate patient accounts.

Let me assure you, Ms. Smith, that if invited to participate as a (name of MCO) preferred group practice, we will offer both stellar administrative and clinical service to your clients and case managers. Our goal is to offer the kind of quality, solution-focused care that will get patients back to maximum functioning in a time-sensitive manner.

I hope this gives you a good overview of our work, and how Active Solutions may fit into the (name of MCO) program. If I may, I'll call you in few days to discuss the next step in the application process. Many thanks for your consideration.

Most sincerely,

Seymour Clients, Ph.D.

Examine this letter carefully. Note how each section addresses specific needs of the MCO and describes how these needs are met by this practice. You can use this as a format for describing your own work to new provider panels in your area. Enclose with the letter curriculum vitae or resume, liability insurance, and licensure of all staff. This technique will distinguish your application packet from the others in the stack. It should significantly increase your chances of acceptance.

If, on the other hand, you talk to an assistant who asks you to just send a letter briefly describing your practice and request an application packet, use the following abbreviated format, highlighting the most important aspects of your practice at a glance:

> We appreciate this opportunity to offer our services as a group practice provider for your network. Active Solutions Counseling Group has been in practice in the Midtown area for over 20 years. The following should give you a brief overview of what we do and how we do it:
>
> - *Orientation:* Brief, solution-focused cognitive therapy.
>
> - *Group Practice:* A professional corporation of eight therapists.
>
> - *Psychiatric Consultation:* Two psychiatrists on staff.
>
> - *Location:* Offices located in the West Midtown and Centerville areas.
>
> - *Managed Care Experience:* Five years experience with many MCO panels.
>
> - *Outcomes Research:* Intake and discharge patient progress measured.
>
> - *Foreign Languages:* Treatment available for Spanish and Korean speakers. Sign language specialist.
>
> - *Specialty Services:* For adults and adolescents; depression and anxiety disorders; chemical dependency; crisis intervention; signing for deaf.
>
> - *Service Availability:* Same-day or next-day appointments; 7-day, 24-hour answering service.

Let me assure you that if invited to become a (name of MCO) provider, we will do a good job offering the kind of quality, outcomes-focused care that will get patients back to maximum functioning in a time-sensitive manner.

I'll call you next week to discuss this with you personally. Thank you for considering Active Solutions for your provider panel.

Most Sincerely,

Seymour Clients, Ph.D.

Using these procedures and adapting these letters to your own practice should increase the probability of your becoming accepted as one of the newest members of their provider network.

What To Do If the Provider Panel Is "Closed"

A chilly reception awaits many clinicians these days at their first call to many MCOs. They are told by a provider relations representative, "I'm sorry but our provider panel is full in your area, but you might check back with us again in a few months." In essence, they are told that the network is closed.

But the term *closed* has more than one meaning. The provider panel is indeed closed to therapists who approach and offer their services to MCOs in the same way most providers do. But "closed" means "partially open" to therapists or groups who are equipped to meet the needs of the MCO in special ways.

When you hear those dreaded words, "The panel is closed," redefine them to mean, "If you present yourself to us in the same way most other therapists do, you don't stand a chance. But if you approach us creatively and strategically, our welcome mat may be out for you."

In *How to Partner with Managed Care*, Browning and Browning (1994a) describe in some detail methods for persuading the gatekeepers to open those gates. Here is a summary of the techniques that have been proven most effective in opening seemingly closed gates to many clinicians:

1. Persevere until you succeed. If there is an MCO you want to join, set your mind on getting your name on their provider list, refusing tenaciously to accept "closed" for an answer. Redefine "closed" as "partially open" and pursue inclusion with unswerving and creative perseverance.
2. Offer your services with tightly focused specialization. Avoid the generic "individual, group, marriage and family counseling" used by other applicants. Instead offer specialities in higher demand; e.g., foreign language therapy, sign language therapy, spiritual issues, ethnic issues, therapy with gays and lesbians, Holocaust survivors, disabled persons, born-again Christians, etc.
3. Form a multidisciplinary group practice, which (a) has a strong solution focused, brief-therapy orientation; (b) offers highly focused specialities; (c) maintains electronic billing procedures; (d) offers services in strategic locations; and (e) routinely performs internal utilization review and outcomes research.
4. Affiliate with a group practice. Join an established multidisciplinary group practice which has positive working and referral relationships with several of the largest MCOs in the area, and which maintains the five criteria in number 3 (above).
5. Plan to "grandfather in" when current patients shift to managed care. Review your current caseload to determine which patients still have indemnity insurance coverage. Within the next year or so most companies will doubtlessly shift to managed care plans. At that time you can aggressively pursue panel inclusion based on "continuity of care" justification with patients you are already seeing.
6. Survey colleagues. Talk to colleagues who are currently panel providers in MCOs and who get regular referrals from them. Learn what approaches opened the panels to them, what areas of specialization the MCO desired most, what locations are most used, and what inside contacts they can recommend to you.
7. Make yourself visible. Learn (through the publications listed earlier) what conferences, workshops, seminars, and meetings the managed care gatekeepers are likely to attend. Attend them yourself. Offer to present a paper at these gatherings. Meet and get to know key gatekeepers and in so doing demonstrate yourself as a knowledgeable, managed care friendly provider.

8. Consider every new patient call a potential opportunity. Don't tell new callers, "I'm sorry, we're not a provider for your plan." Do tell them, "At present we're not on your provider list, but if you'd like to see me, call the provider relations department of your plan and tell them you'd like to see me and how can we become providers on their plan."

9. Let the patient leverage the gates open for you. If the above approach is unsuccessful, encourage the patient to call the person at their company who is responsible for insurance benefits and ask them to request that we be included as a preferred provider because the patient wishes to be seen here by someone within their plan. In many cases the intercession of this person can open closed gates.

10. Utilize the two-step method. If the request for panel inclusion is denied, advise the prospective patient to write a letter to the director of the employer's insurance benefits department. Ask the patient to intercede on your behalf so that the therapist of choice can be seen. The patient should inform the MCO of a visit to their office in a few days to personally discuss this. The letter with the indicated personal visit can enhance the MCO's motivation to follow through as an advocate on the patient's behalf.

11. Repeat step 6 (above) with the director of the patient's EAP or human resources department.

12. Repeat step 7 (above) by having the patient contact the labor union, asking it to intervene with the employer, who then may intervene with the MCO.

13. Use the three-step PEMCO method. Physician → Employer → Managed Care Organization. If the above techniques prove to be of no avail, the patient can be encouraged to contact the physician, indicating that the patient is experiencing increased stress resulting from not being permitted to see a trusted therapist.

14. Join as many of the smaller MCOs as possible. Even though the smaller MCOs will produce few referrals, in time they may be purchased by larger, more successful corporations. Later they may offer provider status to newly acquired plan providers, and with panel status there will be many new client referrals.

BUSINESS BASIC NUMBER III: ADAPTING TO THE NEEDS OF MANAGED CARE: TECHNIQUES FOR GETTING RECOGNITION AND REFERRALS

At this point attitudes have been successfully adjusted and paradigms have been positively shifted. The welcome mat and panel membership have been extended by many MCOs as a result of implementing prudent and persistent approach strategies. The next step is turning panel membership into panel referrals. To get referrals you must first get recognition. Those responsible for making referrals must come to regard you as a team player who provides quality care with an eye toward cost containment. Marketing your value as a provider to managed care personnel requires the use of every professional contact with an MCO as an opportunity to demonstrate excellence with distinction, both administratively and clinically. There are ways to do this effectively.

Profiling for Referrals

All MCOs are not created equal. Some want clinicians to provide updates after the first session, with others after three. Some terminate session certification after an "end date," while others have none. Some want written documentation and others require voice-mail updates. Some authorize sessions liberally; others raise eyebrows after six. Some case managers desire to be actively involved in treatment planning while others defer to the provider's judgment. To succeed in making your practice distinctively managed care friendly, you need to find out what is wanted, then provide it.

To discern the unique, idiosyncratic expectations of various MCOs and the needs of individual case managers, there is a strategic response profile sheet to help clinicians.

Whenever you meet a new case manager, utilization reviewer, or other MCO representative who makes referrals, attempt to learn their likes, dislikes, pet peeves, biases, and the other important "little things" that they require in performing their jobs.

When you consistently tailor your communication according to these special expectations or preferences, you can distinguish your practice from the multitude that shares the provider list with you.

Create a file for the profile sheets, alphabetized by case mangers' names, or by the MCO itself if referrals are made by random case managers or intake workers. Figure 9.1 presents the strategic response profile sheet.

To improve efficiency in providing specific patient information via telephone, voice mail, or written updates, there is a patient update review sheet. With this information handy, you have at your fingertips all relevant data that may be required by case managers and utilization reviewers. When data are requested, it can be provided quickly, easily, and accurately from this one sheet. This conserves your time and theirs, thus enhancing your image as a competent and valued provider.

It is recommended that the information on the patient update review sheet be brought current at the time case charting and progress notes are completed. Figure 9.2 presents a sample of the patient update review sheet to be completed using pencil for ease in updating data.

Making Your Telephone Contacts Effective and Efficient

The most important telephonic communications between clinician and case manager are of two types: (1) direct dialogue in which both parties discuss case issues and treatment planning, and (2) voice mail updates in which the clinician summarizes case issues and progress via recorded messages to the case manager. In either instance it is of the utmost importance that the clinician be well prepared and provide necessary and appropriate information to the case manager in a time-sensitive manner.

The case manager's or utilization reviewer's time is in short supply. They have little patience with vague ramblings by clinicians who make them struggle to get the information they need to update patient files in the computer. The therapist who anticipates these needs prepares in advance for the call, and provides

---

STRATEGIC RESPONSE PROFILE SHEET

CASE MANAGER'S NAME _____ MGD. CARE CO. _____

Phone # _____ Ext. ____ Voice Mail # _____ Pager # _____

Address _____ City _____ State _____ Zip _____

Clients/Locations Represented _____ Fees Paid _____

Best Times To Call _____ Best Days To Call _____ # Sessions Typically Auth'd. _____

Prefers Direct Call ☐ Voice Mail Updates ☐ Written Updates ☐ Faxed Updates ☐ Updates Thru Ass'ts. ☐

Wants Me To Call New Pt. To Set Up First Session ☐   Case Mgr. Asks Pt. To Call Me To Set Up First Appt. ☐

Call Case Mgr. After Pt. Calls To Set First Appt. ☐   Call Case Mgr. If Pt. Fails To Follow Thru ☐

Case Mgr. Wants Update On Pt. _____ Sessions After Intake—By Voice Mail ☐ Written Updates ☐ Direct Phone ☐

What Specific Details Does Case Mgr. Expect Or Desire After Intake?

How Often Are Updates Desired & What Types?

What Does He/She (a) Want On Voice Mail? (b) What's Not Desired?

What Does She/He (a) Want In Written Documentation? (b) What's Not Desired?

How Much DSM Information Required? Preferences & Areas To Emphasize?

Who Does He/She Prefer To Use For: Med. Evals. _____ Hospitalization _____

 Chem. Dep. Detox _____ Chem. Dep. Rehab _____

Psych. Testing _____ Physician Evals. _____

 Outside Support Groups & Resources Preferred _____

PERSONAL PROFILE: Likes/Dislikes. Clinical Orientation. Pet Peeves. Hot Topics. Favorite Books/Authors.
 Resources. People Known In Common. Humorous Topics. Family Profile. Vacations.

Figure 9.1

PATIENT UPDATE REVIEW SHEET

PATIENT'S NAME _____ SOCIAL SECURITY # _____

NAME OF INSURED _____ SOCIAL SECURITY # _____

MGD. CARE CO. _____ CASE MANAGER'S NAME _____

Case Mgr. Phone # _____ Ext. ___ Voice Mail # _____ Pager # _____

MCO Address _____ City _____ State _____ Zip _____

Patient's Address _____ City _____ State _____ Zip _____

Patient's Daytime Phone # _____ Patient's Evening Phone # _____

Date Of First Session _____ # Sessions Authorized _____ End Date _____ # Of Extensions Req'd _____

As Of (Date) _____ How Many Sessions Used _____ Pt. Seen Weekly ☐ /2 Wks ☐ /3 Wks ☐ / Mo. ☐

Pt. In Compliance With Tx: Yes ☐ No ☐. If No, Why _____

DSM IV DIAGNOSIS: AXIS I _____ AXIS II _____

AXIS III _____ AXIS IV STRESSORS _____ AXIS V GAF _____

Ref'd For Meds (Date) _____ M.D. _____ Phone # _____

Reason For Med Eval. _____ Meds/Dosg. Rx'd _____

Any Side-Effects Of Meds. _____ How Meds. Effect'g Symptoms _____

How Symptoms Effect'g Work/School _____ Personal Life _____

Suicidal/Homicidal/Abuse Hx _____

Substance Abuse Hx _____ __

Current Goals _____

Tx Plan & Interventions _____

Problems / Obstacles To Progress _____

Anticipated Discharge Date _____ # Of Sessions _____ Aftercare Plans _____

Criteria For Discharge (Sympt. Reduct'n) _____

Significant Others Enhanc'g Tx _____

Outside Adjunct Resources Rx / Used _____

Results Of Outcomes Research _____

Major Changes Since Last Update & Issues To Bring Up _____

Figure 9.2

TABLE 9.1

Presenting Effective Telephone Updates: A Strategic Checklist

- ☐ Patient's name (correctly spelled)
- ☐ Name and Social Security # of person who holds the insurance coverage (if different)
- ☐ Patient's Social Security #
- ☐ Patient's (or insured's) employer
- ☐ Date of first session
- ☐ Key cognitive-behavioral symptoms causing impaired functioning
- ☐ Any suicidal, homicidal or substance abuse behavior
- ☐ Effect of symptoms on work, personal, relational functioning
- ☐ Current DSM-IV diagnoses (all 5 Axes)
- ☐ GAF scores: Current and past 6 months
- ☐ Number of sessions used to date
- ☐ Authorized end date (if specified)
- ☐ Current goals and interventions linked to them
- ☐ Effects of med, side effects, impact on symptoms
- ☐ Current goals and interventions linked to them
- ☐ Homework prescribed to reduce specific symptoms & compliance
- ☐ Obstacles to attainment of goals
- ☐ Frequency of sessions
- ☐ Total number of anticipated sessions needed to meet goals & discharge patient
- ☐ Anticipated discharge date
- ☐ Use of outside adjunct resources to reduce symptoms
- ☐ Changes in symptoms and functioning due to Tx interventions
- ☐ Request for verbal or written certification, feedback, other Tx suggestions
- ☐ Give phone number and best times to return call, if needed
- ☐ Express appreciation for future referrals

appropriate data before they are requested will quickly distinguish him- or herself from the majority who do not.

The strategic response profile sheet and the patient update review sheet bring together the key ingredients of an efficiently effective phone contact. For convenience, Table 9.1 offers a useful checklist to help prepare a quality phone update. This checklist contains the key times most MCO case managers or utilization reviewers want from a clinician. Not all times will be required in every update by all case managers, but to be safe, it is wise to have them at the ready.

Two typical phone contacts demonstrate incorrect and correct voice-mail updates:

VOICE-MAIL UPDATE—HOW *NOT* TO DO IT: "Hi, this is Dr. Seymour Disfavor and I want to give you an update on Ima Hopeful . . . um, let's see . . . well, I don't have her Social Security number handy . . . uh, hold on a minute. Sorry I can't locate it, but we've discussed her case before. She's making good progress with her depression and her relationship with her husband is improving. She's sleeping better and concentrating better. But I'd like to continue her treatment to explore possible underlying causes of the depression, and to work on her self-esteem. Oh, by the way, I did see her for four sessions already that were not authorized, so I would appreciate it if you would back-cert them? Thanks a lot, goodbye.

VOICE-MAIL UPDATE—HOW TO DO IT *RIGHT*: Hi Carol, this is Dr. Seymour Clients with a brief update on Ima Hopeful, H-O-P-E-F-U-L; her Social Security Number is 123-45-6789; she's a Med-Tech employee. Her first session was on January 27th and she's been seen weekly for 3 sessions now. Her DSM-IV Dx is Major Depression, Single Episode, Moderate 296.23, rule out OCD; current GAF is 55, 6 months ago 70. She reports depressive moods 5/wk with moderate generalized anxiety bouts daily. No suicidal ideation. Obsessive fears about the future. Sleep disturbance 3/wk. Marital conflicts 3–4/wk. Chronic fatigue and forgetfulness daily. Our goals are 1. Refer her to Dr. B. Wellness for med eval to reduce level of depression; 2. Use cognitive reframing to modify self-defeating beliefs to reduce depression; 3. Assertiveness and anger management techniques to reduce anxiety; 4. Rule out any physical causes of depression with M.D.; 5. Conjoint Tx to reduce marital conflicts; 6. To empower pt. to set healthy boundaries, referring her to weekly codependent recovery group; 7. Bibliotherapy homework for spotting relapse triggers. Plan is to see patient biweekly and anticipated discharge date is June 15th. No problems or obstacles. Please fax written authorization for an additional 6 sessions. My office number is (310) 987-6543, beeper (310) 876-5432. Best time to reach me is between 8 and 9 A.M. or at noon. Many thanks for referring her, and for keeping me in mind for future referrals. Have a terrific day!

Obviously, the details provided in the second voice-mail example can be simply shared in person-to-person dialogue with the case manager. The key is to be thorough and succinct.

Some case managers may require less detailed information, while others may require more. Case managers' preferences should be noted on the Strategic Response Profile Sheet and future contacts made to conform to it. Remember: our objective is not to overwhelm case managers with voluminous data to impress them, but to quickly give them enough information to help them do their job efficiently.

Guidelines for Creating Effective Written Documentation

The final step in enhancing your relationship with MCO case managers is to provide treatment reports and other written documentation that demonstrate quality, time-sensitive, solution-focused outcomes. Essentially this means that you prove yourself and your work to be efficiently effective.

Another way of talking about written documentation is "paperwork." Like "marketing," most clinicians find the notion of paperwork anathema. But if you reframe this concept (in classical cognitive fashion) from paper "work" to paper "marketing," then a necessary chore can become a strategic opportunity to further showcase your clinical skills as a brief therapist. Every treatment report not only enables the patient to receive care, but it can also shape the case manager's positive perceptions of you as a preferred referral resource.

There are 20 ways to write a totally ineffective treatment plan which will risk nonauthorization for treatment, incur the ire of case managers, damage your reputation, and repel managed care referrals (Browning & Browning, 1995):

1. Approach the work of treatment planning with an "entitlement attitude" instead of a cooperative attitude. Believe that regardless of the quality of your work, you deserve referrals and are entitled to them.

2. Maintain an attitude that you can be all things for all patients. Believe that a referral to you is the best thing that could happen, and that you can act as the "Lone Ranger" who can do everything for the patient, without resorting to any other adjunctive therapeutic measures (including medication).

3. Be vague about multiaxial diagnoses. Make the case manager look up DSM-IV code numbers. Do not specify criteria of a diagnosis, and ignore GAF scores.

4. Go back 5 or 10 years and mention psychosocial events or issues that were impacting the patient at that time, rather than focusing on stressors affecting the patient now. Make these prominent in your treatment plan.

5. Present a lengthy and rambling history to demonstrate how skilled you are at "packing in the pathology," and how terrible the problem really is.

6. Take a kitchen-sink approach and throw everything you can think of into the treatment plan, hoping something will work and something will impress the case manager with your superior knowledge.

7. Do supportive psychotherapy and emphasize that your relationship with the patient is the most important thing in the world, and in so doing, show that symptom reduction is secondary to building a therapeutic relationship.

8. Give a sketchy, nonspecific description of the patient's symptoms, or give none at all.

9. Consider the use of medication as a "last resort." And when and if you do ask for it, do so only so you can monitor the effect of the medication in a supportive therapy context.

10. If you are an M.D., give inadequate information on medications: what you're prescribing, dosage, frequency, what your plan is, what has been used in the past. Assume that writing "med management" is more than enough.

11. When giving a diagnosis on Axis I, give more than three diagnoses. Or, use V-Codes as your primary Axis I diagnosis.

12. Show catastrophic diagnoses with exaggerated GAF scores. Or do an extreme diagnosis with only a moderate GAF score.

13. Use no outside support or recovery groups. Or show that you recommend support groups or other adjuncts to therapy, but

don't contract with the patient to follow through with these prescriptions.

14. If you do use support groups or adjunctive resources to your treatment, only use them late in treatment, so the transition of life after therapy is abrupt and inadequate, and that relapse is highly probable so that additional sessions will be needed to help with the transition, or to support ongoing med management.

15. Do vague, non-goal-focused treatment and discharge plans, so that when your certification is denied and the treatment ends prematurely, you can blame the "unfairness" of the managed care benefits.

16. Focus on an Axis II personality disorder exclusively with no Axis I disorder teased out as the emphasis of treatment. Ask for authorizations of five sessions per week to deal with characterological defects.

17. Take a psychodynamic approach (but try to pass it off as intensive brief therapy) and do awareness, exploratory, and transference work once a week for several months. Then, when benefits run out and additional sessions are denied and the patient is angry, you can blame it on a stingy, uncaring case manager.

18. Don't mention anything about medication in your treatment plan. Demonstrate resistance to using meds to reduce symptoms, suffering, or length of treatment.

19. Request an extremely high number of sessions, telling the case manager that you can wrap this up in 20 or 30 sessions.

20. Write your treatment plans hastily with no concern about legibility or completeness.

That's what not to do. To successfully avoid these pitfalls, there are specific guidelines for writing effective treatment plans that will win the approval, and the referrals, of even the most demanding case manager. There are 20 simple ways to write effective treatment plans which will get authorizations, win favor with case managers, establish a reputation for excellence, and get more managed care referrals (Browning & Browning, 1995):

1. Approach treatment planning with a cooperative, advocacy, team-player attitude, and one that emphasizes quality,

solutions-focused, time-sensitive care, built around the needs of the patient and the MCO.

2. Throughout your treatment plan indicate that therapy is only one part of a multifaceted plan of intervention to reduce symptoms and return the patient to maximal functioning.

3. Be specific about all five axes of DSM-IV diagnoses, providing accurate code numbers. Be particularly careful formulating and reporting GAF scores. Use specific criteria in the report to justify each diagnosis.

4. Focus on current stressors rather than past traumas. Build your treatment plan around symptoms and problems that impact the patient's life now. Refer to past issues only as they are clearly linked to current dysfunction.

5. Present a succinctly thorough history, emphasizing precipitants that directly relate to symptoms to be addressed.

6. Include in the treatment plan only those issues that a case manager would need to justify necessity of treatment. Impress the case manager with your ability to cut out all extraneous, unnecessary, and unclear information.

7. Report cognitive and behavioral interventions that are unquestionably focused on symptom reduction. Never indicate that you are doing "supportive therapy," but that outside resources are utilized for this purpose.

8. Give precise descriptions of symptoms, from the patient's point of view, and clearly show how they impair functioning.

9. Indicate that you consider the use of psychotropic medication an instrumental part of the treatment plan to more rapidly control symptoms, to restore the patient to maximal functioning. If meds are not used early on, indicate that they will be considered if symptoms do not respond to treatment within 3 or 4 sessions.

10. If you are an M.D., give complete information on medications: what you're prescribing, dosage, frequency, what your plan is, what has been used in the past, side-effects. Writing "med management" is never sufficient.

11. Give no more than three Axis I diagnoses. Never use V-Codes as the primary Axis I diagnosis. V-Codes are acceptable as secondary Axis I diagnoses.

12. Diagnoses, symptoms, and GAF scores should be congruently realistic and appropriate. Never present an extreme GAF score

in order to justify certification. Never minimize GAF scores, as this risks noncertification.

13. Report strong emphasis on prescribed and contracted outside resources to facilitate early and positive outcomes.

14. From the outset of treatment report the reliance on outside resources and homework assignments to reduce patient dependence on the therapy process or on the therapist, to prevent relapse and the need for further treatment.

15. Make treatment plans sharply focused on achievable goals through symptom-specific, active interventions aimed at achieving those goals, and anticipated dates for reaching each.

16. Never seek authorization for treatment based on an Axis II diagnosis exclusively. If there is an Axis II (personality or developmental) diagnosis present, report it honestly. Then ferret out an Axis I diagnosis that is amenable to brief therapy intervention.

17. Commit to and report solution-focused, brief therapy interventions. Avoid exploratory, insight-oriented, regression, or analytical modalities that merit almost certain denial.

18. Throughout the course of treatment reporting, demonstrate continued emphasis on using medications to control symptoms and maintain maximal functioning.

19. Request a conservative number of sessions in which to accomplish the established goals for the patient. Avoid requesting too many extensions. Encourage the patient to apply on his or her own what has been accomplished in treatment before returning for further care, if needed.

20. Carefully craft all treatment plans around the guidelines provided in this chapter. Write succinct, precise reports emphasizing (a) observable, measurable behaviors; (b) definite goals; and (c) cognitive/behavioral therapeutic strategies. Make all reports complete, neat, legible, and easily readable. Provide timely documentation and avoid requesting back certification.

What's at the End of the Tunnel?

Some cynic has said, "Due to financial constraints, the light at the end of the tunnel has been turned off until further notice." This poignant statement could also have been spoken by many a weary and embattled clinician, feeling that since managed care has invaded the land of behavioral healthcare, all hope is gone for survival in private practice. The light may indeed be "turned off" for those who choose to stand and fight, resisting inevitable change. It may also look quite dim for those who decide to give up, abandoning their profession to flee into other careers.

But those clinicians who elect to stay and to adjust their attitudes to today's real-world realities can be assured of peaceful, cooperative coexistence with managed care while working together as a team, providing behavioral health services to needy people in new, prudent, and creative ways.

This chapter presented all the business basics needed to shift paradigms to approach and work effectively with managed care organizations. This author has endeavored to cut out all theoretical "fat" and conceptual "fluff," leaving a marketing blueprint of proven strategies and techniques. The objective was to present methods that could quickly and easily be applied, enhancing survival and success in this dynamic era of healthcare reforms.

If you will go beyond an intellectual consideration of this material, and commit to a persistent, rubber-meets-the-road implementation of these procedures, you may discover something quite exciting: The light at the end of the tunnel is not only still "on," but it's getting brighter!

10.

The Practitioner as Owner

Richard S. Edley, Ph.D.

It is difficult to worry about outcome,
when you are worried about income.
                                    Anonymous

It used to be easy. Historically, the practitioner role was straightforward: provide service. The service was mental health or substance abuse treatment, and it was provided on a fee-for-service basis. If one wanted to practice, the following basic steps needed to be followed: open an office, put out a shingle, build referrals, treat, and collect payment. In following these steps the practitioner could be quite successful, but lived in a vacuum. The "business" of psychotherapy could be left to others. The practitioner could claim to be "business-free," and in one's mind this eliminated any potential business versus treatment conflicts of interest.

The world for this practitioner-owner has changed drastically. One can sum up how the world changed in two words: managed care. While the life of the practitioner in the past may have seemed "pure," it also was without limits. No questions were asked, and cost was rising with little practitioner accountability for quality or effectiveness of service. Soon payers began to question what *value* they were getting for their health dollar.

With managed care came a variety of procedures, all aimed at increasing accountability while decreasing cost: utilization review

(UR), provider panels, case management, centralized patient access and referral, and fee reduction.

The practitioner of old is in trouble. Simply put, those who ignore the "business" of psychotherapy find themselves out of that business. This chapter is written by a psychologist who many years ago enjoyed solo private practice, but seeing the handwriting on the wall, joined a managed behavioral healthcare company (American Biodyne) as a staff psychologist. Soon after he was promoted, and eventually rose to the level of a senior executive. He now is a principal in a newly formed company that aids practitioners in the formation of integrated delivery systems (IDSs).

The practitioner of today is an owner; an owner of a psychotherapy/treatment business. Revenues, expenses, cash flow, authorizations, outpatient treatment reports, panel membership are all part of today's practice.

A practitioner-owner must also be competitive. The solo practitioner cannot survive in today's environment any more than the corner goods store can expect to beat Walmart. Certainly the practitioner can search for a niche, and lay claim to that specific aspect of the market. Beware of this solution: it is far more likely that this is just a form of denial, as with many reactions to severe problems. Unfortunately, denial is far easier to see in a patient than it is within oneself.

WHAT MANAGED CARE WANTS: THE DILEMMA OF THE SOLO PRACTITIONER-OWNER

Given managed care's dominance in the behavioral healthcare market, the practitioner must be alert to the needs of this large payer. While there are providers who claim to ignore or fight managed care in their marketplace this is an extremely risky strategy.

As a practitioner-owner it is far more useful to accept the situation and begin building coping strategies. First, consider what managed care needs:

1. *High quality service.* Most practitioners would state that they offer high quality service. Few, however, can prove it. Payers want to know: (a) are patients satisfied with their services, and (b) are patients getting better with this service?

Given these needs, the practitioner must have in place a mechanism by which to tap in to these two basic quality elements: satisfaction and outcome. The measurement of these elements, however, do not come easily nor are they free. Suddenly the practitioner-owner finds oneself with postage charges, copying charges, secretarial time, and nonclinical (and nonbillable) time.

2. *Cost-effective service.* Just as little work has been done on patient satisfaction and outcome, far less has been done on cost-effectiveness. The vast majority of practitioners have practiced with virtually no eye on cost. This is absolutely unacceptable in today's marketplace. You must know your unit cost, average length of outpatient treatment, and inpatient admission rate. Being the highest quality practitioner in the world (as subjective as that is) is of no use if you cannot get reimbursed for the service.

3. *Geographical coverage.* One of the most important demands in managed care is to cover an entire population in a given plan. In considering this coverage, you would need to look at the size of your practice and its capacity to handle additional patients in this "catchment area." Furthermore, many payers insist on accessibility standards, for example: emergency appointments seen immediately, urgent within 24 hours, and routine within 3 to 5 days.

4. *Specialty coverage.* As with geographical coverage, to provide services for an entire population, a variety (if not all) specialties must be offered. Examples of these specialties would include: age ranges (child, adolescent, adult, geriatric), substance abuse, severe psychopathology, eating disorders, and anxiety disorders. Clearly the practitioner cannot be all things to all patients. When I asked one practitioner recently what his specialty was, he responded, "What do you need?" While having some comic value, his response will not get the business.

5. *Ease of communication with providers.* This area is often overlooked by the practitioner. Communication is expensive. Every time the managed care company or payer needs to speak with the provider, the clock is ticking. Managed care review staff must be hired, appeals staff put in place, and numerous documents and forms must be created. Communication creates administrative overhead, and wasteful communication time represents managed care's greatest problem today.

In order to eliminate this administrative load, communication with the provider must be minimized. Those providers who give accurate and timely information to managed care companies and are available for appointments and referrals have the upper hand. As one colleague put it, "You can squeak by without being managed care friendly, but it is imperative to be managed care competent."

WHAT MANAGED CARE WANTS NOW

As the marketplace continues to change and evolve, additional needs arise. Today, managed care companies and other payers have added two other important elements that are looked for in providers:

6. *Administrative functions.* One of managed care's largest problems today is the administrative cost that is needed to manage care. The practitioner who can assume the administrative functions of the managed care company is attractive in contracting situations with such entities.

For example, utilization review is extremely expensive for managed care. Reviewers need to be hired, expensive UR information systems are needed, and treatment reports continually need to be reviewed. The paper and telephone volume can be staggering. If the provider can prove to the managed care company through objective and clear data that such oversight is not needed, then this cost, too, can be eliminated. The problem with most solo practitioners is that they cannot prove such numbers and, therefore, continue to be expensively and inefficiently managed.

7. *Clinical/financial risk.* Beyond assuming administrative functions, the obvious next step for managed care is to allow the practitioners not only to testify that they can manage themselves, but to ask the practitioners to put their money where their mouth is. In other words, put the provider at clinical and financial risk.

Providers are frightened of taking risk, reflecting their lack of confidence in their own ability to control costs. Their life has been built on providing care and not managing the same. Horror stories exist where providers, and even large hospital systems, have gone bankrupt by assuming ill-calculated risk. Risk, however, is not necessarily bad. In fact, it is the one way for providers to take back control of their own practices and destiny and to eliminate the oversight and management of which they so often complain. What is needed is sound underwriting and risk assessment.

THE INTEGRATED DELIVERY SYSTEM

Given this dire situation, the practitioner, as a business owner, must seek alternatives. As a business owner, the best strategy for survival given these economic conditions of the marketplace is to develop or take part in a larger integrated delivery system (IDS). Of course, this is easier said than done.

To begin with, not every practice group is what managed care would call an IDS. In fact, with the situation today for the practitioner-owner, everyone is running to form groups claiming to be IDSs. One thing for certain is that an IDS is not a simple group practice. A few practitioners who share a secretary may meet their own definition of a "group," but it is not an IDS.

As the term implies, an IDS is a truly integrated system of providers which deliver care in the most clinically and cost-efficient manner. The IDS can further offer geographical coverage, specialty coverage, ease of communication, administrative functions, and the ability to assume clinical and financial risk. For the payer, the IDS represents one stop shopping.

The core of the IDS is providers and group practices that have joined together to share a common clinical, and just as important, economic vision. By joining together they have realized that they can expand geography and specialty coverage, pool resources and capital, spread costs, and increase market share. In doing so, they have dramatically increased their "attractiveness" to the managed care organizations and payers.

The IDS is not to be confused with provider hospital organizations (PHOs), which are an affiliation of practitioners with brick-and-mortar facilities. The problem with PHOs can be seen in the name itself. Managed care has made its mark by reducing and eliminating the importance of hospital-based care. The PHO often revolves around hospital-based practice. It may be a new version of a dinosaur, but it still is a dinosaur.

Take one example of a large PHO that was formed 2 years ago on the East Coast. The driving force behind the formation was the hospital, as it was losing revenue at a rapid pace to managed care. Providers were invited to apply for membership and pay a substantial fee to be part of the PHO. Credentialing criteria were not considered, and the providers invited to join were those practitioners who had supported the hospital in the past by admitting numerous patients. Provider hosptial organization membership, in essence, was a reward for past potentially cost-inefficient practice. Managed care organizations saw the PHO for what it was: one last attempt for the hospital to keep its inpatient revenue. Within 6 months the PHO (which took one year to form) had folded. Providers had lost valuable time and money.

Providers joined without even considering the marketplace, and the PHO had no business to offer. Furthermore, the PHO leadership had not consulted with managed care or other payers to determine how the PHO might be formed and what services were needed. This was a critical mistake, as the only utility of a PHO for managed care is if it solves a problem for that managed care company. In the absence of that criterion, the PHO is no better than any other practitioner in the community.

In sum, a PHO may be an IDS but a PHO is not synonymous with an IDS. It is far more important for the IDS to have hospital affiliations and relationships than it is for the hospital to be a sole driver in the venture.

IDS: 12 Key Administrative and Clinical Functions

For an IDS to be successful, it must take on both the clinical and administrative functions that have been described in this chapter. The goal of the IDS is twofold: to assist managed care where solutions are needed and to replace managed care where their solution is not needed. Overall, then, there are 12 basic points which must be covered for the IDS to develop and thrive:

1. *Legal business entity.* Once the decision has been made by the practitioner-owner to join or form either a group practice entity or a larger IDS, it is naturally important to form the proper legal

relationships. Having legal counsel in such matters is imperative, as certain states have prohibitions as to the type of system that is formed, and as to how the entity can operate and function. There are also important prohibitions as to even the type of information that can be discussed among group members (e.g., provider reimbursement).

2. *One central contact person: one signature needed.* Once the legal entity is formed, it is critical that the IDS have someone in charge. Whether it is the chairperson of a board that is created or simply one elected member who has been legally selected by the group, one signature entity is needed. For the IDS to swiftly move in a marketplace, contracting with MCOs and payers needs to be painless, or the MCO/payer will look elsewhere.

A personal experience is illustrative. I was bidding on a large contract in one particular state, and in my search for an IDS which could effectively manage this business, I was approached by an individual who described just what was needed: a large multi-location IDS with all the elements described in this chapter. I thought I had found the answer. After a series of negotiations, the contractual agreement was prepared. To my surprise, the individual then stated the entire IDS membership needed to approve the agreement and each must sign. He took the agreement for this approval, and never was heard from again. The deal was lost.

3. *Internal credentialing standards, including economic profiles.* Membership in the IDS should be considered a privilege. Unlike the failed PHO described earlier, if an individual provider does not have the clinical or economic profile that is desired they should not be part of the system. The IDS should have an application process in place, including the verification of all applicable credentials (e.g., licensure, malpractice, education). This application process should mirror the requirements of managed care, in that this will save time or even replace managed care processes if done correctly and adequately.

Perhaps one of the most important aspects of credentialing is in the ongoing operations of the IDS. An IDS is only as strong as its ability to be able to exclude practitioners over time who no longer meet standards. This includes economic performance. In other words, if a provider's performance is inefficient and corrective measures do not impact their practice, then they should not be part of the larger entity.

Economic performance is a more complex topic than simple length of stay or admission statistics. Not all that long ago I took part in one study at a managed care company where utilization data across providers and all diagnoses were compiled. The average length of outpatient treatment was a little over eight sessions. Providers scoring 3 standard deviations above the mean were contacted and interviewed. Two distinct sets of providers were discovered: those who were effectively treating the very seriously ill, and those who were rambling inefficiently in the treatment of the less seriously ill. The former are critical to have in a provider network, while the latter are not.

It is a sensitive issue for providers to perform economic profiling on their peers. It is easier when a managed care company excludes someone from a panel. It is not so easy when it is your colleague. Social psychology teaches us that the best way to create a cohesive group is to find a common enemy. Managed care created a lot of cohesiveness among providers. For providers, the enemy is now themselves.

4. *Multidisciplinary and multispeciality staff.* The IDS must be able to handle the full range of clinical presentations. To do this, the various disciplines must put behind them the fights of previous years and find ways to more effectively work together. Many psychiatrists, psychologists, social workers, and other counselors have made careers publicly fighting other disciplines or other "schools" of psychotherapy. Ultimately such fights are meaningless and self-serving in the economically driven healthcare marketplace of today.

As a prelude to failure, there are single discipline groups springing up throughout the country. One such affiliated practice allowed only psychiatrists as members. In their consultation with me, I informed them that they could survive if they (a) build internally the expertise of other disciplines they were excluding, and (b) agree to take home less money because their unit charge would now drop. This latter point seemed puzzling to the group leadership, but it is simple economics. If a master's-level clinician charges $50 less than the psychiatrist for the same counseling service, then the psychiatrist now performing that service will need to drop the fee to that same level. As one managed care executive aptly noted, "The definition of a core provider is one who will take less money for the same service." No one discipline has the answer. The best IDS is one that includes the best of all disciplines and specialties in an optimal clinical and economic mix.

5. *Inpatient and alternative levels of care program affiliations.* The IDS has to cover entire populations and be at risk to be eligible for large pieces of business. An outpatient-only IDS does not offer one stop shopping for the payer and, therefore, is not as competitive as an IDS that covers all levels of care.

The potential failings of PHOs as hospital-dominated systems were discussed earlier. On the other hand, inpatient care, partial hospitalization, and intensive outpatient programs are needed to supply a full continuum of care to the variety of patients that may be seen. The successful IDS must have working relationships with all these and be prepared to enter into risk relationships with them. These relationships need to include both clinical and referral protocols as well as financial arrangements. Legal assistance will again be necessary to assure compliance with local regulations.

6. *Centralized intake: Single point of access.* The cornerstone of an effective IDS is that all patients can easily and efficiently access care. In fact, one of the largest problems in the open provider marketplace is that in the multiple access system, inappropriate care is a rather common occurrence.

Specifically, without a centralized access point patients find care through a variety of mechanisms such as provider lists, telephone directories, and word of mouth. None of these mechanisms do what is most needed: link the patient with the most appropriate provider for what is needed. In addition, once a provider is found in the open marketplace, there is no guarantee they are available. Given this inadequate system, it is very possible for a patient to arrive at a provider who is not appropriate for the presenting condition. For example, an adolescent should not be seen by a provider who has received training only in the treatment of adults. The ethical provider refers the patient to another, more appropriate provider, but time and money are lost. The less (or un-) ethical provider may attempt to treat that patient, and even more time and money is lost, not to mention the quality of care and potential malpractice issues.

Centralized point of access solves this problem. In its most rudimentary form, the single point of access (SPA) provides a telephonic entry point to care for the entire IDS. In this way a patient call immediately accesses all providers in the system and links that patient to the most appropriate provider available. Clinical and cost-efficiency is obtained.

7. *24-hour coverage (including MD coverage).* Too many practitioners today still operate on the notion that they can set up a small office, have an answering machine, and schedule their own appointments; MCOs and payers will no longer tolerate such arrangements, particularly in a preferred provider market.

Patients need intervention at all hours, and answering machines do not address emergencies. The successful IDS provides 24-hour coverage with no answering machines, paging systems, and so forth. A live voice is available, and a clinician can be reached immediately. This includes the ability to address medication issues and admit patients to a facility if needed.

It is common for practitioner-owners to complain to managed care companies about lack of referrals. Understandably, however, the available practitioner will be utilized.

8. *Internal Utilization Management (UM) procedures.* The IDS needs to have a system in place to monitor the clinical practice of its own member practitioners. This is important for clinical quality purposes, and in the case of risk contracting, is essential for financial purposes. The key is not to recreate the inefficient managed care form of utilization management, but rather to use and transform what is already inherent in the IDS practitioner system. In this way, UM is performed but administrative overhead is not necessarily increased.

There are numerous examples of how this may be achieved. In the IDS that has group practices as members, supervision, case conferences, and team meetings are often elements of the already in place daily routine. Typically, however, these meetings focus only on clinical concerns and do not review cost-effectiveness as well. Supervision, conferences, meetings, and so forth should focus on both.

Another UM mechanism that must be employed is the sharing of clinical criteria. Clinical criteria as a whole are probably overrated by managed care companies, but the agreement of a base set of criteria at least allows all practitioners to be working off the same page. In this way, if one practitioner is admitting more patients than others to inpatient settings, their practice can be reviewed using the same standard clinical criteria as with all other IDS members. Further, if all practitioners are trained in and utilizing set practice criteria, there should be (in theory) less need to oversee every clinical act of the individual provider.

9. *Internal Case Management procedures.* As with UM procedures, the IDS also has to have mechanisms to assist in cases that more typically fall through the gaps in a system of care. This is often the case with severe psychopathology, where numerous inpatient admissions and intensive treatment may be needed. What is needed in such cases is for the practitioner to identify the patient as in need of more intensive case management coordination, and to have identified practitioners and programs who are going to be handling these more complex cases. If such a system is not devised, then clinical quality suffers, and the financial cost of such care rises.

10. *Internal quality assurance, including outcome studies and patient satisfaction surveys.* There is a significant movement in managed care toward outcome studies. This is not easy to do, as the entire mental health profession has long failed to adequately and objectively show outcomes of various psychological approaches. It is known, however, that some approaches are generally more successful than others with specific disorders, and that some providers are better than others in offering the treatment. Patient satisfaction and outcome studies begin to narrow in on these two very important areas.

The practitioner system that incorporates outcome studies and patient satisfaction into its own structured routine will have information that will potentially assist in patient care as well as in gaining managed care and payer market share. The marketplace is demanding outcomes; the IDS should deliver.

11. *Ability to contract with alternative reimbursement mechanisms.* A significant trend in managed care is the movement away from traditional reduced fee-for-service arrangements to financial risk agreements with providers. The practitioner-owner has to be ready to meet this trend.

Risk relationships typically fall into two categories: case rates and capitation. Case rates are where providers are paid one flat rate for a patient, regardless of the eventual length of the episode of care. There are many variations of case rates, but regardless of the methodology, case rates work for providers as long as the providers know their unit cost (which is not to be confused with unit charged) and average length of stay. For example, if a per unit cost is $40 and an average length of treatment is 8 sessions, then a $300 case rate will represent a loss unless a more efficient/effective unit cost can be developed.

Capitation is an at-risk arrangement which covers all members of a plan, not just patients who present for treatment. Obviously this requires more sophisticated underwriting and far more potential risk. Capitation also requires that the IDS have funds available should any given month show a loss. In other words, even if an IDS is profitable, a given month might require more spending over capitation revenue. Cash flow can be a serious issue in such cases, and financial resources are the means by which untoward costs in any one period can be paid.

12. *Management information systems (MIS)*. The most overlooked and underfunded area of an IDS is in the area of information systems. Indeed, the vast majority of mental health practitioners do not own more than a personal computer and a fax machine; many do not even have that equipment. The more that the IDS intends to take on in terms of managed care contracting and direct payer-employer contracting, the more sophisticated the system needs to be.

At a base level, the IDS system needs to be able to perform the following functions: call/record tracking, provider database, patient referral data, provider authorization, utilization tracking, reporting, centralized billing, and claims payment.

Many off-the-shelf systems exist today, and not all require the same level of investment. Still, for the developing IDS, assume that sophisticated systems are needed, and these are expensive.

PRACTITIONER-OWNER MARKETING

Marketing for the IDS and group practice is not the same as it was with the solo practitioner-owner of days gone by: yellow pages listings, advertisements, and speaking to other clinicians and physician practices. Many practitioners donated time to speak to local organizations, hoping to then pass out cards to potential referrers or patients. All these antiquated methods aimed at finding ways to get patients to walk through the door were successful in the past.

Today, the focus is not on increasing referrals but on increasing payers. This is a critical shift in mind-set. Getting patients in the door means very little if their insurance coverage does not allow payment for the services once they get there. Unless you as practitioner-owner are interested in donating free time, you cannot see that patient.

Of course there is a subset of practitioners advocating that there is a practice to be made out of self-pay patients. They believe they can buck the trend, ignore managed care and group practices, and just expect patients to pay them out of pocket because of their superior talent. An equally effective alternative strategy would be to take all of your savings to Las Vegas to place on one roulette number, or to the local track to bet on a horse with a familiar sounding name. Your odds of financial survival with these gambles are only a little worse than the self-pay strategy upon which some practitioners are gambling their careers.

The key for marketing success of the practitioner-owner today is in cooperation with managed care and payers. As your group practice and IDS develop, it is important to have contacts with as many managed care companies as possible. Find out what their needs are and fill them. For example, if they tell you that there is a paucity of intensive outpatient programs for adolescents, then you might want to consider building that expertise within your IDS rather than creating a substance abuse program for which they tell you there is a glut in the market. Managed care and payers have often carefully surveyed the provider community in terms of service gaps. Use their knowledge to build your practice.

FINANCIAL RISK

As a practitioner-owner, assumption of financial risk puts you back in charge and offers you opportunities you cannot get through nonrisk reimbursement. Managed care companies fight to gain risk contracts. That should tell the provider community something as to their desirability. Once the practitioner is in control of the dollars, it is the practitioner who decides what services will be paid for and developed and what administrative oversight and overhead is needed. If care is efficient and of high quality, it is the practitioner who keeps the profit. This is exactly what the practitioner-owner should be searching for.

The reason financial risk is difficult for practitioners to swallow is that it is foreign to them. As with many other business topics, finance was not taught in graduate school. Underwriting was a concept left to actuaries at insurance companies. However, as with most mysterious and scary concepts, understanding financial risk is not that difficult once you are armed with the correct core knowledge.

To take on capitation and true risk, there is some basic information needed; e.g., covered lives, historical utilization by level of care and diagnosis, past and current benefit structure, provider network. Most payers will have this information, and if the information on any given data point is not available, your risk is increased proportionately.

Once you feel you have a good handle on the past and the design for the present, you need to next project to the future. Therefore, based on the information gathered you need to chart and predict utilization by level of care. You will then need to determine administrative cost. Much of this is determined by the requirements of the party contracting with you. In terms of underwriting risk, when all else fails, common sense and logic prevail.

MANAGEMENT SERVICES ORGANIZATIONS (MSOs)

The administrative and clinical expertise and infrastructure needed for a successful IDS can be daunting. For many practitioners, the solution in these areas may not be to build, but rather to acquire. Building seems better in that you as the practitioner-owner retain full ownership of the entire IDS structure. Realistically, however, you are aware that you do not have the expertise in nonclinical areas and certainly do not have the time or money to spend on all the nonclinical requirements. Several options exist.

Managed care organizations might be very willing to help. There are examples in the marketplace of MCO/provider partnerships, whereby the MCOs provide the infrastructure and knowledge while the providers do what they do best: deliver care. The advantage to this method is that it is quick and efficient, and also gains immediate access to the lives covered by that particular MCO.

This solution, however, has a major drawback. Once you are a provider partner with one specific MCO, this could very well shut you out of the market with other MCOs and payers. The market is extremely competitive, and if you are identified as the group working with MCO X, then MCO Y will look for alternatives. In other words, if 100% of your practice can be funded by that MCO, then it is a reasonable solution. Otherwise, proceed with great caution. If the market you live in has numerous MCOs and payers, partnering with one may not be the best step.

There are also MCOs, hospitals, and other private organizations which would be willing to buy your practice to infuse capital and infrastructure needs. This seems to be a particularly popular approach today. The advantage is that it gives you as the practitioner-owner immediate cash, and takes away a great headache for you in terms of dealing with the changing marketplace. The downside of selling is that you rarely receive enough cash to make it in the long run. You still will need income from somewhere. In addition, there are often complicated and lengthy earn out periods which will be problematic if the market shifts or your purchaser cannot obtain contracts. As one colleague responds to the question, "Should I sell?"—"Are you ready to retire?"

In comparison to these two options, there is a third one in the marketplace today: the Management Services Organization (MSO). This is a relatively new service, as MSOs work directly with providers in building needed infrastructure. This assistance can take many forms, including a variety of clinical and administrative services.

More specifically, a full-function MSO can offer the provider group or IDS a menu of services to choose from: legal-regulatory, clinical-QI, provider network-contracting, information systems, telephone (including single point of access), financial-budgeting, claims-billing, claims processing, underwriting, and marketing.

The MSO option has a significant advantage for the practitioner. It allows one to quickly provide clinical and administrative infrastructure, while retaining ownership and independence in the marketplace.

SUMMARY

This chapter has focused on the practitioner as an owner of a business in a changing and complex marketplace. Those practitioners who refuse to acknowledge their practice as a business are destined to fail. Furthermore, the economic drivers of health care also make it virtually impossible for the solo practitioner-owner to survive. Partnerships, groups, and the formation of integrated delivery systems are the way of the future and the mechanism for survival.

As the practitioner-owner addresses the needs in the marketplace, opportunities are seen. However, such opportunities exist only for those providers offering solutions to the various payers of the service (e.g., insurance companies, employers, managed care organizations). The solution lies in the provider's ability to increasingly assume nonclinical administrative functions and to provide one-stop shopping of all services for the payer.

In order to do this, the provider group/IDS will need help. It is proposed that the management services organization is one way for the practitioner-owner to keep ownership, grow, and remain independent in the marketplace. The situation may be dire, but the practitioner that understands they are a business owner and makes decisions based on business and economic reality can make it.

11.

Capitation, Case Rate, and Prepaid Health: The Dynamic Balance

Daniel Berman, Psy.D., M.H.A., R.N.

> *Golly, Toto, this sure doesn't look like Kansas.*
>
> Judy Garland as Dorothy
> The Wizard of Oz

Capitation and prepaid health is a concept that instills fear in practitioners. This fear is rooted in both their individual practices and the group and management system with which they are aligned. The fear is that their individual practices and their ethics will be affected. They fear that the patients will *not* receive the care they need. The second fear is an economic one that is driving practitioners to bind together in group practices. The owners of the newly formed groups believe that capitation will force them to choose between economic security versus a desire to give the appropriate amount of care.

This writer, through his consultative work in developing groups, sees the world of capitation differently. This chapter is based upon his extensive consultative experience with colleagues forming group practices, as well as the findings of other experts (Armor, 1994; Freeman, 1995; Zinger, 1994).

Practitioners need to understand and implement the management principles necessary to maintain the dynamic balance.

This article will focus on the positive issues that capitation brings to the new delivery system. The dynamic management model of balance is the key to the success of provider group movement. If the product owned by these groups cannot maintain the delicate balance, their fears of capitation will become reality. If dynamic balance is maintained, there are essential tools of management that will further enable the capitated group to succeed. The product sold in the capitated contract must be balanced among fiscal, clinical/quality, and customer service. Each entity must be addressed with equal, but appropriate emphasis. If one aspect dominates over the others, the balance necessary to service will be lost and the system of capitation will fail.

The other essential management tools that practitioners must master are: (1) the need for outcome research; (2) the need to create a seamless delivery system; and (3) the need to market. The dynamic balance model which involves managing fiscal, clinical/quality, and customer service issues should incorporate outcome research as an integral part of the delivery system. This is as important as having a delivery system that is seamless, and a marketing component that can convey how this group is efficiently and effectively positioned.

Each component must be examined before there is an understanding of how each contributes to the success of the capitated contract:

Fiscal Balance involves not only understanding past utilization, but also how new research employing past and present utilization can predict future use of services. Outcome studies, and the information generated, allows a constant fine-tuning of the delivery system toward efficiency (cost-containment).

Clinical Balance allows the decision makers to assess whether the client's needs are being met, again through outcomes research. Are the patients satisfied with the service?

Customer Service Balance allows the decision maker to determine if the group is meeting the needs of the payer. The future marketing of the group's present contract and future contracts depends on this information.

As mentioned previously, all three forces have to be in equilibrium. Four possible scenarios that could occur and management implications for each are shown in Figure 11.1.

Figure 11.1 Four Possible Scenarios with Consequent
Management Implications

Scenario A

Management Implication—This is the optimal picture for any group.

Scenario B

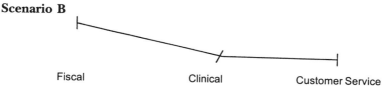

Management Implication—In this scenario, fiscal profit motives have
become the most important aspect of business. Management must pull
back into balance by overemphasizing the other two areas until balance
is restored.

Scenario C

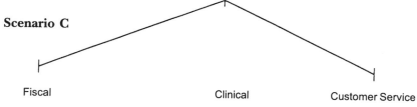

Management Implication—In this scenario, clinical needs have become
the most important. In this case there are some patients that are being
overserved, which causes a financial drain on this contract. Again,
management must overemphasize the other two to bring them into
balance.

Scenario D

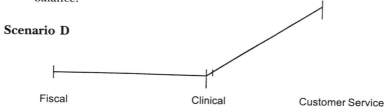

Management Implication—In this scenario, the needs of the payer have
become more important than fiscal or clinical determinants. The
group is probably experiencing fiscal difficulties because they have bid
the contract too low.

Risk factors arise and cause friction among different issues to arise for both management and the direct service providers. Each factor will have an impact:

1. *Morbidity risk* is the true need of services and is called by management "medical necessity." Management wants to limit the service as long as customer service and clinical issues are not affected. The clinician wants only to treat the client while ignoring economic factors.
2. *Demand risk* means that the beneficiaries of the healthcare policy want more treatment than morbidity would allow. Management tends to view this as the beneficiaries indirectly stealing the profits; therefore, the care is limited. The practitioners, because of their own needs, may actually support the beneficiaries in their quest. Actuaries are aware that certain populations demand disproportionately higher mental health services, not only out of morbidity, but also because psychotherapy is fashionable. Examples of such populations are teachers and social workers.

Prepaid health services is a concept by which an organization prepays a fixed sum and the members of the organization can use the services on an unlimited basis based upon a medical necessity determination. The concept of medical determination is complex and is not within the scope of this chapter, but examples of prepaid care are case-rate payment and capitation, with the latter based on per member/per month (pm/pm).

The prepayment of behavioral health is not a new concept. It has been in existence since 1910, beginning with the Western Clinic in Washington State. Other early examples of prepaid behavioral health would be the one conducted by the physician Mildred Shadhid, of Oklahoma City, Oklahoma, and by the Ross-Loos group in Palo Alto, California. On a large scale, prepaid behavioral health began with the Kaiser-Permanente Health Maintenance Organization after World War II. Until the late 1950s and early 1960s, the conventional wisdom was that behavioral healthcare could not be prepaid as it did not conform to recognizable economic factors. This stance began to dissolve with the discovery at Kaiser-Permanente that 60% of physician visits are by patients with no physical illness, and who can be helped by behavioral intervention: the so-called medical cost offset phenomenon (Cummings & VandenBos, 1981).

DIRECT RISKS OF CAPITATION

Behavioral health capitation is best defined as a paid assumption of risk by a provider for the delivery of a set of services. The entire cost of care is contained in one amount. As the risk is shifted to providers, value is increased. Value equals the cost divided by the quality. In other words, in managing capitation cost, quality and value are balanced. Risk to the providers is financial liability for care. There are direct risks of capitation that must be managed.

1. *Morbidity* is the true need for services and may be higher in some populations as indicated above. Some morbidity risk is the result of heredity issues such as bipolar, while others well reflect life-styles or the dangers of living in the inner city. In managing this type of risk one must be skilled in epidemiological population status assessment.
2. *Demand risk* means that the beneficiaries of the healthcare policy want more treatment than they actually need. Beneficiaries may also fail to seek treatment and, therefore, hospitalization becomes necessary and at greater cost.
3. *Utilization risk* is a major problem because clinicians may give greater amounts of care than needed.
4. *Catastrophic risk* results from unplanned, devastating costs as might result with the unexpected protracted hospitalization of the chronically mentally ill.
5. *Price risk* can be a group's worst nightmare. It is the difference between the capitation rate agreed upon and the group's actual cost risk liability, and results from a miscalculation in the contracted capitation rate.

These are called direct risks, and the newly forming groups have objective and effective means of managing these factors. These direct risks are not always under the full control of the clinician or a management that lacks expertise or the authority to mandate the characteristics of the delivery system. For example, in utilization risk the clinician may give more care than needed. For management, this is problematic because managers must take a fiscal and customer service based stand against their own clinicians. On the other hand, the clinicians might oppose management, concentrating on their need to treat, maintain ethics, and have economic security, forgetting that if the capitated system fails they are essentially unemployed.

In catastrophic risk the individual recipients have a large need for services. For example, management might look for clinicians skilled in the kind of outpatient care that will reduce inpatient costs. Again, the danger is that without adequate controls and procedures well in place, the flood gates may be opened and controls may come too late to save the system from bankruptcy.

INDIRECT RISKS OF CAPITATION

1. *Regulatory risk* refers to the financial demands of legislative and regulatory requirements on capitation. These vary from state to state, with overly regulated states imposing costs exceeding those of doing business in other states.
2. *Insurance risk* refers to the additional cost of insurance that groups must maintain.
3. *Liability risk* refers to the cost of lost clinical time resulting from increased services and paperwork needed to protect the organization from litigation. This is often referred to as "defensive practice," and it can be costly.
4. *Contract risk* refers to risks associated with an organization's ability to do business. These could be based on noncompetition agreements, payer cancellations, and the timing of reimbursement mechanisms.
5. *Infrastructure risk* refers to the cost of facilities and mechanisms that must be created to service a contract.
6. *Professional risk* refers to the practitioners' violations of their professional codes of ethics or standards of practice.

In this new environment whereby the outpatient providers are becoming owners and drivers of newly emerging behavioral health delivery systems, developing *groups without walls* or *networks* creates an inherent problem for the evolving clinician managers of capitation. Because they are clinicians first and foremost, there is a tendency to overidentify with their contracted clinicians' needs and thus manage poorly. That is why it is essential for the clinicians to hire a trained healthcare manager to administer any capitated contract. The new owner should give administrative control to this individual so that the *dynamic balance* can be maintained.

The worst fear of any clinician when he or she hears the word *capitation* is that the patient outcomes will be adverse. Therefore, it is essential that management develop a comprehensive outcome study program. This program need not be expensive and it can develop its own tools, or employ off-the-shelf software. The program should include a customer satisfaction survey as well as a measure of therapeutic outcome. The best outcomes research is so well integrated into the delivery system that practitioners and patients are not directly aware of its presence. In other words, it does not interfere with the delivery of services by intrusiveness.

The payer and referral services, if different, should also be surveyed to determine satisfaction with management's services. This should include management's responsiveness along with outcomes of services.

Patient outcomes research is extremely important, if not paramount. It demonstrates to the contractor that care is being delivered efficiently and within contract boundaries.

In provider owned groups, another dynamic will inevitably emerge. When delivering services as a provider, there will arise instances when the provider's advocacy for a patient may place him or her in direct conflict with the part of the same provider that is also a provider-owner.

The procurement of capitated contracts involves the use of a knowledge base and understanding of financial mechanisms. A group can obtain a capitated contract directly from an HMO/Payer, behavioral managed care company, or an employee assistance program which is at risk. There are basically three types of at-risk bidding. They are:

1. *Case rates.* The provider group is given one fee to manage one episode of care, or a sum to manage a set number of referrals over a one-year period.
2. *Capitation.* The provider group is paid a flat fee per month for each beneficiary to provide all the necessary care. The capitation rate represents a per member/per month amount, referred to in the health industry as "pm/pm."
3. *Withhold.* This is used to reward a provider group for low utilization, normally 0 to 15%, which is then returned in part to the group in accordance with prior agreement. In this arrangement the provider is sharing in the cost saving.

All three are financial bidding mechanisms. In principle, the group must be knowledgeable enough to predict costs and skillful enough to control costs. Without the ability to predict and control costs, there can be no accurate capitation rate.

PLANNING AND DEVELOPMENT

The integrated behavioral group must develop and implement certain systems and skills before it is ready to bid for contracts. They are as follows:

1. The group must examine its clinical philosophy. It must make certain it is utilizing the least restrictive site and the best frequency of care.
2. The group's chief financial officer must develop actuarial tables and claims utilization rates.
3. A working knowledge of the population served is important to understand utilization review patterns for different ethnicities, diagnoses, genders, socioeconomic categories, etc.
4. A working knowledge of employer benefit design with specific numbers of service units to be utilized must be acquired.
5. The group must be aware of legal issues and be protected with internal standards as well as liability insurance.
6. The group must be prepared to provide the full continuum of behavioral health services.

Responding to RFPs for Capitation and/or Case Rates

After obtaining the opportunity to bid on a contract, the group must write a proposal or answer a request for proposal (RFP) which should include a description of the organization, including administration and management information systems (MIS), as well as clinical services. This latter section must include the entire clinical process, including a description of the scope of services, a complete description of the MIS system supporting the clinical process, and a delineation of outcome studies which show the survey tools to be utilized. The calculated cost saving and how it will be accomplished is called the "value added" factor. For early managed behavioral healthcare companies, the "value added" was the savings resulting from lowering psychiatric hospitalization rates, often as much as 95%, by substitution of intensive outpatient care and medical necessity standards for inpatient admission.

The next step is rate and bid calculations. There are several assumptions that must be made in bidding. It should be emphasized that these assumptions are subject to variability from contract to contract.

1. Regarding utilization, people use an average of 30 I/P (inpatient) days and 200 O/P (outpatient) visits annually per 1000 enrollees of a benefit.
2. The net cost is $500 per I/P day and $80 per O/P visit.
3. Administrative costs are 40% of gross contract amount.
4. Profit margin is 10% of the gross amount of the contract.

The following are real examples of calculating a capitated bid:

Example A: 15,000 enrollees in an insurance plan.

Step 1: There is a 7% utilization of O/P behavioral health; therefore, 1050 enrollees will use O/P behavioral health.
Step 2: 1050 times an average of 7 sessions = 7,350 sessions annually.
Step 3: The cost of these visits is 7,350 × $80 = $588,000 annually.

Step 4: $588,000 divided by 15,000 enrollees will equal $39.20 annually, or $3.27 pm/pm (per member, per month).

Example B: 115,000 enrollees in an insurance plan.

Step 1: There is a 9% utilization of O/P behavioral health; therefore, 19,350 enrollees will use O/P behavioral health.
Step 2: 10,350 times an average of 6.5 sessions = 67,275 sessions annually.
Step 3: The cost of these visits is 67,275 × $80 = $5,382,000 annually.
Step 4: $5,382,000 divided by 115,000 enrollees will equal $46.80 annually, or $3.90 pm/pm.

In the development of a proposal for a capitated contract, the final calculation is always expressed in pm/pm (per member, per month), with $1.00 to $1.50 added for administration. The components of a proposal are:

1. The introduction
2. The summary of services
3. The scope of services, which always includes:
   Cost breakdown
   Utilization expectation
   Role changes
   Program evaluation and outcomes

Capitation has resulted in a need for, and drive toward, multispecialty groups that provide the continuum of services. Ultimately capitation, with its need for financial integration, may accelerate the process of clinical integration with seamless delivery of services.

From a consumer point of view, capitation has caused providers to handle care in a different fashion, as prepaid behavioral health services are now offered only in managed care networks. This has resulted in a consolidation of provider groups with private practitioners binding together to form networks that can handle capitation. The survival of such groups is essentially dependent upon their ability to develop a seamless delivery system, meaning eventually a multispecialty group that provides the entire spectrum of health services.

For now, the elements of a seamless delivery system are: (1) 24-hour accessibility to services, with professional handling of intakes, the ability to triage care based on emergency, aesthetically pleasing offices, the ability to interface with primary care physicians, the willingness to be customer responsive, and the ability to interface with other providers so that the full continuum of behavioral health services can be delivered. (2) Quality management, which requires a written definition of medical necessity, a process to review high-risk utilization, patient satisfaction surveys, and referent satisfactions surveys. (3) A solid administrative infrastructure with the ability to assume financial risk, a communication channel to payers, a defined appeals process, prompt claims processing, customer service, a provider relations department, and a responsive human resources system. (4) An MIS that is tied to the payment of claims, benefit structures, patients, quality control, clinical decisions, and the provider.

MARKETING

Although the next logical step is the marketing of capitated contracts, experience shows that provider groups mistakenly market before they fully understand capitation or have the ability to quickly mobilize the necessary infrastructure. It is recommended that marketing and the infrastructure be created at the same time. Most often administrative expertise must be hired from outside the clinical group.

Once a potential group understands capitation and case rates, it can organize an integrated behavioral delivery system, with varied programs that cover the complete continuum of care. It can market to the following:

1. *Employers* that have the ability to directly contract with employees.
2. *Labor unions'* health and welfare funds.
3. *Health insurance carriers*, including insurance companies and Blue Cross/Blue Shield plans.

In marketing for capitation, there are several elements a group must have:

1. Sophisticated public relations material demonstrating that the group has the appropriate expertise.
2. A complete business plan with market and income projections.
3. A market analysis with target business.
4. A working knowledge of competitive bidders.
5. Key business contacts.
6. A showcasing of key clinicians with specific expertise.

Clinicians often mistakenly assume that managing cost control is simple. It is highly recommended that no capitation be sought until there is a sufficient knowledge base in the areas previously discussed: an understanding of capitation, a network in place, an adequate MIS, sophisticated administrative systems, and a capacity for outcomes research.

If the provider groups follow the procedures outlined, capitation is attainable and profitable. Some provider groups mistakenly choose not to become involved because of ethical issues. As long as provider groups do the following ethically appropriate actions there should be no difficulty:

1. Follow professional codes of ethics and accepted standards of practice.
2. Honor the spirit of MCO contracts.
3. Treat clients as humans in need of care.
4. Provide the highest quality services.
5. Provide financial data, and be responsible clinicians who do not "overtreat."
6. Always explain benefits.
7. Abandon no patients.

CONCLUSION

This author has outlined a financial, clinical, and administrative system that, if implemented, makes capitation extremely profitable. If the clinicians follow the ethics outlined, as well, there should be no problems. Capitation and prepaid health have created a tremendous opportunity for behavioral health groups.

The opportunity will only be fruitful if the provider group maintains the dynamic equilibrium among fiscal, clinical/quality, and customer service issues. Fiscal responsibility addresses costs within the clinical/quality need to provide ethical and effective care, while customer service must be responsive to both the preceding as well as the requirements of the customer-payer.

12.

The Search for Capital: Positioning for Growth, Joint Venturing, Acquisition, and Public Offering

Nicholas A. Cummings, Ph.D., Sc.D.

An empty sack cannot remain upright.
Baron von Rothschild

In the race between practitioners seeking to form practitioner owned regional group practices and the managed care organizations (MCOs) which look tó form or acquire their own captive (company owned) groups, the latter currently have the cash in hand while the former scramble to find capitalization. The inability to find start-up money will severely hamper or prevent the evolution of practitioner-equity regional group practices, yet the capital is there. Unfortunately, mental health practitioners seldom know how to position themselves to attract capitalization. The purpose of this chapter is to enable practitioners who want to launch their company to position themselves appropriately. It is not intended to be an extensive description of a complex financial area. It will be necessary to retain appropriate help. The novice entrepreneur who confronts the subjects of attitude, positioning, and risk within oneself, will be able to differentiate expertise from

205

the many marginal consultants who would take advantage of fear, indecision, and lack of knowledge.

OVERCOMING RISK AVERSION

Many venture capitalists have confided in the author that their decisions are based only 25% on the excellence of the idea, and 75% on the ability and confidence of the founder(s) to pull it off. The ideal entrepreneur is a David Packard working 18 hours a day in a rented garage because he was too poor to rent an office-workshop. It is now history how Packard, with his partner Hewlett, went on to form one of the Fortune 500 companies. Few practitioners can match the dedication of Dave Packard, Steve Jobs, or Bill Gates, and venture capitalists really do not expect this ideal. Yet they are put off when the would-be entrepreneur desperately retains his or her faculty position, V.A. appointment, or other full-time job. This behavior telegraphs to venture capitalists that the psychologist has little confidence in his or her own ability or idea, and the concept has been relegated to the status of an exciting hobby which deserves capitalization.

When the author was founding American Biodyne he was interviewed for over 2 hours by the legendary venture capitalist Arthur Rock who capitalized Apple Computer and reportedly over 600 other successful start-ups. A small excerpt from the interview is illuminating:

Mr. Rock: You are 62. Isn't that a little old to be founding a company, to say nothing of creating a whole new industry?

Dr. Cummings: I don't think so. Armand Hammer was 62 when he founded Occidental Petroleum (a Fortune 500 company).

Mr. Rock: If you fail, you will lose everything and be too old to recoup. Doesn't that frighten you?

Dr. Cummings: No, I know I can do it.

Mr. Rock: But what if, for whatever reason, you can't pull it off?

Dr. Cummings: This is such a good idea that if I don't pull it off I deserve to live my old age in poverty.

Five years later when American Biodyne completed a very successful Initial Public Offering (IPO), Arthur Rock confided that this 2-minute interchange was the deciding factor in his becoming an investor.

There is no start-up without risk. The greater the potential reward, the more likely the risk. Look risk directly in the eye, assess it, and learn to live with it. Your risk aversion is contagious to anyone considering investing in you.

WHAT ELSE DO VCs LOOK FOR?

Overcoming risk aversion is only the first, yet critical, step. No matter how much confidence is exuded, however, the idea must have merit and the founder, or preferably founders as a team, must have the track record that would indicate their ability to successfully implement the idea. The overwhelming majority of venture capitalists (VCs) distrust "Lone Rangers." They look for a team whose various competencies complement each other. So make certain your team covers the parameters. Look beyond the few good colleagues who merely share your vision and give you encouragement. This is not a team; it is a social club, or even worse, a support group.

Venture capitalists like big problems, because this signals the potential for big solutions. Behavioral healthcare is a $60 to $80 billion industry, with several times that amount in such annual costs as suicide, absenteeism, disability, and human suffering. There is room for big companies providing big solutions for big problems. So think big.

Your company must have this ability to grow. The law in biology which states that when an organism stops growing it begins to die is also true in economics: companies that stop growing soon disappear. The more rapid the growth potential, the more attractive your start-up is.

In selling to venture capitalists you must have a compelling and understandable story. You must be able to ignite enthusiasm in someone who knows nothing or little about the industry you are entering. If an analogy can be made to a known success story, do so. But you must also be able to straightforwardly discuss the negatives, such as barriers to entry and the competition. The compelling story will show how you can overcome the barriers to entry, which will be an advantage over those who lack ability to do so. Stress your advantages over the competition, and demonstrate your stamina and staying power.

Be aware that venture capitalists tend to specialize, such as in technology or in healthcare, as two examples. For some VCs some industries will be shunned, while these same industries will be favored by others. Do your homework and make certain the VC you are addressing is a good fit. The most compelling story will fail before a VC who does not capitalize within the business sector you represent.

Venture capitalists range from those who choose an investment and then trust their judgment by staying out of management's way, to those who are very intrusive. A seat, or even seats, on the board of directors is a frequent demand, and the history of startups reveals that the venture capitalists are often instrumental in dislodging and replacing the founder. Some VCs have the reputation of replacing 95% of the founding management, while others would rarely, if ever, so intrude. In their rush to cash in, some VCs pressure management into premature IPOs, when waiting one or two more years would have resulted in greater market valuation for the company. Clearly there are great differences in degree of intrusiveness among VCs, and entrepreneurs need to assess investors with whom they might have to live for a number of years.

Some investors require two forms of stock from the outset: common stock for the founders, and *preferred stock* for the investors. This arrangement usually requires that, if a distressed company is liquidated, the preferred stock (investors) will be paid first. This is a reasonable arrangement and contributes to the peace of mind of the investors. When a company goes public the preferred stock is automatically converted to common stock.

THREE TYPES OF REGIONAL GROUP START-UPS

There are essentially two strategies in starting up a regional practice, with the third strategy being the ability to change from the second strategy to the first.

Start-Up With Exit Strategy

Most start-ups, whether a regional group practice or a more general type venture, have as a goal an initial public offering (IPO) within five years. Venture capitalists insist on this as the best means to cash-out. It also makes the founders' stock liquid, raises a warchest to use for acquisitions, finances expansion, and wipes out debt. At this point ownership shifts from a closely held private company to one that is publicly traded, in our industry usually on the NASDAQ.

A company can do an IPO only if it is successful. It is the culmination of several years of growth and stability which have resulted, in the estimation of the underwriters, in the company having value on the open market. Going public is a costly, enormous undertaking, with legal, accounting, and other costs ranging from $500,000 to $1 million. It is important to position the company from the very beginning so that this exit strategy is enhanced. It is also important to realize that an IPO will most definitely effect the control and complexion of the company forever, often to the dismay of the founders.

Other exit strategies include mergers and acquisitions. These in a privately held company are voluntary, and may be done because a company is doing so well that it is attractive to another company, or it may be done because a company is not doing as well as it might and merging or being acquired would better position it. A hostile takeover is not possible in a company that is not publicly traded, but the word *voluntary* is used advisedly. A company may be pressured to merge or be acquired by the venture capitalist investors, often to the displeasure of the founders.

Start-Up in Perpetuity

Although the preceding strategy is sought in almost every start-up, there is an unusual kind of group, seemingly limited to healthcare, where the goal is one of perpetuation without an exit strategy. The outstanding examples are the several Permanente Medical Groups that contract with the nation's original and largest HMO, the Kaiser Health Plan. The purpose is to provide a stable, practitioner owned environment in which to practice for one's entire career. Each practitioner is a shareholder, but the share cannot be sold. A practitioner is selected by the group for participation, at which point he or she fulfills certain requirements and acquires equity. Upon retirement this equity is sold back to the corporation in return for a comfortable retirement.

The first of these groups was founded in 1945, and although in the past 50 years practitioners have entered while others have retired, the group practice is stable and permanent. More recently the physician-equity model has been exemplified by the Mullikin Group on the West Coast which demonstrates the phenomenal growth characteristic of well-run groups in which the doctors are working for themselves.

Options Open Strategy

In a third type of start-up the original intent may be to have a group practice in perpetuity, but the company can be positioned from the beginning so that it can keep open the option of being acquired or going public. The Permanente Medical Group is an example of the first, and it would be very difficult, if not impossible, to go in a different direction than the physician-equity regional group practice in perpetuity. On the other hand, the Mullikin Group was positioned from the beginning to keep its options open, and in 1995 it did change direction when it elected to be acquired by MedPartners, Inc.

INCORPORATION

It seems obvious that a regional group practice should be an incorporated entity, but it is a fact that many mental health professionals do not comprehend the difference between a corporation and a partnership. Once they realize the need to incorporate, they hire a lawyer in their state who never mentions the advantages of incorporating in either Delaware or Nevada. A lawyer cannot perform this service outside the state in which he or she practices and thus cannot earn a fee from you. If your regional group practice is, or intends to be multistate, it can be incorporated in either Delaware or Nevada, taking advantage of congenial corporate statutes, without actually doing business there.

The author, in Founding American Biodyne, first incorporated in California, possibly the worst of all choices along with New York and Illinois. Once realizing the severe disadvantages of being a California corporation, it took over two years to extricate and re-incorporate in Delaware. Since that time Nevada has begun offering advantages above and beyond those traditionally offered in Delaware.

It must be emphasized that this is not a tax avoidance strategy. The profits will be taxed by each state in which they are earned, and in accordance with the tax laws of the respective state. The advantages are far too complex for discussion here, but can be explained by any good Nevada or Delaware lawyer. They could also be explained by the lawyer in your state, but it is unlikely she or he would be so inclined. Rather, your home state lawyer will even attempt to dissuade you using a series of flimsy arguments.

CAPITALIZATION: AVOID GOING BACK TO THE WELL

Overcapitalizing a company can be almost as bad as undercapitalizing it. In the latter, the company will run short of operating capital and find itself having to go back to venture capitalists and suffer dilution. In an overcapitalized company the temptation is to make expenditures prematurely or unnecessarily. This too can result in having to seek additional capital. Two actual cases in which each company took a different course from the other will illustrate:

Company A

This company believed in the notion of being "lean and mean." It created only the necessary infrastructure, used good off-the-shelf software, and shortly after its founding signed two excellent contracts that allowed the company to be profitable from the first quarter. Current revenues financed each future expansion, and two years after the founding, the company still had intact its original capitalization. It used this to acquire and rehabilitate at a bargain two floundering competitors.

Company B

This company believed from the start that infrastructure should be put in place to accommodate growth before it occurred, the very opposite of company A. Revenue lagged and soon it resembled a Cadillac engine powering a skateboard. Even worse, it embarked on developing an extensive computerized system that experienced one cost overrun after another, and was obsolete before it was completed. Management had to seek additional capital on three subsequent occasions, experienced considerable dilution, and was forced by its venture capitalists, who now controlled the company, to sell itself to a competitor.

There are legitimate reasons to return to the well, the most important of which are to finance expansion or an acquisition. But if management looks for more capital because the company is burning cash, dilution is the consequence. Such successive dilutions can severely cripple a company.

THE BUSINESS PLAN

The business plan with its financial projections is integral to the start-up. Most mental health practitioners have never so much as seen a business plan, and fortunately there is now software which will help you organize and prepare it—but it cannot write the plan for you. This business plan must tell a compelling story. It must showcase the founders, emphasize the competitive edge, and have numbers that will make sense when the VCs crunch them. It must clearly determine the mission, goals, and strategies of the company, and honestly present problems and how they will be surmounted. The author has seen great ideas with poorly constructed business plans, and poor ideas with excellent business plans, neither of which is viable. The business plan must be the best presentation of an excellent idea, a competent management team, along with believ-able but optimistic financial projections.

Venture capitalists will not go beyond the business plan. If it is lacking either in presentation or conceptualization, they will distance themselves without ever telling you why. It is literally the *key* to your start-up.

THE IPO PROSPECTUS

If your company is successful and you elect to do an initial public offering, you will have to prepare a prospectus which is to the IPO what the business plan is to the capitalization. However, by this time you will have an extensive and expensive team of lawyers, accoun-tants, underwriters, and gophers to help you. The frightening as-pect of the prospectus is its liability to a stockholders' suit should the price of your stock, following the IPO, drift downward. There are legal firms, mostly based in New York, that buy a few shares in each IPO. Then they wait for those stocks to lose value, at which time they may well file a class action stockholders' suit alleging the prospectus was inaccurate. Once the suit is filed, the stock plunges downward and the allegation becomes a self-fulfilling prophecy. In 1996 federal legislation was enacted to render such frivolous lawsuits more difficult, and only time will tell what positive effect the new law will have.

The author spent more time on the American Biodyne pro-spectus for the IPO than on the business plan for the initial capi-talization. It must be drawn with meticulous accuracy, disclosing anything that later might be considered as having been purposely withheld, and after this is done the lawyers fill the document with blood-curdling disclaimers. One wonders why anyone would buy stock, except that knowledgeable investors ignore the boiler plate legal disclaimers and evaluate the company.

Criteria for considering an IPO are formidable and usually require 5 years of successful operation. Among these are three consecutive quarters of profitability, with the fourth quarter dem-onstrating a projected annualized income of at least $1 million. The growth in revenues and income should resemble a staircase; that is, it should demonstrate an overall upward trend even though at points it is flat. The initial market capitalization should be at least *$40 million in an industry that is on the scale of at least $1 billion.* The company should also be experiencing at least 35% annual growth with increasing margins. These criteria will bring the required institutional support for the IPO.

The market valuation of the company after 5 years is based on a complex formula which begins with something in the neighborhood of 20 times projected earnings, then discounted by 25%. Underwriters who earn substantial fees through the IPO must be certain the valuation will comply with market expectations. Even after some of the most meticulous planning and numbers crunching, a last minute rumor or disclosure can be disastrous.

But the process does not stop with the IPO. Management must constantly educate stock analysts about the company so as to assure proper analyses of the stock. A negative analysis can immediately weaken a stock. The corporation must become quarterly report oriented. Optimistic projections boost a stock, but falling short of expectations will naturally suppress it.

THE FOUNDERS: BEYOND THE IPO

The attributes that make a successful entrepreneur are often the opposite of those that constitute a good ongoing manager. The author, who has founded a number of organizations and companies, all of which remain highly successful, has had to face this fact concerning his own personality and leave the institution at the point in which the start-up has been completed.

The successful entrepreneur must possess the propensity to disregard the advice swirling about him or her because the preponderance of the advice is that "it cannot be done." The entrepreneur must doggedly work toward the goal, turning away the nay-sayers; otherwise, he or she would become discouraged and demoralized. This attribute becomes the entrepreneur's undoing once ongoing management must assume the reins. A manager must listen to everyone, the very opposite of what makes the risk-taking entrepreneur.

Some VCs systematically replace 95% of the founders once the company is established. Others wait and play it by ear, moving as necessary. This latter procedure has produced many an unfortunate sequence, like the VCs' forcing a genius of the magnitude of Steve Jobs, the founder of Apple Computer, out of his own company. The talented entrepreneur must be sensitive to, and accepting of his own limitations. This author has had no difficulty with this, relishing the excitement of starting new ventures as opposed to the dullness (to him) of ongoing management.

VESTING

The purpose of allocating shares of ownership to the founders and management is the "sweat-equity" concept. A start-up cannot afford high initial salaries. Those who come on board are substituting the promise of an eventual reward. Also, the sweat-equity principle gives the incentive to struggle together to make the company succeed. The stock position is further a way of retaining necessary and good management. By creating a vesting period of three to five years, those who are making the venture work must see the enterprise through in order to gain the big reward. It also allows those who do not work out to be let go without their walking away with founding stock positions. Typical vesting schedules allow no vesting in the initial period, regular proportional vesting in the second period, and total vesting in the third period. Vesting schedules may be based on two, three or five years, with total vesting occurring if an IPO is completed before the designated schedule is completed.

SUMMARY AND CONCLUSIONS

This chapter has sought to give a succinct overview of the entrepreneurial function. A primmer of the financial markets in this regard is beyond the scope of this section. Rather, the author has attempted to give the reader a working acquaintance with the procedures so the novice entrepreneur may proceed with some confidence in acquiring the necessary additional knowledge, consultation and help.

There have been enough successful practitioner entrepreneurs to date to make it clear that entrepreneurship and practice are not at all incompatible. A number of attitudes, however, must be addressed:

1. The practitioner must accept educated risk and learn to live with it.
2. The financial markets are not mysterious and comprehended only by Wall Street types. They are understandable to anyone taking the time to learn.
3. Practice is a business. Once the practitioner is comfortable with this fact, it is only a matter of deciding how large and how successful the business of practice might be.
4. The business of practice can be constructed to allow a cashing in for the founders, or a perpetual environment for those equity practitioners who want to work for themselves in an atmosphere of authority and dignity.

Finally, as an addendum, there is a rule-of-thumb for ownership in an entrepreneurial endeavor. This applies, of course, to those ventures with the reasonable exit strategy. In such start-ups one-third of this ownership is relegated to the idea and the doer (the principle founder or founders), another one-third for the investors who capitalize the venture, and a final third for all management and possible dilution up to the point of the execution of the exit strategy.

PART IV

Practice, Outcomes, and Informatics

13.

The Toughest Transition: Outcomes Strategies and Patient Functioning

Michael S. Pallak, Ph.D.

> *Quality is the engine that drives the company to the bank.*
>
> K. R. Bhote

For most clinicians, it is a great transition to shift one's clinical perspective from the traditional long-term treatment approach (with, arguably, 100 years of tradition) to a managed care approach, often employing brief treatment and time efficient procedures for many patients. However, it has been my experience that the shift to an outcomes perspective is an even greater transition for most providers.

There are a variety of factors that impede or facilitate a shift to an "outcomes" perspective as part of one's clinical approach. A major factor is simply reframing the issue, i.e., what do we mean by outcomes? Many of us have watched a transition from utilization review to quality assurance (QA), to some form of continuous quality improvement (CQI) and so forth—a lot of jargon in the approaches for tracking care. Yet only in a limited sense do these systems touch on the issue of outcomes. These systems are only designed in my view to assess the service delivery system: did the system (and the participants) deliver the usual and consensually

219

determined care (however defined) in an appropriate (however defined) fashion at an appropriate (however determined) time in treatment? These systems focus often on negative events (e.g., mortality, extreme waiting time) in which something occurred beyond previously specified operating parameters. Upon discovery of negative events or a pattern of negative events, something in the care delivery system is changed in the belief that the change lessens the probability of those negative events. The care delivery system is monitored and the amount of change in the pattern is assessed with other changes following if determined to be necessary.

Yet this admittedly stereotyped approach fails to assess patient outcomes in clinically relevant terms for the patient or the provider. The key definition of outcomes approaches in a simple fashion is whether the patient improved on dimensions important to the patient. In a more sophisticated definition, outcomes are any data that let us answer the question: "Under what conditions do patients improve?" In the QA approaches, the emphasis is often upon the delivery system and some patients may have received care in the system that was in some fashion not appropriate or within specified limits. In an outcomes approach the emphasis is upon whether the care delivered, in fact, helped the patient improve and under what conditions did that improvement take place. Reframing the outcomes issues in this fashion brings a much broader array of considerations to bear in thinking about the clinical process.

First, the outcome approach is patient focused and obviously clinically and socially eclectic. It is clinically eclectic because the emphasis is upon "what works for this patient" rather than how to formulate and fit this patient into a particular theoretical or conceptual system. As a social psychologist, I have always been struck by the fact that graduate training socializes students into particular definitions of the treatment process that are often maintained by a social and professional milieu so that one's treatment concepts are maintained (or changed) in part by a social process. The socially eclectic outcomes approach means that one looks at what is happening with a patient rather than only applying the lens of one's professional colleagues, theory, or culture. Moving to brief therapy approaches in a managed care system involves a major conceptual and social shift in how one thinks about the process of treatment to one that can be aided and enhanced by appropriate evidence that the patient improves.

Second, the outcomes focus places the patient in the context of other patients and data where patient variables (demographics, diagnosis, severity) may interact with provider variables (clinical training, clinical orientation, social skills, cultural background), with service delivery variables (private practice, group practice, HMO, integrated continuum of care) and with other exogenous variables such as benefit design, treatment financing, etc. Ideally, providers have access to a (growing) database regarding patient outcomes that is organized along the dimensions above. Thus, the provider can make an approximation as to where the specific patient falls in relation to combinations of the variables above in order to provide maximally effective treatment as rapidly as possible. Over time treatment outcomes evidence enables the development of treatment protocols that incorporate the most effective approach for a particular patient.

Providers may be hindered in making a transition to an outcome perspective for at least three reasons. First, as with issues of the healthcare policy context in which we operate, traditional training typically does not prepare providers to think much beyond the specific patient, i.e., we are rarely socialized in psychology to think about ourselves as acting within various systems that effect what we do with patients. Second, most clinicians are not particularly familiar with research and evaluation strategies and often think about these issues in a very stereotyped fashion. The stereotype contains elements suggesting that "good research" is only defined as the elaborate, randomized and controlled clinical trials suitable for academic publications. As a result, the stereotype continues, "I can't do research based evaluations because they wouldn't be 'real' research" and, finally, "It is too complicated and I don't know what to do anyway."

As a result, a substantial body of psychotherapy research may be only minimally incorporated into one's clinical outlook, and may be dismissed as "too theoretical" to be of use in thinking about "my particular, complicated patient today." The substantial body of therapy research literature largely addresses conceptual and theoretical issues related to the treatment process and delineates variables, processes, and conceptual frameworks that may have value in thinking about a specific patient in the process of developing treatment specific to the particular patient. Because of the stereotypical thinking, providers may simply think that outcomes considerations are beyond their pale.

Third, because of the profound differences in orientation between the clinical and research cultures in which we were all socialized in the training system, clinicians rarely see themselves formally testing hypotheses as to what might be happening with a specific patient while considering information from the patient in evaluating the worth of the hypothesis. Yet, ironically, this process of formulating a hypothesis and examining information about what happened in order to assess the hypothesis is the core process in research. Without realizing it, clinicians do this all the time. Similarly, because clinical work is often dismissed as "subjective" in the culture of psychology, our culture fails often to adopt an outcomes perspective because clinical work appears not to be open to rigorous, empirical analysis and evaluation.

Also, ironically, I have met few clinicians who can't tell me if or when a patient has improved and why the patient has improved. In my experience, it is a profound realization for clinicians when I point out that they have been continuously engaged in outcomes thinking at least at the first level of "does the patient improve?" Thus the third component of the outcomes perspective is simply that of more objectively documenting the improvement rather than simply relying on the clinician's subjective assessment. In short, the outcomes perspective uses measures, usually questionnaires, that capture the dimensions along which patients do or do not improve and helps quantify the clinician's judgment.

At a broader level, transitions to operating in an outcomes perspective have been facilitated by some managed care operations. In my experience at American Biodyne (1988–1991), it took about one to two years for traditionally trained providers to make the transition to a managed care approach in a clinically competent and comfortable fashion. There was about a 35% attrition rate among clinicians during a 2-year period. An outcome perspective was implicit, as well as explicit, in the clinical milieu at a patient by patient level. The constant theme in supervision, observation, training, audits, and case conferences was always that of "what works best for this patient?" The core of the clinical approach was "did the patient improve?" Over time and over patients a range of treatment approaches was modified, enhanced, and developed by clinical experience aggregated across patients and clinicians, constituting an outcomes based approach to clinical services.

There are at least two other factors that either hinder or facilitate a transition to outcomes based approaches as part of the clinical perspective. The first is the corporate milieu in which clinical operations take place. Originally, the drive for CQI and some form of outcomes assessment in the industry was motivated in response to the charge that managed care represented truncated, inadequate, and inherently inferior care relative to traditional long-term approaches. Within the industry, these issues were put forward as a basic attitude within the several provider groups. Thus the drive was to show that managed care patients were no worse off and just as satisfied as patients in more traditional service systems. Thus in the early days of managed care, the corporate culture supported some form of outcomes assessment but largely to meet corporate marketing needs to answer critics and to assist in gaining new contracts. The view at that time was based on the belief that since the clinical providers said patients were progressing there was little need to document or quantify objectively that progress. Hence early outcomes strategies were often less clinically driven. Increasingly, however, groups in the industry are moving to more systematic efforts to assess outcomes of treatment (Trabin, Freeman, & Pallak, 1995).

The second factor is that the national healthcare context is changing. As Cummings has so eloquently argued (cf. Cummings, this volume), the ongoing healthcare revolution will force a much greater emphasis on outcomes results and clinical systems management by clinical outcomes. As the need for time efficient and cost effective treatment increases, clinical outcomes results will provide the basis for treatment protocols derived from what works best for patients under varying combinations of documented variables (above). In addition, healthcare financing in general, and behavioral healthcare in specific, will shift increasingly to capitated systems for defined populations. This shift means that successful managed care organizations (MCOs) will need to know much more about the health status of their covered populations. This information will be critical in order to bid on contracts, to plan levels of clinical resources, to integrate treatment systems most effectively, and to improve health status through prevention, early intervention strategies, and disease management. These are all necessary in managing the system to provide effective services and to enhance profitability. A key element will be outcomes evaluations as the key basis for managing the system. As this shift takes place, MCOs will need to move to more routine outcomes efforts as a major part of the delivery system milieu in order to survive and to compete effectively for capitation contracts.

One consistent dilemma that I've encountered among groups who are in the early stages of thinking about outcomes is what to measure or evaluate and how to implement the outcomes measurement process. Again it is useful to distinguish between outcomes research designed for theoretical reasons and outcomes research that provides a basis for answering the question of whether patients improve (and under what conditions). The goal is using empirically quantifiable measures rather than relying only on the clinician's "subjective" judgment—in short to document empirically and to inform the clinician's judgment. In the "real world" of clinical service delivery, measures need to be meaningful and relevant to the patient's experience and useful to the clinician in monitoring progress and outcome.

There are a variety of general measures of functioning and well-being as well as condition specific measures (Andrews, Peters, & Teeson, 1994). In assisting clients with outcomes efforts, I've found that patients in distress are able to fill out measures in such a way that diminished functioning and well-being are reflected. They respond in ways that are pertinent to them, regardless as to the exact nature or specific cause of distress. In a somewhat useful analogy, patients with a bacterial infection (regardless of the nature) present with fever (and can relate that they have a fever) and one indication of successful treatment of the infection is the diminution of the fever. Similarly, when asked a series of questions about how they are feeling and how they are functioning, patients readily indicate distress and restricted functioning, regardless of the specific cause of the distress. Successful progress in meeting the distress is then reflected in positive changes in the general level of distress and functioning reported.

In general, the evaluation strategy operating in the real world involves measures that are time efficient. About 15 minutes plus or minus is about the maximum that patients are willing to devote to evaluation in behavioral health settings, if there is minimal intrusion into the treatment process. Usually it is administered at the point of service and perhaps during treatment, depending on information needed about the course of treatment. Patients receive the measures at the end of treatment and possibly at some point after treatment. This basic case study design (and we've all been taught to dismiss case studies as unscientific) is useful to the clinician and the MCO if the results are not overinterpreted and overgeneralized. They should be seen as one set of information from treatment that forms one piece of an overall mosaic. The case study approach is more useful if the measures are anchored in a psychometrically sophisticated database providing normative information that can be disaggregated; e.g., provide normative distributions for demographics (age, gender, etc.), clinical condition (normative for confirmed diagnoses and severity, etc.), as well as normative data for nonmorbid populations. One can look at the patient's results in relation to the norms, and the level of distress can be expressed in terms of where the patient's results fall in the percentile ranking relative to the morbid and nonmorbid population. For example, a profile may fall at the 28th percentile of the general nonmorbid population and about average for the morbid population with the same or similar diagnosis. In short, the profile informs the clinician, documents level of severity in a quantifiable fashion, and provides an empirical starting point for the beginning of treatment.

In this strategy, patient progress and outcomes at any given point in time can be assessed by readministering the measure and comparing the current profile with the initial profile. Similarly the patient's progress during the episode can be compared to that of other patients with similar conditions providing some relevant evidence about treatment efficiency. In turn, by examining the patient's progress and comparing it to available data in relation to the constellation of patient variables, provider variables, etc., we begin to the development of an answer to the question of "under what conditions do patients improve?" Similarly, as the outcomes results accumulate across patients, we begin an approximation of the answer to the question of, "What is the optimum combination of variables for this patient with this condition with this therapist?"

AN OUTCOMES CASE STUDY

Let me move to some recent case study data for outpatient treatment that illustrate a number of these issues.

Protocol and Method

Patients were from two employer groups who presented for outpatient treatment during an 18-month period and there were no reliable differences between the two groups. Network providers received a step-by-step protocol and after treatment authorization received an informed consent form and the primary measure of functioning and well being, the SF-36.

The SF-36 Questionnaire: The SF-36 (Short Form—36 items) has been extensively developed and normed (Ware, Snow, Kosinski, and Gandek, 1993) for the United States (U.S.) General Nonpatient population, for groups with minor and major medical problems, and for groups with confirmed psychiatric diagnoses. The SF-36 measures eight dimensions of functioning and well-being:

1. *Physical functioning.* Measures the patient's limitations due to health in performing various physical functions, e.g., running, climbing stairs, walking a mile, etc.
2. *Role physical.* Measures the patient's limitations in work and other activities due to physical problems.
3 . *Bodily pain.* Measures the presence and level of bodily pain and how much pain limits work or other activities.
4. *General health.* Measures perceptions of current health, perceptions of health status relative to other people, and expectations about health improving or declining.
5. *Vitality.* Measures the extent to which patients feel energetic or "worn out."
6. *Social functioning.* Measures the extent to which health or emotional problems interfered with usual social activities including those with family or friends.

7. *Role emotional.* Measures how much emotional problems interfered with work responsibilities or other activities and whether patients accomplished less due to emotional problems.
8. *Mental health.* Measures how the patient feels in term of nervousness, feeling downhearted or "blue" and/or happy, calm, or peaceful.

We made the decision to use the SF-36 rather than other measures that might be more directed to specific conditions. Based on the literature, people in emotional distress reflect lower levels of functioning relative to the Nonpatient general population regardless of the specific cause of distress or specific problem.

A total of 474 patients filled out the measure at the first presentation for treatment, and 252 patients completed the measure at the end of treatment. Finally a total of 67% (N = 78) of the 25% follow-up sample (3–5 months after the treatment episode) returned the mailed questionnaire. Within the overall sample of patients, a total of N = 142 completed the measure both at Pretreatment and End of Treatment, while N = 38 completed the measure at the End of Treatment and at Follow-up. These latter let us look at change scores using the patient as their own control. The residual represents independent samples of patients who completed the measure at each of the three time points. Data are not disaggregated here in terms of demographics, diagnoses, severity or utilization.

As an aside, the diminished number of patients who completed the SF-36 at End of Treatment reflected the difficulties that occur in the real world of data collection. Similarly in managed care settings, the clinician may not know that the last session is in fact the last session since a formal termination may not occur. Thus, participating clinicians may have been unable to administer the measure for some patients.

RESULTS

Overall, 47% of those who completed the questionnaire at some point were female. About 68% were in the age range of 19 to 44 years and the remainder in the range of 45 to 65 years. A

10-session benefit limit could be expanded upon review and authorization.

How Did Patients in the Present Study Compare to Other Normed Groups?

The results summarized in Table 13.1 reflect nationally normed groups for the SF-36 as well as from the 474 pretreatment patients in the present study, thus enabling a comparison of profiles. For each dimension and for each identified group, we present the mean, the percentile ranking of the score in terms of the U.S. general Nonpatient population (first column).

The SF-36 was constructed so that the highest score of 100 represents the absence of a negative state (limitation, disability, distress). For example, the 50th percentile (median) for the Physical Functioning scale is a score of 90 in the U.S. Nonpatient population. These scales were designed to discriminate among patients at the lower end of the distributions rather than to produce unit-normal or "bell-shaped" symmetric distributions. The exception is the Mental Health scale which is designed as bi-polar, so that someone reporting little distress would have a score of 50 rather than 100. For the Mental Health scale the 50th percentile (median score) is 80 with a mean of 75 (which represents the 39th percentile) for the U.S. Nonpatient population.

From Table 13.1, the U.S. general nonpatient population had means, respectively, for the three physical dimensions (Physical Function, Role Physical, and Bodily Pain) of 84, 81, and 75, representing the 34th, 30th, and 48th percentile for these distributions. Similarly, patients with Minor Medical conditions did not differ (other than nominally) from the U.S. General Nonpatient population for these three dimensions of physical health.

In contrast, means for patients with Major Medical Conditions (Table 13.1) were reliably lower (Ware et al., 1993) for each of these three dimensions, as one would expect. The respective percentile rankings were at the 14th, 19th, and 33rd percentile for Physical Functioning, Role Physical, and Bodily Pain, respectively.

Patients with confirmed Psychiatric Diagnoses and patients in the Current Study (Table 13.1) did not differ from the U.S.

TABLE 13.1

SF-36 Norms (mean, percentiles, median) from a U.S. General Nonpatient Population and from Patients with Minor Medical Diagnoses, Major Medical Diagnoses, Psychiatric Diagnoses, and from the Current Study Group of Outpatient Mental Health Users

SF-36 Dimensions	U.S. General Nonpatient	Minor Medical	Major Medical	Psychiatric Diagnoses	Current Study
Physical Function					
Mean	84	80	59	80	85
Percentile	34%	28%	14%	28%	34%
Median	90				
Role Physical					
Mean	81	70	45	58	66
Percentile	30%	25%	19%	21%	21%
Median	100				
Bodily Pain					
Mean	75	75	65	62	70
Percentile	48%	48%	33%	32%	33%
Median	74				
General Health					
Mean	72	65	50	59	66
Percentile	50%	30%	14%	23%	38%
Median	72				
Vitality					
Mean	61	60	50	45	41
Percentile	48%	48%	32%	23%	20%
Median	65				
Social Functioning					
Mean	83	90	80	55	51
Percentile	42%	48%	41%	18%	16%
Median	100				
Role Emotional					
Mean	81	82	78	40	40
Percentile	75%	75%	73%	18%	18%
Median	100				
Mental Health					
Mean	75	81	79	55	45
Percentile	39%	58%	55%	14%	9%
Median	80				

Note: The first four columns are adapted from Ware et al. (1993). The means represent the mean score on the respective dimension with a score of 100 representing the best functioning. The "%" entries represent percentile ranking for each mean based on the distribution of the U.S. General Nonpatient Population. "Median" represents the median (50th percentile) for the U.S. General Population norm group.

General Nonpatient population for Physical Functioning and there was no reliable difference between the two groups (28th, 34th percentile, respectively). Similarly, these two groups were only nominally different from the U.S. Nonpatient population for Role Physical, and Bodily Pain and were at the 33rd percentile level.

All groups were nominally lower in perceptions of General Health relative to the U.S. General Nonpatient population.

For these physical dimensions of functioning and well-being, patients in the present study had profiles similar to patients with confirmed psychiatric diagnoses. Both of these two groups were similar to the U.S. Nonpatient population for Physical Functioning and were higher than the Major Medical Condition group.

For the Vitality dimension, the Psychiatric Diagnoses and Current Study group were at the 23rd and 20th percentile reliably lower than the U.S. Nonpatient norm group. Similarly these two groups were reliably lower than the U.S. Nonpatient group in terms of Social Functioning, Role Emotional, and Mental Health status (see Table 13.1).

In short, patients who presented in the Current Study had profiles similar to the Psychiatric Diagnoses group for each of the four dimensions most closely related to emotional status. Both were reliably lower than the U.S. Nonpatient norm. Clearly patients who presented for treatment were experiencing high levels of emotional distress and poor levels of functioning and well-being. The profiles generated here illustrate the usefulness of this approach in terms of documenting patient status at the beginning of treatment.

Did the Current Study Outpatients Improve in Functioning and Well-Being?

The results summarized in Table 13.2 describe the overall means from the Pretreatment, End of Treatment and Follow-Up administration of the SF-36. These results were analyzed by two independent strategies:

Change Scores: A subset of patients (N = 142) filled out the SF-36 both at Pretreatment and End of Treatment A mean change score for each of the eight dimensions is summarized in Table 13.3 In

TABLE 13.2

SF-36 Means and Percentile Rankings for the Present Outpatient Mental Health Study Group from the Pretreatment, End of Treatment, and Follow-Up (3 to 5 months) Administrations of the Questionnaire

SF-36 Dimensions	Pretreatment (N = 474)	End of Treatment (N = 272)	Follow-up (N = 78)
Physical Function			
Mean	85	86	84
Percentile	34%	35%	29%
Role Physical			
Mean	66	76	76
Percentile	21%	30%	30%
Bodily Pain			
Mean	70	76	72
Percentile	33%	49%	40%
General Health			
Mean	66	71	73
Percentile	38%	38%	48%
Vitality			
Mean	41	55	58
Percentile	20%	39%	48%
Social Function			
Mean	51	71	77
Percentile	16%	28%	36%
Role Emotional			
Mean	40	68	67
Percentile	18%	30%	30%
Mental Health			
Mean	45	63	67
Percentile	8%	26%	28%

addition, a subset of patients (N = 38) filled out the SF-36 at both End of Treatment and at Follow-Up and the change score indexes any change that took place following treatment (Table 13.4).

Independent Samples: The remaining patients responded to the questionnaire only at the Pretreatment (N = 332), the End of Treatment (N = 130) or at the Follow-Up (N = 40) stages. The results from these three independent groups are summarized in Table 13.5. We would expect the means to be consistent with the results from the change scores in Table 13.3 and Table 13.4.

TABLE 13.3

Mean Change and Reliability for SF-36 Dimensions from Pretreatment to End of Treatment for N = 142 Patients Who Answered both Administrations (pre and post)

	Pretreatment (N = 142)	End of Treatment (N = 142)	Change (Pre-End) (N = 142)
SF-36 Dimensions:			
Physical Function	85	86	+ .92 ($p < .5$)
Role Physical	67	74	+ 7.00 ($p < .05$)
Bodily Pain	71	75	+ 4.00 ($p < .03$)
General Health	68	71	+ 3.00 ($p < .07$)
Vitality	41	54	+13.00 ($p < .00$)
Social Functioning	50	68	+18.00 ($p < .00$)
Role Emotional	40	65	+25.00 ($p < .00$)
Mental Health	44	61	+17.00 ($p < .00$)

Note: Table entries represent the mean score on the respective SF-36 dimension for that administration. Change is from pretreatment to after the last treatment session (end of treatment). Reliability of the change score is tested against zero change; "$p < .00$" means "$p < .0001$."

The change score results (Table 13.3) reflect several important trends:

Physical Functioning: There was no reliable change (Pre- to End of Treatment, +.92, $p < .5$) as one would expect since patients were not presenting for physical problems.

Role Functioning—Physical: Patients reported improved Role Functioning with less limitation due to physical distress (+7.00, $p < .05$), i.e., the obtained change score was reliably different from zero change. Thus patients moved from the 22nd percentile (Table 13.2) to the 28th percentile (Table 13.3) relative to the U.S. General Nonpatient population.

Bodily Pain: Patients showed reliable positive improvement (+4.00, $p < .03$) moving from the 34th percentile to the 48th percentile relative to the Nonpatient group.

General Health: There was a small unreliable increase in perception of general health (+3.00, $p < .07$).

TABLE 13.4

Mean Change and Reliability for SF-36 Dimensions from the End
of Treatment to Follow-Up (N = 38).

	End of Treatment (N = 38)	Follow-up (3–5 months) (N = 38)	Change
SF-36 Dimensions:			
Physical Function	86	86	+0.00
Role Physical	74	68	−6.00 ($p < .19$)
Bodily Pain	75	75	+0.00
General Health	71	70	−1.00 ($p < .46$)
Vitality	54	55	+1.00 ($p < .77$)
Social Functioning	68	74	+6.00 ($p < .16$)
Role Emotional	65	66	+ .90 ($p < .88$)
Mental Health	61	64	+3.00 ($p < .35$)

The remaining four dimensions were more directly related
to emotional and mental health functioning and reflected substantial change:

Vitality: Patients showed reliable improvement in perception
of vitality (+13.00, $p < .0001$) and moved from the 20th percentile
to the 38th percentile relative to the U.S. Nonpatient norm group.

Social Functioning: Patients showed reliable improvement (+18.00,
$p < .0001$) and moved from the 15th to the 29th percentile of the
Nonpatient group.

Role Functioning—Emotional: Patients showed reliable improvement (+28.00, $p < .0001$) moving from the 18th to the 30th percentile of the U.S. General Nonpatient group.

Mental Health: Patients reliably improved (+17 00, $p < .0001$) from
the 8th percentile up to the 26th percentile of the U.S. Nonpatient
population.

In summary, while patients showed some modest improvement on three of the physical functioning dimensions, there was

TABLE 13.5

SF-36 Means from Patients Who Responded Only to the Pretreatment or the End of Treatment Administration but not Both (Independent Samples) and Reliability of Differences

	Pretreatment (N = 332)	End of Treatment (N = 130)	Difference
SF-36 Dimensions:			
Physical Functioning	85	86	+ 1.00 ($p < .9$)
Role Physical	66	78	+11.00 ($p < .02$)
Bodily Pain	70	77	+ 7.00 ($p < .02$)
General Health	68	70	+ 2.00 ($p < .28$)
Vitality	41	55	+14.00 ($p < .00$)
Social Functioning	51	75	+24.00 ($p < .00$)
Role Emotional	39	71	+32.00 ($p < .00$)
Mental Health	45	64	+19.00 ($p < .00$)

remarkable improvement on the four dimensions most related to emotional and mental health status. In terms of the metric provided by the Nonpatient norm group, patients showed improvement on Vitality, Social Functioning, and Role Emotional that was about double their initial percentile ranking and about triple for the Mental Health dimension.

Follow-Up Results

The results presented in Table 13.4 reflect change from End of Treatment to Follow-Up (3–5 months after conclusion of treatment). There were no reliable changes for any of the eight dimensions of the SF-36. Based on these results, patients neither deteriorated nor improved following treatment. Thus patients showed substantial improvement in dimensions related to emotional status and functioning and that the improvement was stable during the follow-up period. In addition one can argue that change during the follow-up period reflects the test–retest reliability of the measure for these patients. That is, the unreliable change in the follow-up period may reflect the stability of scores over a time period similar to that of

TABLE 13.6

SF-36 Means from Patients Who Responded Only to the End of Treatment (N = 130) or the Follow-Up Administration (N = 40) but Not Both (independent samples)

	End of Treatment	Follow-up (3–5 months)	Difference
SF-36 Dimensions:			
Physical Functioning	86	80	−6.00 ($p < .2$)
Role Physical	73	71	−2.00 ($p < .5$)
Bodily Pain	76	73	−3.00 ($p < .5$)
General Health	70	70	0.00
Vitality	54	56	+2.00 ($p < .5$)
Social Functioning	70	73	+3.00 ($p < .5$)
Role Emotional	66	69	+3.00 ($p < .5$)
Mental Health	62	64	+2.00 ($p < .5$)

the Pretreatment and End of Treatment time period. It will be recalled that the analyses compared obtained change with zero change. To the extent that change in the Follow-Up period reflects change that would have obtained in the absence of treatment, we may compare Pre- to End of Treatment change with change in the Follow-Up period.

There was no reliable difference between change scores for the two periods for the Physical Function dimension. For each of the remaining dimensions change in the treatment period was reliably greater than change in the follow-up period. While this is not a statistically pure approach, it provides some assurance that the change obtained that was correlated with treatment was in fact reliable; i.e., was greater than change that would have been obtained with a no-treatment control group.

Independent Sample Results

The results in Table 13.5 and Table 13.6 are from patients who responded to the questionnaire only once during the process and hence formed independent samples for each time point in the process.

First, Pretreatment means for each SF-36 dimension were not reliably different between the independent sample and the sample in the change score analysis. Thus differences between those who responded only at the Pretreatment point and those who also responded at End of Treatment were not related to level of functioning or well-being.

Second, there were no reliable differences between means from the End of Treatment for the independent sample (Table 13.5) and from the End of Treatment means from the change score sample. Taken together these two sets of results provide increased confidence that the outcomes obtained thus far did not result from differential failure to fill out the questionnaire, biased sampling or self-selection by patients.

From Table 13.5, there was no reliable difference between Pretreatment and End of Treatment means for the Physical Function or General Health dimensions ($p < .9$, $p < .28$, respectively), a pattern similar to the change score analyses (Table 13.3).

As with the change score results (Table 13.3), the End of Treatment sample means were reliably higher than the Pretreatment sample means for the remaining dimensions: Role Physical ($p < .02$), Bodily Pain ($p < .02$), Vitality ($p < .0001$), Social Functioning ($p < .0001$), Role Emotional ($p < .0001$), and Mental Health ($p < .0001$). As can be seen by inspection, these results were consistent with the change score analyses and reflected similar levels of improvement.

Finally, there were no reliable differences (Table 13.6) between the means from the independent samples at End of Treatment and at Follow-Up for any of the eight dimensions, consistent with the change score analyses (Table 13.4). These results also increase our confidence that the improvements associated with treatment were stable.

DISCUSSION

Note that while patients showed improvement, they remained in the lower ranges relative to the healthy Nonpatient norm group. Without the change scores and norms the naive critic might assume that treatment was a failure since patients were not "cured";

i.e., did not move up to at least the average for the Nonpatient group. Rather, for those of us trained in the intermittent treatment model, patients aren't "cured" but instead received treatment that resulted in improvement and may continue the work of treatment at some future time as they continue to work on their problems. Similarly, about 85 to 95% of patients reported satisfaction with treatment and that they dealt with their problems more effectively as a result of treatment.

Of course there are some limitations that should be noted here. Since this is a case study, there is no way to guarantee that the patients in the independent samples were all similar in profile prior to treatment. However, the cross-comparisons among the patients in the change score analyses and the independent sample patients provide greater confidence that this was not the case. Case study research is limited by the absence of an appropriate control group, thereby permitting the alternative hypothesis that these patients would have improved anyway regardless of treatment. However, the fact that improvement obtained appeared stable in the follow-up period makes it more likely that the improvement was in fact associated with treatment. Nevertheless, since we don't know what factors may have motivated patients in the Follow-Up to return the questionnaires it is possible that some bias was operating and that responders were somehow different from nonresponders. Countering this, however, is the fact that 67% of those receiving Follow-Up questionnaires returned them.

One advantage of general rather than condition specific measures and of the SF-36 specifically is that it permits assessment of the health burden due to both physical and emotional distress in terms of profiles. The ability to profile across the full range of morbidity has important clinical implications. People in emotional distress often present or manifest distress in physical terms. Similarly people with physical health problems often have accompanying emotional distress and/or sequelae that, if unrecognized and untreated, complicate and prolong treatment. Such measures, if incorporated in a routine screening process, enable early recognition and referral to appropriate treatment sources.

General measures such as the SF-36 may provide a useful tool, as a result, when capitated systems are fully integrated in terms of medical and behavioral health. For example, coupled with the general norms noted here we should be able to develop more detailed norms for a covered defined population and hence guidelines for appropriate referral and consultation by a range of providers. Equally importantly we will be able to assess the value of that referral and treatment in terms of how well the patient progresses in both physical and emotional functioning and well-being.

In addition, such quantifiable and normed instruments offer the potential for our greater integration in the health system by establishing a common outcomes language useful for both medical and emotional health problems. Coupled with studies and data regarding medical services utilization (Pallak, Cummings, Dörken, & Henke, 1994), we will have the basis for a fully comprehensive outcomes strategy in terms useful and meaningful to both the patient and to the clinician. Aside from these broad considerations, measures such as the SF-36 enable individual clinicians to track their own patients' treatment outcomes.

14.

The Practitioner as Informatics Expert

Dennis P. Morrison, Ph.D.

*In the future there will be two kinds of
people: those that understand numbers and
everybody else.*

Alan Toffler

The use of computers in behavioral healthcare is over 30 years old
(Overall & Hollister, 1964; Piotrowski, A., 1964). However, behavioral healthcare practitioners have generally adopted computerization at their own rate and usually for administrative or
management tasks such as billing or scheduling. The administrative needs will not abate, but clinical computing will likely increase.

Three trends will significantly change the way behavioral
healthcare practitioners conduct their business: (1) increasing
knowledge about the clinical efficacy of behavioral healthcare;
(2) the availability of powerful desktop computers used alone or
in networks; and (3) payers' requests for accountability. These
three trends form the core of the revolution in behavioral informatics.

This chapter will focus on the first two trends, their interaction, and the opportunity available to behavioral healthcare practitioners who take advantage of these two trends in their practices
to respond to the third. To establish a common language, this
chapter will also discuss some of the rudiments of PC-based

information systems. Since Windows-based personal computers make up the bulk of the PC market, this chapter will focus on those systems and appendix A provides a list of management and clinical information vendors.

Personal computers are becoming ubiquitous. The speed of evolution and the value available (in terms of processing power per dollar) have led to rapid adaptation of computers and, as a consequence, to automated information.

Professionally, Rosen and Weil (1995) reported that a survey of licensed psychologists in California showed that 72% had a computer and that nearly all used them exclusively as word processors, hardly the full potential of the computers.

Given the rapid changes occurring in the information systems arena, it would be futile to try to identify the correct computers or even the correct levels of computing power that the reader should consider. Some estimate that the computing power available to the consumer doubles every 18 months (Wilcox, 1995). Consequently, this chapter will focus on what clinical information systems should do for the user and provides recommendations of resources when seeking specific information.

There are some general caveats that seem to remain relevant regardless of the size, cost, or scope of an information systems project. They are: (1) It costs money to get information in a usable fashion; (2) Any information systems project will take longer than you or your consultant expects; and (3) Be prepared to experience "buyer's remorse."

Developing systems that convert data to information or aggregate existing information in new ways always has both start-up and ongoing costs associated with it. It takes time and money to get data into a computer and information out, particularly for "getting data in."

The fact that it always takes longer than expected seems inherent in the computer business because of "creeping elegance," which occurs when a project begins rather simply and then gradually evolves into a much more sophisticated project. ("Why don't we add . . ." and "For just a little more time/money/effort we can . . .").

Purchasers of personal computer equipment should be prepared for "buyer's remorse" because of the speed with which computers evolve. Whatever you buy today will be replaced by something twice as powerful in about a year and a half.

FOCUS ON DATA

In general, providers will do well if they purchase software and hardware that allow them to grow as their information needs increase. Keep in mind that the real value of an automated system lies in the data residing on that hardware and software. A significant hedge against obsolescence is to purchase systems that allow data to migrate to future systems. Organizations frequently make the mistake of buying a proprietary system that is not based on an "open architecture," so the data in the computer are not readily available using standard "off-the-shelf" software tools.

The core of any information system is a database. That database should be a relational database that is written in the highest standards that are currently available. At the time of this writing, relational databases written in a fourth-generation language (referred to as a 4 GL) is the standard. Standard database formats should likewise be used wherever possible. These can be identified by the one-to-three letter appendage to the right of the period in a file name. For example, a de facto standard in the PC database industry is d-Base. Database files using the d-Base standard have a three-letter suffix, .dbf and can be read by many software products.

INFORMATION NEEDS VARY BY THE SIZE
OF THE ORGANIZATION

As organizations grow they need varying types of information (Alter & Currie, 1995). However, regardless of size, a comprehensive information system should have these features (adapted from Currie, 1994): (1) a "one write" system that eliminates redundant data entry; (2) a user friendly system employing standard graphical user interface tools such as Windows; (3) able to automatically generate, submit, and process claims; (4) able to provide automated quality checks on the clinical record and prompt

providers to operate and document within standardized ethical/
legal requirements; (5) extensive user customizable report generation; (6) able to insure confidentiality and informational security; and (7) electric data interface; i e., use open architecture.

Structural Integration

Solo or small-group practices are usually very homogeneous entities with basic information concerns such as electronic claims submission. A variety of vendors provide electronic claims submission
services or offer ways in which information can be submitted electronically. However, many small-group practitioners are surprised
when they learn that managed care companies do not fully support
electronic claims submission. Despite their size and wealth, the
managed behavioral care companies are still relatively young, and
many evolved from fairly small operations. Consequently, most practitioners would be surprised at the lack of information systems sophistication in even some of the major managed care companies.

Another area that is of concern for small-group practices is
outcomes management. Measuring outcomes becomes more important to these organizations as they take on more managed care
contracts (Mirin & Namerow, 1991) (the topic of outcomes is addressed in chapter 13).

Also of concern to small-group practices is scheduling. As the
size of the practice grows and as clinicians are added, electronic
scheduling becomes more attractive.

Small Multispecialty Practices

As small groups grow into multispecialty providers, they frequently
take on more capitation or subcapitation which causes them to
become more like managed care companies and less like private
practices. In addition to utilization management and tracking,
these practices now have to devote resources to issues such as
credentialing and treatment authorization tracking for various
specialties. While these are important for small-group practices,
both can usually be handled without a sophisticated information

system. However, with larger multispecialty practices, tracking these areas becomes much more important and difficult.

Independent Practice Associations

As multispecialty clinics evolve into independent practice associations (IPA), their information systems needs take on a qualitative change. Because they are usually geographically diverse, networking and telephone issues become important. The transfer and integration of information among practices becomes important, and work flow automation starts to become more important. For example, how does one automate the transfer of information from a local IPA site to a centralized site for claims payment and aggregation? Specifically, what steps occur to make this happen?

Integrated Multispecialty and Integrated Delivery Systems (IDS)

As organizations grow into large multispecialty organizations, they need to address the problem of wide area networking. These wide area networks (WANs) are essentially the integration of many local area networks (LANs). Frequently, the organizations that participate in integration at this level have different software platforms at different geographic sites. For example, one organization may be running a Macintosh network while another runs a mainframe system with "dumb" terminals, and a third has a Windows™ NT system. All of these must be integrated if the organization is to function as one unit. As a result, the management of capitation becomes an interesting challenge since many of the participants may be using different utilization, accounting, and software systems that must also be integrated.

Population Size

Just as the organization needs vary according to the size of the practice, the number of lives covered will drive the needs of the information system's area.

For contracts with fewer than 30,000 lives, organizations typically can exist on fairly rudimentary information systems technologies. This number of lives can literally be run using stand-alone personal computers and off-the-shelf or homemade software.

When the number of lives increases to between 30,000 and 60,000 lives, organizations frequently begin looking at commercial accounting software. It usually is at this size level that ad hoc queries become more important as questions develop that are not answered by standard reports provided by the system. Consequently, the organization has to be able to answer those questions through special reports or other outputs and new corporate customers may ask for data not historically reported.

As organizations grow from between 60,000 and 200,000 lives, providers typically become more interested in client server networks. At this level "pods" of computers begin to cluster into departments and queries that were previously all ad hoc in nature become automated and routine while telephony and connectivity issues between departments and remote sites become more important.

When the number of covered lives passes 200,000, wide area network issues begin to emerge. It becomes important for multiple types of local area networks to be able to communicate effectively across wide areas geographically (hence, the name *wide area network*). Sophisticated payables and receivables systems begin to be implemented and specialized information processing tools are developed.

Smith (1995) divides information needs for managing managed care into six areas: (1) client demographics, (2) client insurance, (3) client treatment, (4) provider performance, (5) treatment cost and outcome, and (6) client satisfaction.

Currie (1995) suggests the critical functions that must be addressed by a comprehensive information system include: provider credentialing, primary source verification, peer review, client contracting, payer and benefit registration, marketing and referral tracking, patient registration and enrollment, authorization management, appointment scheduling, clinical record, fee-for-service and capitation management, claims adjudication, robust report generation, utilization review, case management, risk management, continuous quality improvement, and outcomes research.

Planning

Before starting on a computer project, the first thing to do is to understand exactly what the desired outcome will be and what problems you are trying to solve. In reality, however, information systems only can do three things:

1. *Increase speed.* This is often the reason providers look to computers as a solution since doing things more quickly is attractive to them. But speed is helpful only if the targets of computerization are *ready* to be computerized. Otherwise, "When you automate a mess, what you get is a very fast mess."
2. *Improve quality.* The things computers do better than human beings usually have to do with repetition, detail, and numeric analysis. Computers are better than humans at sorting through thousands of records. If providers plan their automation strategy, they often find there are better alternatives to solve a problem than computers. It is usually a good idea to be sure that the processes used to accomplish tasks within an organization are well known, or else automation will cause more problems than it will solve.
3. *Change paradigms of information flow.* Perhaps the most valuable benefit of developing an automated information system is that it forces the user to ask difficult questions about why they do certain things and why they do them the way they do. Providers have the opportunity to rethink what they're doing and to identify better ways to get their needs met.

Clinicians know the importance of clinical progress notes. In the behavioral healthcare business, these notes are usually in narrative, free-form text. In today's managed care environment, there is a need for outcomes and measurements of all types, but narrative data do not lend themselves to analysis. "Buried" in the clinical note are bits of information that, if structured differently, could be quantified. For example, consider this hypothetical narrative note:

10/20/95   50 minute session
Mrs. Jones is progressing well in her treatment. Her affect has improved as have her coping skills. She has returned to work

and expects to be ending treatment soon. Will see again in 2 weeks. In that time, she is to practice the positive "self-talk" exercises as her homework.

Imbedded in this progress note are several things that could be quantified. Compare this note to the structured progress note in Figure 14.1.

The structured note lets the clinician quantify several of those aspects of care that were mentioned in the narrative example. By structuring the information, the practitioner has set up a data acquisition system that lends itself to computerization and the development of outcomes measures. Rather, structuring the data starts a path that puts the data in a format that *can* be automated. The measures on this form include things such as changes in functioning, progress toward goals, and other items that most clinicians already capture during the course of treatment but do so in an unstructured and, therefore, unusable fashion.

This business of structured data is critical. Weed (1969) advocated a more structured language to help quantify or at least standardize the information being captured in the medical record. As Hill (1995) noted, "The behavioral healthcare industry, providers, managed care organizations, and payers can and must agree upon standard data content and standard formats for electronic data communications covering the majority of transactions." Others (Axelson, 1995; Geraty, 1995) have taken similar positions. The National Academy of Sciences Institute of Medicine has been working on the development of a Computer Based Patient Record (CPR) (Ball, 1995). Naturally, there are concerns about the confidentiality and security of such a record (Donaldson, 1995). But the need for structure is evident if automation is to occur.

The problem of standardization is a problem for the entire computer industry. For example, how does one assure that a text document developed on one computer will look the same on another one? One solution was described by Silverman (1995), "A universal language is needed that can describe any document to every computer. Right now the leading candidate . . . is SGML (Standard General Markup Language)." SGML is a structured method of constructing text documents so different computers can read them and format them as intended by the author. SGML

Progress Note

Patient Name _____

ID | | | | | | | | | |

Date | | | | | | | |

GAF | | |

Homework Assigned? (N) (Y)   Progress toward Goal

Describe: _____

_____

_____

Goal No.	Percent 0	25	50	75	100
1					
2					
3					
4					
5					

_____ Note: _____

_____

_____

_____

_____

_____

Service (CPT): | | | | | | Therapist ID | | | | | | | | | |

Next Appt: | | | | | | | | |

_____

Therapist Signature

Figure 14.1 Structured Progress Note

is not a substitute for structured data. It only structures the format or layout of text. It does not help in the search for quantifiable elements of that text.

Developing standardized languages means developing generally agreed upon definitions of familiar facets of one's business. This is not as easy as it might appear. Gather several clinicians together and try to seek consensus on (1) what constitutes an "episode of care"; and (2) who is the customer in the behavioral healthcare business.

The paradigm shift in the case of our structured progress note is an important one that should precede the implementation of information systems in general and particularly clinical information systems.

Management Information Systems

Management information systems (MIS) are not new to the behavioral healthcare business. Most of us have worked in organizations that had administrative and managerial computing capabilities as well as utilization information systems. In this section, we will discuss various types of computing systems and describe some of the advantages and disadvantages of them.

As noted above, the size of the organization frequently dictates what type of computing capabilities are needed. It is rare that a practitioner-based system would need something larger than a minicomputer and extraordinary if they would ever need a mainframe computer. All but the largest Integrated Delivery Systems can run on a networked system. Even if an organization has minicomputers or mainframes, most are interacting with them via PCs in networks. Because of this, the personal computer is still the interface with which most clinicians will work, probably in a client server network.

What is Client Server? In this context, clients are computers that are attached to other computers, called servers, so computing responsibilities can be shared or distributed. In general, client server systems work on local area networks (LANs) or wide area networks (WANs). The jobs of "clients" and "servers" in client server systems are as shown in Table 14.1.

TABLE 14.1
Functions of Client-Server Computers

Client	Server
• User interface	• Data updates
• Pick lists	• Data integrity
• Data validation	• Data extraction
• Second-level sorts	• System/network administration
• Local area networks	• Wide area networks
ad hoc query/reporting	• Production reports
	• Electronic data interface transfers

The client server networks harness the power of several personal computers together. The PCs are connected to each other and to servers or to minicomputers or mainframes. Obviously in this context it makes sense to have these different types of computers doing the things at which they excel. Servers, minicomputers, and mainframes are good at large-volume transaction processing of a routine nature. Consequently, the things listed under "Server" in Table 14.1 are those things that are done on a more or less routine basis. Personal computers, on the other hand, are usually much more user friendly and are designed to respond to the arbitrary desires of the user. As a result of this division of labor, the PC network capitalizes on each computer's strength (Derfler, 1995; Nance, 1994).

Network Types. The types of networks available vary according to the size and needs of the organization. They usually fall into four categories: (1) peer-to-peer networks, (2) small server-based LANs, (3) multihub networks, and (4) wide area networks (WANs) (Lowe, 1995; Derfler, 1995).

See Figures 14.2 and 14.3 for diagrams of peer-to-peer networks. The difference in the two networks has to do with the way the computers are connected to each other. (This is called the "topology," and a "star" topology is the most common.) Notice in Figures 14.2 and 14.3, no computer controls another; each runs autonomously. The only function of the network is to allow all of the independent computers to communicate and to share files and other resources. The computers all have network interface cards (NIC) which are electronic devices to which the communication

Dennis P. Morrison

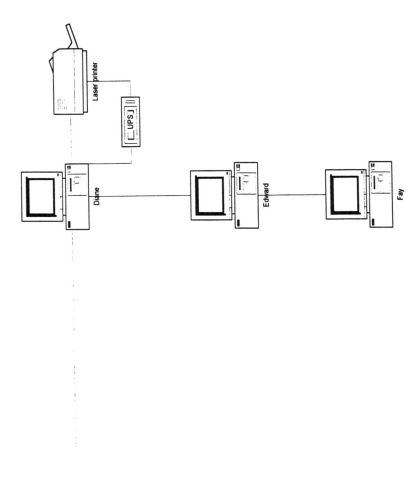

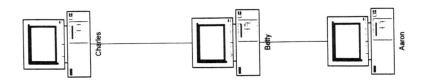

Figure 14.2 Peer to Peer LAN Bus Topology

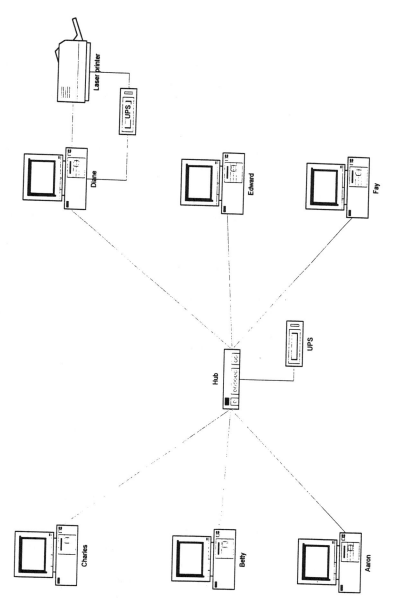

Figure 14.3 Peer to Peer LAN Star Topology

cables are connected. These cards (called PCMCIA cards or PC cards) are standardized so they fit in all laptops that have the necessary slots. There are several uninterruptable power supplies (UPS) in this network in case of a catastrophic power failure. One computer (Diane's) is running an uninterruptable power supply because this computer controls a printer which is shared by all of the members of this network. Notice also that the wiring of Figure 14.3 resembles a star with a wiring "hub" at the center and all of the computers branching from that hub, which allows information to be directed from one computer to another.

Another important issue in this networking business is the protocol, or "language," that is, the set of communication rules that allow computers to communicate. A standard in the computer network business is the ethernet protocol. For this system to work correctly, each computer must be running software that has the ability to work on a network. An inexpensive solution for the software in this case can be found in Windows for Work Groups 3.11, Windows 95, or Novell Personal Netware. In the case of Windows for Work Groups and Windows 95, the software is built in and available to the user without any modifications to the computer itself (a network interface card is still needed). An add-on package like Novell Personal Netware is available at a nominal cost and also works well in peer-to-peer networks.

Figure 14.4 looks very similar to Figure 14.3 because both work on a star topology. In this case, though, the wiring hub serves not only to direct information among the different PCs on the network but also to shunt messages to and from the server. What's usually being "served" are various files that all members of the local area network must access. This is different from the peer-to-peer LAN where no single computer holds the files needed by the other computers. The difference between a peer-to-peer LAN and a server-based LAN is roughly analogous to a peer support group in behavioral healthcare which has no identified leader versus a therapist-led group in which the therapist coordinates much of the activity in the group. Both types of groups have their purpose and do their jobs quite well, but the patterns of communication in them are different.

Compare Figure 14.3 to Figure 14.4 and note how all the hardware used in the peer-to-peer LAN can be migrated to a more

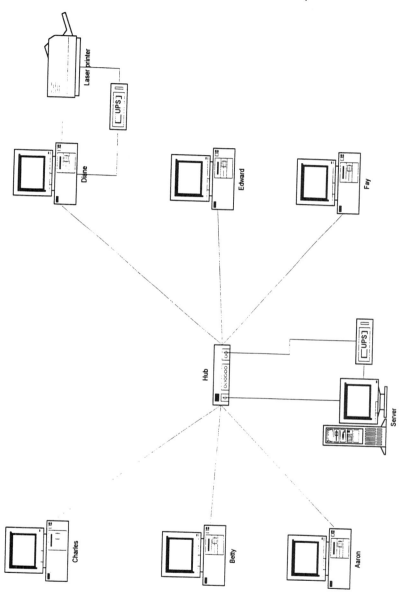

Figure 14.4 Small Service LAN Star Topology

robust server-based LAN. All the wiring, hubs, and network interface cards can still be used for this new type of network. In this case, most of the software can also be migrated. In the peer-to-peer LAN, Windows for Work Groups or Windows 95 was recommended for the personal computers. That software can still be used to access a local area network. However, the server will need some special software called a network operating system (NOS) provided by Novell (NetWare) and Microsoft (Windows NT). Note that there are several other types of networks and network software, but Ethernet is the most common.

If a practice moves from a peer LAN to a server LAN, there will likely be an increased investment in support personnel and consultants available to assist in the implementation and in the management of these systems. There are a variety of good references to learn more about local area networks. One is *Client/Server Computing for Dummies* by Doug Lowe (1995). (Incidentally, there is a whole series of ". . . *for Dummies*" books on a variety of computer topics. The books are highly informative, humorous, and not at all demeaning as the title might suggest.) Also consider *Networking Windows for Work Groups* by Barry Nance (1993). Both of these references are written at a beginner's level that someone new to the issue of networks will understand.

Data Acquisition: People who are building information systems frequently underestimate the problem of how to get data *into* a computer. When developing an information system, it is helpful to think how information flows through the entire system.

The purpose of an information system is to collect, store, and analyze, and report on data. This process can actually take up to five steps: (1) data capture, (2) data transmission, (3) data entry, (4) data analysis, and (5) report generation.

Data Capture: We routinely capture data every time we ask a patient to fill out a form. That paper form is, in fact, the data capture "device." However, if a patient sits at a computer and takes an on-line administered psychological test, the data from the test (e.g., the item responses) are being captured directly by the computer. In this case, the "device" allows data capture, transmission, and entry to be compressed into one step. Data from clinicians must likewise be captured either on paper or by dictation equipment and must be somehow entered into a computer, usually through a keyboard.

Data Transmission: In most organizations, data that have been captured in one place must be "transmitted" to another. If a patient fills out intake forms in the waiting room and then hands them to a receptionist, the receptionist must physically carry them to a data entry clerk, or the receptionist might fax them to a centralized location. Both are examples of data transmission.

Data Entry: Data are entered into a computer system through various means, but the most common is via keyboard. When data are entered into a computer, they usually go into a file of some sort that is represented in the computer either as an electronic record or a database.

Data Analysis: Once entered in a computer, the data can be summarized into understandable groups and reviewed for trends, outliers, and other anomalies using standard database, spreadsheet, or statistical analysis software. At this point, data are converted into information.

Report Generation: Presenting the information that was generated through the analysis phase is report generation developed directly out of software products doing the analysis or with dedicated software.

Capturing data into a computer has numerous clinical, administrative, and financial ramifications. In this section, we will review five methods by which data can be captured into a computer:

1. *Direct input.* Any system that allows the source of data (patient's or clinician's) to directly interact with the computer can be considered direct input. For example two direct input methods are touch screen technology and pen pad technology. Touch screen allows the user to enter data by touching the screen instead of the keyboard. Pen pad technology is usually seen on hand-held computers called personal digital assistants, or PDAs. These devices usually have fairly large liquid crystal display (LCD) screens on

which a user can "write" using a penlike stylus. An advantage of touch screen technology is that it does not require a keyboard for data to be captured.

As noted elsewhere in this chapter, computers can do many things, but the thing they do the best is to change paradigms. The advantages of going from a free text information system to a structured data system are numerous from an information systems point of view. Just as one should move from free text to structured data on a paper document (so the data can be captured easily in another format), so it is with pen pad computers. The reader might remember several years ago when the Apple Newton™ was introduced with much fanfare. The Newton is arguably the best known of the pen pad devices. However, the Newton was roundly criticized for its inability to correctly recognize words and letters when printed on its screen. The other unfortunate part of this is that it did not encourage the users to change the paradigm in which they worked. Rather, it encouraged them to continue to use a free text data capture methodology onto a computing system.

Like touch screen technology, the data input process for pen pads is transparent and, consequently, more efficient. Pen pads also are more expensive than sheets of paper, and they represent relatively new technology. However, both touch screen and pen pad have a place in the healthcare delivery system.

2. *Key entry.* Key entering data via keyboard is the data entry method that is probably best known and is an expensive process. When one commits to key entry as the only means of entering data into a computer, one has in effect made a choice to incur fairly high and ongoing costs for data entry. The good news about key entry is that the materials are inexpensive. Anybody can design a form and photocopy as many copies as they like to capture data on those forms.

3. *Optical Mark Recognition (OMR).* Next to key entry, optical mark recognition (OMR) may well be the one that is most familiar to most of us. Anyone who has ever taken a multiple choice test in high school or college has filled out one of these forms. Optical mark recognition scanning is also very fast and very accurate but has the disadvantage of high initial costs. Optical mark recognition scanners start at around $3,000 for a basic model.

The type of scanners used to score OMR forms are devices dedicated to this purpose. These scanners have to be purchased from a company specializing in this business such as National Computer Systems and ScanTron and each OMR form costs 25 to 40 cents. Depending on the volume, this could result in a high ongoing cost and OMR can only recognize "bubbles" and not hand printed characters. The forms used in OMR must be customized, adding to the cost of this system. While limited customization by the user on a personal computer is possible, the systems are fairly limited, ultimately requiring users to customize most forms through the vendor.

Despite these disadvantages, OMR should be seriously considered if fast, accurate processing of discrete (noncharacter based) information is your need.

4. *Optical Character Recognition (OCR).* This form of optical technology is significantly different than OMR. Optical character recognition uses the types of scanners advertised by your local computer store, which resemble a copier in operation, and are relatively inexpensive ($300 and up). They can be used to scan almost anything into a computer, including pictures and other graphical data. We focus on two types of optical character recognition software that can be used to get data (not pictures) into a computer.

When an optical character scanner "scans," it produces a picture of the original document. Once scanned, the software "tries" to interpret the text, and it can then treat the text as if it had been typed into the computer. The advantage of this is that a machine (the scanner) has replaced the key entry person. There are other software products that will take forms that are scanned and enter the text on the form into a database, thereby automating data entry.

This technology continues to improve with up to 99% recognition rates. Unfortunately, forms developed for OCR applications are not compatible with OMR scanners nor are OMR forms typically used for OCR.

One obvious advantage of OCR technology over OMR is that the software can interpret characters and enter them into databases automatically. Some information (such as someone's name) is much easier to capture by printing than by filling out bubbles. One should expect that all software (including the OMR system noted above) have some form of human editing capabilities since the computers are limited in their "intelligence."

Optical character recognition with fax input is another type of optical character software that provides the user all of the features available through OCR scanning but adds the ability to use a fax machine as the data input device in addition to or in lieu of a scanner. This provides an interesting opportunity for organizations that have several clinics or other, remote sites where they capture data (e.g., fill out forms) but they also want to build a centralized database from the information on those forms. One company specializing in this market is Cardiff Software. Their product is called Teleform™.

The reader should invest in dedicated OCR software if interested in pursuing this technology. The software is available for a few hundred dollars from computer stores. The fax-based product can be purchased for approximately $1,500. In both cases, the software has the ability to both design and interpret forms.

5. *Voice Recognition.* Voice recognition software allows the computer to literally interpret one's voice as it is spoken into a microphone connected to the computer. This is fairly new technology that is improving. For environments that require a limited vocabulary, such as an assembly line where users need only to tell a computer whether a part is "good" or "bad," the system is quite accurate. For nonstructured environments, the software is still not accurate enough or easy enough to use. The software for these systems is still fairly expensive, ranging from a few thousand dollars to tens of thousands of dollars for sophisticated systems, but continues to evolve.

See Table 14.2 for a comparison of these different data entry technologies across seven clinically relevant domains.

CLINICAL INFORMATION

Compared to traditional management information systems, clinical information systems are relatively new. The impetus for clinical information has come from the need for outcomes data. However, there is already a huge amount of evidence showing what does and does not work in behavioral healthcare. Note the following: "The point has been reached where certain findings about comparative outcomes and the relation of various facets

TABLE 14.2
Relative Comparison of Six Methods of Data Acquisition
(1 = worst, 5 = best)

	Cost	Compliance	Accuracy	Flexibility	Speed	Clinical Impact	Proven Technology
Direct Input	2	2	4	2	3	1	5
Key Entry	1	5	4	3	4	4	5
OMR	2	4	5	1	5	3	5
OCR	2	4	3	3	2	4	3
OCR with Input	3	5	3	4	4	4	4
Voice Entry	2	4	2	3	3	1	2

Cost = total cost to implement the system

Compliance = likelihood the system will be used

Accuracy = how well does the system interpret the input

Flexibility = how easy is it to modify the system and data

Clinical Impact = the extent to which clinical processes must be modified to accommodate the technology

Proven Technology = new technology versus established and mature technology of process to outcome are so well replicated that they can be accorded the status of established facts. Clinicians and healthcare managers who choose to remain ignorant of the facts will increasingly put their professional competence at the risk" (Orlinsky, Grawe & Parks, 1994). For a more complete treatment of this issue, see Bergin and Garfield's (1994) *Handbook of Psychotherapy and Behavior Change.*

One could argue that traditional psychological tests are the original clinical information tools, but test publishers have not led the development of tools to provide accurate and accountable information (Moreland, Morrison, & Maruish, 1995). Many new companies have formed in response to the market's demand for automated clinical information technology (see Appendix A for a list of some of these vendors).

What to Measure

The development of a clinical information system starts with measurement. Consequently, the first question is: "What does one measure efficiently to develop usable clinical databases?" While there are a variety of instruments available (see appendix B), the most popular tend to cluster into three categories: (1) symptomatology, (2) functionality, and (3) satisfaction.

Symptomatology measures have been around for some time. The Symptom Check List-90, Revised (SCL-90-R) and its shorter variant, the Brief Symptom Inventory (BSI) by Len Derogatis, are two examples. Users need relatively short instruments that assess a variety of domains that capture "snapshots" of the individuals' symptomatology and are brief, minimizing intrusiveness in the clinical process. A list of commonly used clinical information measurement tools is Appendix B.

If clinicians are the primary users of symptomatology measures, then certainly payers and employer groups are most interested in functionality. Those who pay the bills or manage the health benefit are concerned about returning the patient to a healthy level of functioning. Perhaps the most commonly used functionality measure is the Global Assessment of Functioning Scale (GAF) used on Axis V of DSM-IV. Capturing, analyzing, and reporting symptomatology and functionality information should be an integral part of a good clinical information system.

Finally, satisfaction is frequently asked as a way to substantiate a patient's perception of helpfulness of the services and the service provider. Aside from issues of customer service, satisfaction has clinical ramifications as well (Morrison, 1991; Morrison, in press a) in that it provides a reliable predictor of patient adherence (Meichenbaum & Turk, 1987, p. 63). Although frequently measured, there is a paucity of instruments with psychometric rigor with three exceptions: (1) the Client Satisfaction Questionnaire-8 (CSQ-8) (Attkisson & Greenfield, 1994; Attkisson & Zwick, 1982); (2) the Service Satisfaction Scale (SSS) (Attkisson & Greenfield, 1994; Greenfield & Attkisson, 1989), and (3) the Mental Health Corporation of America (MHCA) Customer Satisfaction System (MHCA, 1995). The CSQ is a unidimensional instrument measuring general satisfaction with services. The SSS is a multifactorial extension of the CSQ by some of the same authors. The MHCA Customer Satisfaction System is a very comprehensive product with two measurement tools at its core. One tool measures the clients' satisfaction with care on a multidimensional system. Since MHCA has rightly identified referrers as customers as well, the second tool measures their satisfaction. Information from these instruments can be captured using scanable (OMR or OCR) forms, and the data can be mailed or transmitted to a central database. Participants can then get reports comparing the satisfaction of their clients and referrers with other organizations (see Appendix B). Further information about automating outcomes assessments can be found in Morrison (in press b) and in the May/June 1995 issue of *Behavioral Health Management Magazine.* Ward (1993) discusses information systems in a clinical quality improvement system.

Internet

By now most readers have been exposed to the Internet in some fashion. Krul (1994) provides a good source of information about the Internet. As clinicians access "the Net," their work could radically change by improved communication and by accessing standardized databases.

One accesses the Internet in one of three ways: (1) Connect your computer to a local area network that is an Internet host; (2) Dial into an Internet host using the standard protocols; and (3) Dial into an online service that provides Internet access (such as CompuServe, America Online, Prodigy, or Microsoft Network) (Olsen, 1995). See Appendix C for a list of Internet sites of potential interest to clinicians.

Human Factors

Computers have to do with the automation of information management. Whatever unhealthy communication habits an organization has developed before automation will be made worse when computers are introduced.

Computerization is a people-oriented process. Davenport (1994) notes, "effective information management must begin by thinking about how people use information—not with how people use machines." If organizations exert control through information, the computer enhances the ability to do so. Conversely, organizations that share information openly can also increase that skill as well. In fact, successful computerization of an organization has relatively little to do with machines at all. "Indeed, the solution that most reliably leads to successful [Information Technology] implementation is also the hardest one to carry out: Changing an organization's information culture" (Davenport, 1994).

CONCLUSION

The speed with which behavioral healthcare has evolved has been eclipsed only by the information revolution. Fortunately, these two trends covary. The brief psychotherapy models proposed by Cummings and VandenBos (1979) and later by Bennett (1984) helped set the stage for a more accountable behavioral healthcare system. The complexity of psychotherapy requires computerization if honest measurements of change and value are to be made. We have seen significant progress in the measurement of behavioral healthcare (Bergin & Garfield, 1994). Clinical information systems have been used effectively with many populations, including the seriously mentally ill (Vieweg & DiFranco, 1995).

Yet with all of that, what is needed now is someone who understands the human impact of information systems. Cummings (1995b) has predicted that doctoral-level clinicians will assume more supervisory and management responsibilities and less direct therapy work. The clinician-manager will need to understand information systems, how information flows, and how people use information. How to accrue information will not be as important as knowing what to do with it once you've got it. As Greist (1982) observed: "We don't need another generation of computers or even programming languages. We need a generation of clinicians who will be able to take the powerful tools presently available and apply them with care, ingenuity, diligence, and patience to difficult mental health problems which will gradually yield to our steady efforts" (p. 3).

PART V

The Practitioner as Clinician

15.

The Practitioner as Clinician: The Business of Practice

Scott O. Harris, Ph.D.

> *There is no more powerful cost reduction tool than quality improvement.*
> K. R. Bhote

As the era of managed care is well upon us, psychologists are strategizing as to how to position themselves best in a rapidly changing mental health market. What the old and new clinician must ask is how to become and remain successful, efficient, and progressive in a market that is predominantly managed care. In looking into the future with what crystal balls are available, the solo practitioner is becoming the dinosaur and more and more clinicians are banding together to huddle around a fire that is precious and not too plentiful! As groups are securing and maintaining more of the mental health marketplace, the question becomes how one develops and creates a practice that is on the cutting edge while maintaining clinical quality and integrity, positioning oneself for the present and future of an ever changing market (Austad & Berman, 1991; Cummings, 1986; Cummings, 1995a).

The author sees himself first and foremost as a clinician. All the other roles are secondary. There was nothing more sacred upon graduating from graduate school than the thought of practicing psychotherapy and helping those who are in need. With managed care, PPOs, and HMOs, clinicians continually ask if they can continue to maintain quality and integrity and experience fulfillment as caregivers.

This chapter describes a model group practice. Anecdotal descriptive material will be offered to illustrate development and design. The practice described is the Center for Behavioral Healthcare (CBH), a practice the author established and codirects in Southern California. Illustrations will provide the thinking, planning, and development of this group practice by two psychologists with managed care experience. As psychologists educated some 15 years ago, the author and his colleagues never took business courses or received training in that area. The orientation was as clinicians within the scientist–practitioner mode, but with more of an emphasis on practice.

CBH was founded when two psychologists with different experiences and expertise put their heads together to create a group practice. After many breakfast meetings a vision for a group practice was born. The two partners created a union of hospital and managed care organizational experience, and joining forces resulted in a single vision of group practice. Many details consumed these meetings, from finding a location, to real estate, to malpractice insurance, and the hiring of office staff, as well as a myriad of accounting, tax, and other business issues.

As psychologists begin to take on new roles to face the challenge of the industrialization of mental health (Cummings, 1995b) there can be noted seven qualities or roles of the new psychologist. These roles are necessary in the era of survival and change: (1) innovator, (2) entrepreneur, (3) clinician, (4) case manager, (5) businessperson, (6) leader, and (7) visionary.

As many colleagues know and remember, good clinical work is not only rewarding and fulfilling but useful, necessary, and an important health service for millions of people. Does this mean that things are not changing for mental health practice? No! What it does mean is that good clinical work will always be needed (Harris & DeMayo, 1991). Here is the case example of John that illustrates the use of a managed care system within the context of good practice:

John is a 56-year-old recently widowed civil engineer. An unlikely and improbable candidate for psychotherapy, John was referred to his employee assistance program by his supervisor, who was concerned about John's wish to return to work 2 days after the death of his wife of 28 years. The supervisor was also concerned about his forgetfulness and lethargic manner. Recently, John had a physical examination from the family physician who could not find anything physically wrong with him. Confused about the purpose of his initial visit, John described the multitude of tasks he needed to complete. Only with some prodding was he able to speculate about his supervisor's concern. He acknowledged his occasional forgetfulness on the job in the preceding weeks as his wife's condition deteriorated. He began to talk fondly about his marriage, as well as his anger at his wife's doctors who appeared unable to prevent her condition from worsening. Grudgingly, he agreed to try therapy for a few weeks and to take some time off work. After two sessions he phoned to cancel further appointments, stating he had decided to return to work, and would be too busy to attend therapy. Two weeks later the therapist received an emergency call from the patient who was panicked to discover he had forgotten to check a basic safety feature in his work that afternoon and had potentially put other coworkers at risk. He was seen twice a week for the next few weeks while on medical leave from work. In these sessions he began the grieving process he had been so rigidly avoiding. After 4 weeks he was ready to work, and decreased the frequency of his appointments to once per week. After two additional months he terminated treatment and had no further contact with the therapist until the following year when he telephoned his therapist on the anniversary of his wife's death. He requested a session and came in for only two more sessions in which he focused on the task of reestablishing his relationship with his only child, a daughter who had been more closely attached to her mother.

In the case of John this therapy under managed care was the same as that which would have been optimal before the era of managed care.

What is the future for psychologists? They have to redefine their roles and position in mental health. There are a number of new roles that doctoral-level psychologists must serve since they will not be primarily psychotherapists; master's-level clinicians will be providing the front-line treatment. Psychologists must demonstrate leadership in group practice in keeping pace with healthcare trends.

PSYCHOLOGIST AS INNOVATOR

Psychologists have to be in control of their own destinies, as this author discovered in his own professional experiences. Four years ago I decided to leave a position working for a national managed care organization. Before that I had always worked in solo private practice and was planning to return to that mode. However, I decided to enter into a partnership for the future by building a group practice. This was a vision, a creation of a business practice that would combine clinical quality and integrity, and become a fruitful business enterprise. Many hours were spent in brainstorming what would make up a state of the art group practice, planning and strategizing the development of this creation. Our plan was to create a state of the art group practice that would run efficiently, that could grow in size, stature, and reputation, and that would have quality and integrity in the clinical work itself. The practice would develop into a business that could provide some security and financial rewards in an ever changing healthcare market.

Many of our cherished beliefs and attitudes had to be reexamined. The Boulder model of scientist-practitioner could now be revised and construed as a businessperson-practitioner model. This new model places psychologists in business as never before. In order to build a practice one has to create a vision of tomorrow that incorporates practice trends, new technology and systems, as well as the warmth and empathy needed to deliver quality service. An idea or creation is only as good as the motivation, determination, and drive behind it. Becoming an innovator in managed care is like running in a 5 or 10K race. You may not come in first, but you need to keep up, finding a way to persevere!

PSYCHOLOGIST AS ENTREPRENEUR

In past clinical practice, we have not thought of ourselves as creative and entrepreneurial. However, we had not considered ourselves to be in the business of practice either. Now we must. Business and practice are synonymous entities whereby new ideas and plans need to be continually created and executed. Becoming an entrepreneur is in a way similar to the way an artist creates a painting. You take from experience, hone your skills, work hard to create a vision of something that only you can see. As we created CBH the practice, we had to draw from the expertise of various professionals. However, the foundation must be constructed with an emphasis on good clinical work.

Over 4 years ago my partner and I created a vision and a plan while we met for breakfast at the same restaurant for months. We now have three office sites, 30 clinicians, and a very busy group practice. As many entrepreneurs before us, my partner and I have done everything from cleaning to carpentry to consultation to buying office supplies. We have put as much sweat into contracts as putting desks together. We have put our blood, sweat, and tears and fears into our practice along with our reputations. Service and delivery have been key. Quality and reputation are what sells a mental health group practice. Psychologists in this respect must maintain a good name, a quality service, and a reasonable business.

PSYCHOLOGIST AS CLINICIAN

In developing a managed care practice, some colleagues may think we've sold out, jumped ship, or have forsaken our clinical values and integrity in exchange for a managed care business and its income. However, this is definitely not the case. One can develop a business, a strategy, and an operation and at the same time provide excellent clinical services. Our clinical staff have all been handpicked based upon their backgrounds, experience, and areas of expertise. The new clinician needs to have solid clinical skills, case management knowledge, and the ability to work collegially in a group practice setting, as well as a keen awareness of managed care philosophy and parameters. This means a working knowledge of the terms and definitions of medical necessity, scope of benefits, utilization review, quality assurance, etc. This clinician needs to know how to provide brief solution focused treatment and must be a good communicator both clinically and administratively. The new clinician manifests many roles, such as diagnostician, trainer, case manager, and crisis intervention worker. The diagnostician completes the assessment and provides the most appropriate level of care plus adjunctive supports. The trainer provides direction, support, and guidance in the practice for the other clinicians. The clinician who is providing crisis intervention needs to be available in times of escalation, trauma, and increased symptomatology in order to assess the situation and to provide the most appropriate intervention. Within the group practice the new psychologist must be able to provide appropriate triage. The case manager considers an overall perception of the case as it applies to the managed care benefit. The supervising psychologist is the case manager for all the clinicians who work within the group practice. The following is the case of a patient well managed in a managed care system:

Leo is a 53-year-old married engineer, referred through his employee assistance program in an aerospace firm. A hard-working, dedicated employee for 27 years, Leo became distraught upon facing a work project which required multiple public presentations before groups of other engineers. Feeling terrified at the thought of public speaking, yet unable to assert himself and decline the assignment, within a week Leo became panicked, confused, and frightened. He began to experience heart palpitations, undue anxiety, and uncontrollable episodes of crying. Leo remembered a strikingly similar response 8 years ago when confronted with a task he felt incapable of completing. At that time his problem escalated for approximately 3 weeks before he sought help from a psychiatrist recommended by his family physician. The psychiatrist immediately hospitalized Leo and he remained in the hospital for 7 weeks! In contrast to the episode 8 years ago, Leo's current difficulties came to the attention of the employee assistance program within 3 days. The EAP evaluator in turn referred the patient directly to a clinical psychologist who began treatment immediately. After consulting with the utilization management department, the psychologist began seeing the patient two times per week while Leo was on temporary medical disability. Simultaneously the patient was referred for a medication consultation to a psychiatrist. After 3 weeks of intensive treatment, the patient requested a decrease of therapy sessions to one a week and was ready to return to work. The return to work proceeded well, although not without some anxiety as the patient has begun to assert himself with his supervisor for the first time in his career.

This case demonstrates the efficacy of managed care in preventing 7 weeks of probably unnecessary hospitalization. The least intrusive care was in the best interest of the patient.

PSYCHOLOGIST AS CASE MANAGER

Clinicians are now required to provide case management for their patients, as the following vignette illustrates. A 42-year-old patient presents for the first time as a severely depressed person with vegetative signs. He has just received an eviction notice from his landlord. He further complains of severe stomach pains. The therapist must make an early decision. Does he or she:

1. See him for psychotherapy?
2. Refer him for a medication consultation with a psychiatrist?
3. Refer him to his family practitioner?
4. Refer him to a legal aid clinic?
5. Suggest books on depression?
6. All of the above?

The answer of course is all of the above! What also comes with these recommendations is the coordination of care for this patient. The clinician who serves as a case manager for his or her patient has to be familiar with managed care systems as these facilitate appropriate, comprehensive care.

Case management involves the planning of discharge from the point of admission, which will involve several variables such as community resources and family support.

The notion of case management means interfacing with other individuals and coordinating care in a professional and collegial way. This case management is essential to good quality care and cannot occur without an appropriate group practice. Solo practice lacks the resources for this kind of integration. Case management involves:

1. Overseeing the course, direction, and progress of the treatment.
2. Monitoring the need for an increase or decrease in the level of care, as well as the utilization of community support and resources.
3. Maintaining a relationship-dialogue with the treating clinician that is collegial, helpful, and constructive.
4. Ensuring movement and progress of the treatment.
5. Providing feedback-consultation for a difficult system or clinical issue.

THE PSYCHOLOGIST AS SUPERVISOR

In group practice, the psychologist is looked upon to administer and monitor treatment, consultation, and supervision. Although the staff is trained, licensed, and experienced, in the supervisory role the psychologist is shaping the clinical quality and reputation of the practice. We have learned to identify the attributes and qualities of clinicians that fit into the model for CBH. These would include:

1. Experience in crisis intervention.
2. Brief solution-focused treatment expertise, knowledge, and experience.
3. Reliable, responsible, and conscientious skills regarding patient care, phone calling, and paperwork.
4. Ethical, dedicated, and committed professionalism.
5. Verification-documentation of license, malpractice, and work experience.

As a supervisor in a group practice one must continually monitor treatment, looking for acuity, level of care changes, need for medication consultations or community support referrals. Most group practices incorporate a structured quality assurance process and procedure, but in the final analysis a practice is only as good as the quality of care. The case of Jorge illustrates how these needs can be met in a managed care system.

Jorge is a chronically depressed 22-year-old Hispanic male employed as a maintenance man by a local municipal government. Born to a 16-year-old mother who was unable to care for his basic needs, Jorge was placed in a foster home at the age of 2. Due to severe behavior problems, Jorge went through a series of foster homes prior to placement at the age of 12 in the home of a paternal uncle. Unable to read, he received failing grades and dropped out of school at the age of 14. By the age of 16, he had experimented with a wide range of drugs and had become a functional alcoholic by the age of 19. Despite several reprimands for tardiness and frequent absences, Jorge had managed to hold down a job for the past year. Unable to read his benefits pamphlet, Jorge was told by a fellow employee about a "counseling program" for which the city would largely pay. Referred by the managed care company, in his initial therapy appointment the patient commented that this was the first time he had seen a "private doctor." Previously he received all of his medical treatments at county facilities. Initial sessions were focused on establishing a therapeutic alliance and addressing the patient's denial of his substance abuse. The patient was referred to a local AA meeting to which he was surprisingly receptive. Simultaneously continuing in AA and in the therapy, the patient began to confront the issues which his substance abuse had suppressed for many years.

This patient was seen in a managed care system and provided with good clinical care. Community resources were utilized and integrated into a reasonable treatment plan. Care was not compromised and a positive outcome was obtained.

PSYCHOLOGIST AS BUSINESSPERSON

In my first job as a psychological assistant, I was told to carry a brief case instead of my traditional graduate student knapsack. I was supposed to look and feel that part. Today being a businessperson is necessary for survival. The service that one provides in one's practice is the only product that the psychologist as businessperson can sell. Service involves clinical quality, accessibility, reliability, professionalism, and outcome. The product must be marketed, sold, and accounted for. In order to be in business the practice must have efficient systems, enabling the group to predict and control costs. A check list of necessary systems would include:

1. Computer(s) with management information systems (MIS).
2. Intake and referral systems.
3. Emergency/crisis services.
4. Scheduling procedures (i.e., patient access).
5. Logging-accounting of services.
6. Patient filing and records.
7. Authorization and treatment planning.
8. Financial: bookkeeping and accounting procedures.
9. Quality assurance and utilization review.
10. Orientation and training.

In running a group practice the psychologist as businessper-son needs to be the marketer. Unless one has the capital to hire consultants and all sorts of business personnel, the proprietor be-comes the jack of all trades and does everything from intake to emergency. The goal is always to be able to provide quality service that is comprehensive, accessible, and professional. Effectiveness in providing psychotherapy is not only producing some change and/ or alleviation of symptoms, but also: (1) service delivery, (2) docu-mentation, (3) quality assurance and outcome, and (4) office sys-tems. The need to obtain new business contracts is a never ending process, which involves continually marketing one's practice and reputation.

PSYCHOLOGIST AS LEADER

Psychologists are in a unique position to provide leadership in the evolution of managed health care (Cummings, 1995b). In our prac-tice we remain vigilant regarding changes in healthcare policy and trends and feel it to be necessary to remain on the cutting edge of group practice. Our business is only as good as the reputation that precedes it. We teach and train our staff and clinicians who de-liver our product. We work hard to perpetually develop, modify, and shape our practice. We are forever looking for new ideas or ways to promote our practice. We would like to believe we lead by example. Thus the psychologist takes a leadership role in this mar-ketplace, positioned to provide and manage clinical services in what is becoming the business of practice.

PSYCHOLOGIST AS VISIONARY

In taking a prominent role in the forefront of the managed care evolution, the psychologist needs to be able to develop a vision of the future. That vision combines caring for people with building a business. As the psychologist attempts to keep up with trends, it is clear that diversification is key. The psychologist as clinician and businessperson wears several hats but must still provide meaning-ful clinical care. As was stressed previously, the best product you can sell is based upon your reputation. As trends shift toward extending more risk and responsibility to the clinicians with case rates and capitation, psychologists are searching to see what type of delivery systems work best. Group practices of several forms (staff model, IPA, super IPA, hybrid models) are being tested. Alliances between groups of clinicians and managed care organizations are being formed to provide not only service to patients, but also a method of survival for practitioners in an ever changing market.

HOPES FOR THE FUTURE

Some psychologists hope that managed care will just go away and not come back another day. However, managed care is constantly evolving and changing, which means that it can be shaped and molded with some impact by practitioners. Those in practice do not have magical powers to look into a crystal ball and predict the future, but we are trained as scientists to look at the data in a systematic way. Psychologists cannot provide mental health services in a vacuum. As healthcare changes, the psychologist has to begin to work more closely with individual physicians, medical groups, and medical structures. Group practices have begun to contract with medical IPAs to provide treatment, and carve-out companies are changing in shape and form. As mental health treatment is being redefined, it is clear that there still exists a need for psychological services. A commitment to one's work and to quality of clinical care shapes the practice reputation in the marketplace. The work of the practitioner within the scope of a group practice is still important and essential work.

CONCLUSIONS

Practitioners can still practice with integrity. There are now more roles than ever, much to the surprise of some providers. We have outlined seven roles practitioners need to maintain in clinical group practice. There are, indeed, other roles and positions in the areas of research, management information systems and consultation. There are positions available with managed care organizations, insurance companies and quality assurances firms. The scientist-practitioner is becoming the businessperson-practitioner with new challenges in the business of healthcare. Mental health treatment has become a product, a commodity. However, since it is the practitioner who is creating and developing service delivery systems and busy group practices, it is still possible to provide good clinical treatment in what must remain a caring behavioral health profession.

16.

Managing Suicidal Patients: The Ultimate Test in Overcoming Outmoded Attitudes

Janet L. Cummings, Psy.D.

I want to live so that my life cannot be ruined by a single phone call.
Federico Fellini
La Dolce Vita

Although most therapists do their best to make accurate diagnoses and develop effective treatment plans for all their patients, even the most skilled therapists occasionally find that treatment of a particular patient is ineffective and that they need to rethink the diagnosis and rewrite the treatment plan. However, the therapist managing a suicidal patient may not have the luxury of reevaluating the diagnosis and treatment plan. There is no second chance following a patient's suicide. An error in the treatment of a suicidal patient can be lethal to the patient, as well as devastating to the patient's loved ones and to the therapist.

Most therapists who mismanage suicidal patients do so because of their belief in one or more of four outmoded attitudes. These outmoded attitudes will be discussed, along with shifts in thinking which are necessary in order to effectively manage suicidal patients.

OUTMODED ATTITUDES

Everyone Who Threatens Suicide Needs to be Hospitalized

In trying to avoid the loss of human life and the devastation which follows, many therapists err by relying too heavily upon psychiatric hospitalization for suicidal patients. Some therapists routinely hospitalize any patient who expresses suicidal ideation with even the vaguest plan. Even though only one out of 23 patients who threaten suicide is truly lethal (Cummings & Sayama, 1995), many clinicians hospitalize all patients who threaten suicide because of their own inability to differentiate the lethal from the nonlethal patient.

Many therapists have hospitalized patients unnecessarily in order to hide their own incompetence and insecurity about managing suicidal patients. Rather, it should be the therapists' obligation to hone their skills so as to be able to differentiate the lethal from the nonlethal patient and to treat each appropriately. This will take practice and, most likely, further education. However, even a therapist who can accurately assess 12 out of the 23 suicide threatening patients as nonlethal will reduce her unnecessary hospital admissions for suicidality by over 50%.

Unnecessary Hospitalization Can't Hurt, so Better to be Safe

The routine hospitalization of patients threatening suicide is extremely inefficient from a cost-containment standpoint, as individuals and insurance companies are paying for 22 unnecessary hospitalizations for each necessary one. More importantly, however, unnecessary hospitalizations do a disservice to many patients, not just economically, but psychologically, as well. For example, unnecessary hospitalization of histrionic patients causes them to think of themselves as much crazier than they really are. Unnecessary hospitalization of borderline patients teaches them to continue using suicidal threats to manipulate their therapists; in other words, the therapists give these patients a trump card which they can pull out and use against their therapists at any time. Borderline patients look for a ticket into the hospital whenever life becomes stressful and, with repeated hospitalizations, lose all motivation to learn to handle problems outside of the hospital. For these reasons, unnecessary hospitalization can be deleterious to further treatment or can actually increase lethality in previously nonlethal patients.

Case Illustration: Tony: At the age of 17, this high school student was lying on the couch in his parents' family room one day feeling sorry for himself and lamenting the day he had been born. His mother, aware of the high teen suicide rate in recent years yet failing to consider Tony's rather melodramatic personality style, feared that he might want to kill himself. She rushed him to the nearest psychiatric hospital. Although Tony denied any plan or intent to harm himself, he was admitted to the hospital as a precautionary measure. He was released 5 months later. (Apparently, Tony's parents had either lots of money or very liberal insurance.)

After his 5-month hospital stay, Tony was convinced that he was crazy and lived in terror that he might try to hurt himself at any moment, even though he really did not want to harm himself. He sought outpatient therapy, thinking that anyone who had spent 5 months in the psychiatric hospital must be crazy enough to need life-long therapy to avoid repeated hospitalizations.

Tony's new therapist helped him to see that nearly everyone, especially in the teenage years, wishes they were dead at times. The therapist also helped Tony to see his own strengths and to choose to view himself as a healthy young man rather than as a chronic mental patient. Tony soon went to college, seeing his therapist approximately once every 3 or 4 months while in college. After completing his university degree, Tony felt comfortable terminating therapy in order to relocate for his new job.

Although Tony's story has a happy ending, his unnecessary hospitalization was very destructive to him. He was lucky that he serendipitously found a therapist who was able to put his problems in their proper perspective and recognize that the 5-month hospital stay was both unwarranted and deleterious.

The Best Intervention Is to Take Responsibility for the Suicidal Patient's Life

Most people who suicide do so *at* someone. By taking responsibility for a suicidal patient's life, the therapist volunteers to substitute for the person at whom they wish to suicide. Then, the patient can suicide *at* the therapist.

Case Illustration: Evelyn: This patient, a homemaker in her mid-forties, entered therapy because of depression as a result of feeling trapped in her marriage. The patient was quite angry at her husband, who made all the major decisions in the family. She felt that her husband treated her like a child, often telling her what to do, and requiring that she obtain his permission on any course of action she might take. Most recently, he had refused to allow her to return to work, which she wanted to do now that her children were grown. Although Evelyn was furious at her husband, she repressed her rage at him and was experiencing a reactive depression rather than being aware of her anger.

When Evelyn told her therapist about her suicidal ideation, the therapist insisted that she be hospitalized. Although Evelyn protested, she soon acquiesced to her therapist's request, just as she generally acquiesced to her husband's demands. Following her release from the hospital 10 days later (when her insurance benefit for psychiatric hospitalization was exhausted), Evelyn told her therapist that she still felt suicidal and that she had been stockpiling prescription medication on which to overdose.

The therapist insisted that Evelyn bring her collection of medication to her next session to surrender to him and that she give consent for him to contact the prescribing physician to urge that no further prescriptions be issued to her. As usual, the patient acquiesced. However, immediately following the session in which she surrendered her pills, she purchased some over-the-counter medication and used it to commit suicide.

The therapist involved in this case made some critical errors which resulted in Evelyn's death. Most importantly, he took responsibility for the patient's life rather than helping the patient decide to live. Furthermore, the therapist treated Evelyn very much like her husband did by taking responsibility for her and telling her how to behave. For example, even though insisting that the patient surrender lethal means may be a good intervention for some patients, it was clearly an error in this case. Thus, Evelyn displaced her anger at her husband onto her therapist and suicided at him.

Evelyn's therapist later told this author of his own devastation following the suicide and that he had learned some very painful lessons. However, these lessons came too late for Evelyn.

Call a Psychiatrist because Nonmedical Practitioners Cannot Handle Suicidal Patients

Although it is appropriate to contact a physician when a patient is in need of medication, it is not necessary to involve physicians in every case where a patient threatens suicide. Nonmedical practitioners, with the proper training and experience, *can* manage suicidal patients.

Most therapists who wish to manage suicidal patients effectively will need additional training, as trying to learn by trial-and-error can be deleterious, or even lethal, to patients. The remainder of this chapter will serve as an illustration of what can be done by competent therapists in the management of suicidal patients. However, it is not meant to provide exhaustive training on the subject, and most therapists will need to get additional training, more extensive than this illustrative chapter.

It is this author's intention in the remainder of this chapter to outline the suicidal process, discuss treatment strategies for lethal patients, and offer some strategies for treating nonlethal patients.

THE SUICIDAL PROCESS

Most suicidal persons follow a distinct three-stage process (Sattem, 1989). (Paranoids are a marked exception to this rule and, therefore, will be discussed separately, later in this chapter.) During this process, suicidal persons choose the time, location, and method of their own deaths. The suicidal process can be interrupted at any point with intervention. However, if the process runs its full course, the end result is a suicide attempt or completion.

As individuals move through the suicidal process, they often exhibit the following verbal, nonverbal, and tactile indicators of lethality (Sattem, 1989):

Verbal Indicators

Most suicidal people tend to be more open to discussing their lethality earlier in the process. They tend to talk about their lethality less later in the process, as others may have indicated they are tired of listening or as the suicidal individuals feel that others don't understand or care. Suicidal people commonly talk about death and suicide in general, but don't always readily tell others of their own suicidal ideation.

As people move through the suicidal process, their verbal expression becomes increasingly right-brain dominated. They often talk of being overwhelmed with feelings and unable to concentrate. They may seem increasingly less logical and more emotional and creative in their speech or writing.

Case Illustration: The Poetry Man: A middle-aged man was depressed with suicidal ideation following a number of losses in his life. He had always been a very logical, rather unemotional man. However, as he progressed through the suicidal process, he began writing very creative poetry (something he had never done previously). Although he did not talk openly about suicide, he wrote a poem about birds. The poem talked about how beautiful birds are, but ended by saying that there are so many birds in the world that nobody really misses one when it falls from the sky and dies. A family member recognized this poem as an expression of suicidal ideation and helped the poetry man enter psychotherapy.

Nonverbal Indicators

Suicidal persons continue listening to or performing their usual styles of music. However, they narrow their focus more and more, until they are listening to or performing only very few songs, or perhaps only one song. Their choice of focus has meaning to them and will generally tell something about their pain source.

Suicidal persons' artistic expression tends to focus on themes of death, suicide, pain, and hopelessness. In drawings, the body size of figures may be quite reduced, reflecting low self-worth, and the necks or wrists may be omitted or slashed. Dark colors or heavy lines are often used.

Case Illustration: The Girl Who Was a Speck: A teenage girl who had expressed suicidal ideation was asked by her therapist to draw a picture of her family. The therapist saw all of the members of the girl's family in the drawing except the girl herself, and asked why she was not in the drawing. The patient responded by pointing to a speck in the corner of the drawing and saying, "There I am." This was a clear indication of her low self-esteem.

Tactile Indicators

Although not all suicidal persons exhibit tactile indicators, these signs are quite powerful in those who do show them. Suicidal persons can selectively hide their verbal and nonverbal indicators from others, yet have much less ability to prevent tactile indicators from becoming apparent to those around them.

Suicidal persons often stop touching other people and stop allowing others to touch them. They often avoid touching themselves, as is often evident from their neglect of grooming and personal hygiene. Some suicidal people rest or sleep in the fetal position. Others experience a number of injuries, as they become less careful and more accident prone. In some cases, suicidal persons exhibit nervous touching of their wrist and neck areas, as these areas become irritation points for them even if they are not considering a suicide method involving these areas.

These verbal, nonverbal, and tactile indicators of suicide differ greatly from individual to individual. Some suicidal persons exhibit a number of these indicators, whereas other persons may exhibit relatively few. However, the following three-stage process applies to all suicidal persons except paranoids. Some suicidal people are very open to talking about their suicidal ideation with friends, family, or therapists, whereas others are reluctant to discuss their lethality. Unfortunately, some people never warn anybody before their suicides.

Stage I: Ideation

People at this beginning stage in the suicidal process are considering suicide as a possible solution to their problems and relief from their pain. They may spend a lot of time thinking about death and suicide, but are generally afraid of suicide. Because of this fear, they have a difficult time planning their suicides and are likely to think about a number of possible methods. They often fantasize about dying from natural causes or wish they would be killed in an accident.

In stage I, people commonly verbalize their feelings of ambivalence, talking about both their desire to die and their fear of death. However, the tactile indicators are still absent or minimal while the nonverbal indicators may just begin to be evident.

Stage I generally lasts at least several months and can go on for years (Sattem, 1989). Some people spend most of their adult lives toying with the idea of suicide and are chronically in this stage. People in stage I may or may not move on to subsequent stages.

Stage II: Planning

In stage II, the attraction to suicide becomes more salient than the fear of suicide, although these people still have not decided to die. An individual in this stage is able to formulate a very specific plan for his suicide, choosing the exact time, location, and method of his own death.

A person who is very seriously contemplating suicide will generally select a very lethal method and will choose a time and place for his death which affords minimal chance that someone will find him, intervene, and thwart the plan. On the other hand, the person whose plan includes less lethal means and great likelihood of rescue may make suicidal gestures but is unlikely to be lethal. The noteworthy exception to this rule is the histrionic personality, who tends to miscalculate the rescue and sometimes dies from what was intended only as a gesture (Cummings & Sayama, 1995).

As a person moves through stage II, he likely will show a decrease in verbal indicators with an increase in nonverbal and tactile indicators. Stage II generally lasts at least a few weeks and sometimes months, but rarely over a year (Sattem, 1989). Once the individual has made specific plans, he feels tremendous pressure to decide either to die or not to die.

Stage III: Autopilot

A suicidal person moves from stage II to stage III at the moment she decides to suicide. Instantly upon making the decision to die, that decision becomes repressed, or unconscious, and the person goes on "autopilot" (Cummings & Sayama, 1995). Whereas people at stage I and stage II in the process are not lethal, those who reach stage III are lethal, even though they are no longer aware that they have decided to die.

In stage III, there is generally a complete absence of, or at least marked decrease in, the verbal, nonverbal, and tactile indicators previously discussed. The person on autopilot will inevitably show a dramatic elevation in mood, with remission of depressive symptoms, as she feels a tremendous sense of relief having made the decision to suicide. She will, however, give someone a clue that she has decided to die, but these subtle clues are seldom recognized by loved ones or by therapists.

Stage III seldom lasts over 48 hours (Sattem, 1989). Even though an individual may wrestle for some time with the decision to suicide, once the decision is made she tends to carry out her decision quickly.

INTERVENTIONS FOR LETHAL STAGE III PATIENTS

As was mentioned previously, persons in stage III usually give someone a clue that they have decided to suicide. In cases where the suicidal individual has been discussing his ideation and planning with a family member, close friend, or therapist, he will inevitably give that person a clue that he has decided to die. The human will to live is so powerful that, even though the decision to die has been made, the individual gives one final opportunity for intervention.

Unfortunately, however, these clues are more often than not overlooked until after the suicide. Because stage III brings an elevation in mood and remission of depressive symptoms, family, friends, and even therapists tend to breathe a sigh of relief. They fail to look for clues to lethality or consider the possibility that the suicidal person is on autopilot.

Case Illustration: The Last Supper

A man in his early forties had been depressed with suicidal ideation for some months. As his depression worsened, he became increasingly withdrawn from his wife and three sons. He eventually refused to leave his bedroom, stopped dressing and grooming himself, and would not speak to his family.

One evening, the man surprised his family by showing up at the dinner table dressed and groomed. He seemed upbeat and was quite talkative. His family was delighted to see this sudden change, thinking that his depression had finally ended.

After dinner, the man kissed each of his family members. He told his eldest son that he would be the man of the house, should anything ever happen to himself. Because the family was so overjoyed to see their husband and father acting like his old self again, they failed to realize that he was saying good-bye to them and placing the eldest boy in charge of the family. The man soon returned to his bedroom and suicided by gunshot.

Case Illustration: Marie

Marie had been seeing a therapist for several months because of depression with suicidal ideation. Neither psychotherapy nor antidepressant medication seemed to be helping her, and the therapist began to worry that Marie might commit suicide.

The therapist felt relieved when Marie arrived for a session in good spirits. She said she felt much better and thanked the therapist for being very helpful. Marie asked to cut the session a bit short, stating very matter-of-factly that she needed to keep an appointment with her attorney to update her will. The therapist did not recognize this as a clue that Marie intended to get her affairs in order before her death, and dismissed the patient from the session. Marie did see her attorney to get her affairs in order. She committed suicide before her next scheduled therapy session.

As these cases illustrate, the lethal stage III patient often goes undetected. Knowing this, it is imperative that the therapist working with suicidal patients take the following steps (Cummings & Sayama, 1995):

1. Be alert when a depressed patient who doesn't seem to improve suddenly gets markedly better, especially if there is an absence of any psychological reason for the sudden improvement. Recognize that the patient may have decided to suicide and is on autopilot.
2. Instead of relaxing when a depressed patient finally seems to get better, the therapist should become more vigilant than ever and look for any words or action that might be a clue of a decision to suicide.
3. If there is any suspicion that a patient may be on autopilot, the therapist should forcefully confront him by saying, "When and how did you decide to kill yourself?" The question should be repeated as many times as necessary until the patient convinces the therapist that he has not decided to die (which will be the case two out of three times) or until the patient can no longer remain on autopilot and confesses his plan and intent to suicide. Remember, it is better to apologize to those two out of three patients for falsely accusing them than to risk a suicide by failing to take this step.
4. If a patient on autopilot, when confronted, remembers and confesses his decision to suicide, the therapist should discuss his plan with him. This discussion should be meticulous and cover every detail of the plan. It is best to repeat this discussion as many times as necessary for the therapist to be certain the plan can no longer become unconscious.

Case Illustration: A Success Story

Bill, who had been in therapy for depression for several months, arrived at his therapist's office happy and full of energy. He talked excitedly about how much better he was feeling, casually mentioning that he had given his cherished stamp collection to his favorite nephew. The therapist suspected that Bill had made the decision to suicide and was on autopilot, and that the passing remark about the stamp collection was a clue.

The therapist forcefully confronted Bill, repeating the question, "When and how did you decide to kill yourself?" until the patient remembered his decision to suicide. Bill looked stunned as he told the therapist in near disbelief, "Oh, my God! I bought some rope so I could hang myself. I have the rope in the trunk of my car."

The therapist meticulously went over Bill's plan with him several times until it was apparent that he was fully aware of every detail of his plan. Bill talked about buying the rope without realizing he planned to use it to hang himself. He confessed that he had planned to hang himself from the rafters in his garage that very evening while his wife was out of the house at her weekly women's club meeting. The therapist asked Bill many other details of his plan, such as what type of knot he planned to use in forming the noose and what he planned to stand on while placing the noose around his neck.

Shocked to see how close to death he had come, Bill felt a renewed will to live. He decided that he wanted to live a meaningful life and began working harder in therapy. Over the next several months, Bill's depression gradually improved.

MANAGING LETHAL PARANOID PATIENTS

Paranoid patients warrant a separate discussion because they do not follow the same three-stage suicidal process that other suicidal patients follow and because they require much different intervention. Paranoids use projection as a defense mechanism and, in so doing, are unaware of their own suicidal feelings. These patients do not need to go on autopilot in order to carry out a decision to suicide; they are unaware of their suicidal ideation long before they are ready to carry out their plan. Furthermore, they may not view suicide as death, but rather as achieving invulnerability to life's problems by going on to a higher plane.

Because lethal paranoids express their suicidal ideation via projection rather than directly, many therapists fail to recognize their lethality. When a paranoid says that someone (the CIA, space aliens, or "they") plans to kill her, she really is planning to kill herself but is projecting her suicidal feelings onto the CIA, space aliens, or whomever else. Likewise, if a paranoid says that she is aware of a plot to kill someone else, it means that she herself is experiencing homicidal ideation toward that person.

Many suicide notes from successful suicides have a paranoid quality to them (Cummings & Sayama, 1995). Furthermore, many dual deaths (i.e., one or more homicides followed by a suicide) are perpetrated by paranoids who believe they are helping themselves and their loved ones go on to some higher existence where they can be together without the problems of this world.

Case Illustration: There's No Divorce in Heaven

Sandra, a paranoid schizophrenic in her late twenties, learned that her husband planned to divorce her and seek custody of their 5-year-old child on the grounds that Sandra's mental illness made her an incompetent mother. Sandra believed that the local police were brainwashing her husband to make him seek a divorce. After trying to no avail to convince her husband that he was being brainwashed by the police, Sandra shot her husband, her child, and herself. She believed that the family would then remain intact in heaven, where there is no divorce and where the local police would be unable to use their brainwashing techniques on her husband.

Although the intervention of contracting with patients to abstain from suicide for specified periods of time will be discussed in the next section of this chapter, it is important to note here that such contracting is ineffective with paranoids. These patients do not recognize themselves as being suicidal in the first place.

Furthermore, they generally do not believe in death but, rather, in some higher level of existence. Paranoids simply do not keep contracts.

Reasoning with a paranoid is also ineffective. Trying to talk him out of his delusion will only convince him that the therapist is in collusion with whomever he believes wishes to harm him. Although the therapist must ask very specific questions to get information from a paranoid, the information can be elicited without causing him to distrust the therapist.

Case Illustration: The Plot against Paul

Paul, a paranoid schizophrenic in his thirties, told his therapist that some people were plotting to kill him. Many people were part of this plot, and Paul was somehow able to distinguish them from people not involved in the plot. The therapist asked Paul when the plot would be carried out. He responded that it probably would not be soon, as the plot was still in the early planning stages. The therapist knew that Paul was not in immediate danger.

A week later, Paul seemed very agitated as he told his therapist that the people plotting to kill him had gotten him fired from his job. When the therapist asked again when the plot to kill him would be carried out, Paul indicated that it could be any day now. The therapist recognized that Paul was imminently suicidal and hospitalized him immediately.

Paranoid patients in imminent danger of suicide or homicide must be hospitalized immediately and stabilized on antipsychotic medication. Other interventions, no matter how effective with nonparanoid patients, will fail when used with a lethal paranoid.

INTERVENTIONS FOR NONLETHAL PATIENTS

Although this chapter has outlined very specific interventions for lethal stage III and lethal paranoid patients, the number and diversity of interventions which can be effective with nonlethal patients are virtually unlimited. For this reason, working with nonlethal suicidal patients can be challenging and enjoyable, as the therapist has the flexibility to tailor interventions to each specific patient. In developing an intervention, the therapist can consider whether the patient is in the suicidal process or merely making manipulative threats, as well as the patient's personality style, diagnosis, and world-view. Although an exhaustive list of interventions would be impossible, the case illustrations which follow should provide examples of some possible interventions.

Case Illustration: The Contract

The patient, a man in his midtwenties, told his therapist of suicidal ideation since the recent loss of both a job and a significant relationship. The therapist judged that the patient was in stage II of the suicidal process, as he was actively developing a plan for his suicide. The therapist also noted that the patient was still afraid of suicide.

The therapist used the patient's fear of suicide to encourage him to make a suicide abstinence contract. Knowing that the patient could at any time move into stage III, the therapist suggested a short-term renegotiable contract rather than a long-term one. That is, rather than ask the patient to agree not to suicide for the duration of therapy, the therapist suggested contracting until the next face-to-face or telephone contact.

Each time the contract was renewed, the therapist asked the patient how long he felt he could agree to abstain from suicide. The next contact was scheduled accordingly. During a brief period when the patient was particularly distraught, he was seen each morning and had a telephone contact with the therapist each afternoon and each evening. The patient was given permission to contact the therapist through a 24-hour answering service should he at any time feel unable to keep his contract.

Gradually, the patient was able to contract for longer and longer periods of promised abstinence from suicide. Eventually, his suicidal ideation remitted entirely. Meanwhile, the patient learned to use resources outside the hospital setting to manage his crisis.

It should be noted that the suicide abstinence contract can be a very effective intervention for nonlethal suicidal patients if the contracts are negotiated for periods of time which the patient can manage. However, contracting is ineffective with patients who are unable to keep contracts and, in these cases, serve only to give the therapist a dangerous false sense of security. Stage III and paranoid patients do not keep contracts. Patients with organic problems often do not understand and remember contracts, and substance abusing patients forget or ignore contracts when under the influence of a substance (Cummings & Sayama, 1995).

Case Illustration: Finding a Better Way to Get Even

A woman in her early forties was angry at her husband because he left her for a much younger woman. She was considering suicide as a way to punish her husband and was enjoying fantasizing about the remorse he would feel after learning of her death. Because the patient did not have a specific method in mind, the therapist judged her to be in stage I.

The therapist took the enjoyment out of the patient's fantasy by explaining that her husband probably would experience a brief bout of guilt, but would then be free to live life with his new lover unencumbered by divorce proceedings and alimony payments. The therapist further shattered the patient's fantasy by mentioning that her husband's lover would finish raising her two adolescent children after her death.

The patient decided that suicide would not adequately punish her husband. With her therapist's help, she decided to punish him by staying alive long enough to seek her rightful share of the family's assets as well as alimony and child support.

Case Illustration: Histrionic Helen

Helen, a woman in her thirties with histrionic personality disorder, threatened to commit suicide by overdosing on alcohol and tranquilizers following the most recent break-up in a long succession of failed relationships. Helen had recently begun to notice a few gray hairs, which further convinced her that her life was over.

Helen's therapist knew that she had chosen overdose as a suicide method because it would allow her to die as she had lived, neatly and attractively dressed and groomed. He also knew that a histrionic would rather die than be disfigured (Cummings & Sayama, 1995). Therefore, he convinced Helen that her plan might disfigure rather than kill her. He described how neurological damage might cause her to appear following a failed suicide attempt: unable to stand and walk erect, incontinent, and lacking the intellect and fine motor coordination to apply makeup and style her hair. He also mentioned that she might look unattractive even if her plan succeeded because the coma she would experience prior to death would distort and disfigure her facial muscles. The muscle distortion, if severe enough, could not be corrected, and all who viewed her at her funeral would see her disfigurement.

Helen quickly and readily gave up the idea of overdosing. She decided instead to work with her therapist to find ways to make her life meaningful.

Case Illustration: The Zero to Ten Scale

A man in his late thirties with borderline personality disorder had been chronically suicidal for most of his adult life. He had seen numerous therapists over the years, many of whom had hospitalized him because of his suicidality. The patient was often terrified by his suicidal ideation and frequently called his therapist or the crisis hotline in a panic.

Because of a change to a new insurance plan, the patient began seeing a therapist who was able to recognize that he was not lethal and not in need of hospitalization. Instead of asking whether or not the patient felt suicidal (as he almost always did), the therapist asked him at each contact to rate his suicidality on a scale of zero to 10. In so doing, the therapist was able to help the patient realize that not every suicidal thought was cause for alarm. The patient agreed to call the therapist or crisis hotline only if his suicidality rating got above an 8 on the zero to 10 scale. The patient's telephone calls to the therapist and crisis hotline decreased by 90% within a few weeks.

Case Illustration: Staying a Step Ahead

The patient, a woman in her late twenties with borderline person-ality disorder, threatened suicide whenever life didn't go her way. She was fearful of suicide, and needed to feel that her therapist was stronger and wiser than she in order to feel safe.

Knowing this, the therapist learned to foresee instances when the patient might threaten suicide and began raising the issue before that patient had the chance. For example, the patient had often threatened to go to a nearby 24-hour pharmacy to buy pills on which to overdose. Therefore, when the therapist believed the patient might be leading up to a suicide threat, she asked if she had visited the 24-hour pharmacy yet. The patient smiled, feeling relieved that the therapist was one step ahead of her, and said she had not visited the pharmacy and probably would not do so any time in the near future.

The patient once mentioned in passing that her insurance benefit for prescriptions had changed. She would need to get pre-scriptions filled at Walgreen's rather than the independent phar-macy she had been using. Seizing this opportunity to show that she was still one step ahead of the patient, the therapist interjected and said, "I'm sure you've already found the nearest 24-hour Walgreen's just in case you ever need it." The patient laughed with delight that the therapist was a step ahead of her. She admitted that she had located the nearest 24-hour Walgreen's, but assured the therapist that she really had no intention of buying pills on which to overdose.

Case Illustration: Mobilizing Support for Sam

Sam, a widower in his sixties, was very depressed and suicidal. He had formulated a well-thought plan and was wrestling with whether or not he wanted to implement the plan. Clearly, the patient was in stage II.

The therapist learned that Sam was a member of a church with about 200 members, even though he had recently become very iso-lated and had stopped attending services. With Sam's permission, the therapist was able to mobilize support for Sam through his church rather than hospitalize him. The pastor arranged to have various parishioners prepare meals for Sam, while others stayed with him on a rotating basis to lend support.

Sam felt so touched by his church's care for him that his depression began to remit. He began attending church regularly again and involved himself in various church social activities. He developed a very strong support system upon which he continued to rely. Sam could not have developed such a lasting support system in the hospital.

Case Illustration: A Paradoxical Intervention

This author was working with a female borderline patient in her late twenties who often attempted to control her treatment and manipulate her therapist with threats of suicide. The therapist was able to diffuse the patient's manipulative power using a paradoxical intervention.

The therapist told the patient, "I'm currently authoring a chapter on suicide for a book. However, I have never actually experienced a suicide and am having difficulty coming up with dramatic examples of how suicides are carried out. If you are going to be my first suicide, the least you can do is come up with something dramatic enough to make my chapter incredibly interesting." The therapist then gave the patient the homework assignment of deciding upon a suicide method which would be worthy of a prominent place in the chapter, to be discussed at the next session.

The patient came to the next session and described her plan to jump off a high bridge. The therapist responded by saying, "I'm disappointed. That's been done and overdone. I grew up in San Francisco, where I heard of more suicides by jumping off the Golden Gate Bridge than I can count. You need to come up with something better than that." The patient was given the homework of thinking of a more worthy plan.

The patient returned for her next session with a new plan, which the therapist again deemed unworthy. The patient was again asked to improve upon her plan before the next session. After a few more such rounds, the patient admitted that she really did not want to commit suicide and never again used suicide threats in an attempt to manipulate her therapist.

This intervention may not work for every therapist, as it was borrowed from one therapist's current experience. However, the idea behind this intervention of paradoxically prescribing the symptom can be adapted to fit a particular therapist's and patient's personalities. As with most interventions for nonlethal patients, the therapist is free to be creative and innovative.

APPENDICES

Compiled by Dennis P. Morrison, Ph.D.

Information System Vendors

Abacus Software, Inc.
  Bruce Kantelis
  2600 McCormick Drive,
    Suite 200
  Clearwater FL 34619
  813-726-6511

**Advanced Institutional
Management Software, Inc.**
  Mark Bohlmann,
    Vice President
  5151 Reed Road, Suite B-220
  Columbus OH 43220
  614-457-6630
  516-496-7069 fax

**Boston Technologies
Incorporated**
  Director, Behavioral Health
    Software Development
  620 Landis Avenue,
    Third Floor
  Vineland NJ 08360
  609-692-4958
  609-691-8160 fax

Breakthrough Data Systems
  Jack Manuel, President
  PO Box 890189
  Houston TX 77289

CATOR
  Norman C. Hoffman, PhD
    Executive Director
  17 West Exchange Street
  St. Paul MN 55102
  612-221-3155

CMHC Systems, Inc.
  Clarence Reed
  5500 Frantz Road, Suite 150
  Dublin OH 43017
  614-764-0143
  614-764-0362 fax

Community Sector Systems
  Duncan West,
    Research Analyst
  700 Fifth Avenue, Suite 5500
  Seattle WA 98104
  206-467-9061

Creative Socio-Medics Corporation
Director, Behavioral Health
Software Products
146 Nassau Avenue
Islip NY 11751
516-968-2000
516-968-2123 fax

ECHO
Director, Behavioral Health
Software Development
PO Box 540
Center Conway NH 03813
603-447-5453
603-446-2037 fax

Foundation Data Systems
Roger Dunigan
PO Box 463
Traverse City Ml 49684
616-929-9225
616-929-9268 fax

Hill and Associates
Joseph Naughton,
Vice President
One Industrial Drive
Windham NH 03087
603-893-3115
603-898-3115 ext 103 fax

InStream
Jesse Kalfel, Director
Product Development
300 Unicorn Park Drive
Woburn MA 01801
617-935-2100
617-935-2103 fax

Interactive Health Systems
Roger Gould, MD,
President
1333 Ocean Boulevard
Santa Monica CA 90401
310-451-8111

Lavender and Wyatt Systems
Director, Behavioral Health
Software Development
5805 West 12 Street
Little Rock AR 72204
501-664-7039
501-664-7518 fax

Logical System Solutions, Inc.
Ben Borenstein
343 Panorama Drive
San Francisco CA 94131
415-641-7060

Management Information Systems (MIS), Inc.
Joe Braga, Vice President
Sales and Marketing
Echo Management Group
1620 Main Street
Center Conway NH 03813
800-635-8209
619-447-2037 fax

MEDecisions, Inc.
Tom Davis, Vice President
Sales and Marketing
1436 Lancaster Avenue
Berwyn PA 19312
610-648-0202
610-889-1775 fax

Medipay
James S. Coke, President
620 SW Fifth Street,
Suite 610
Portland OR 97204
503-227-6491
503-299-6490 fax

Mitchell and McCormick, P.C.
Shawn Stone
4271 First Avenue
Tucker, GA 30084
800-551-0775
404-938-9193 fax

NCS Assessments
Jeffrey Sugerman, PhD
Vice President &
Publisher
5605 Green Circle Drive
Minnetonka MN 55343
612-939-5126
612-939-5099 fax

The Psychological Corporation
Aurelio Prifitera, PhD,
Director
Psychological
Measurement
555 Academic Court
San Antonio TX 78204-2498
210-299-1061
210-270-0327 fax

PsychResources Group, Inc.
Geoffrey V. Gray, PhD,
President
6 Devine Street
North Haven CT 06473
800-357-1200
203-230-0045 fax

Strategic Advantage, Inc.
Murray P. Naditch, PhD,
President
1784 Dupont Avenue South
Minneapolis MN 55403
612-374-5995

Strategic Decisions Systems, Inc.
Gary Long, President
5575-B Chamblee-
Dunwoody Road
Atlanta GA 30338
404-551-9763

UNICARE Systems
Les Frahm
3150 Livernois,
Suite 115
Troy MI 48083
810-689-9890

Wenzel Group
Lee Wenzel
8666 West Wind Circle
Eden Prairie MN 55344
612-944-2699

Frequently Used Clinical Information Instruments

Addiction Severity Index (adult)

Description: 45 minute interview measuring problem severity in seven areas relating to addictions and relapse. Widely used in substance abuse treatment and research.

Dimensions: Severity of patient problems in the areas of drug, alcohol, medical, employment/support, legal, family/social, and psychiatric.

Source: Treatment Research Institute
One Commerce Square, Suite 1020
2005 Market Street
Philadelphia PA 19103
800-335-9874

BASIS-32 (adult)

Description: Brief self-report measure of symptoms and problem difficulty administered at admission, discharge, follow up, measuring level of functioning and symptom severity.

Dimensions: Interpersonal relationships, daily living, role functioning, depression, anxiety, impulsive/addictive behavior, psychosis.

305

Source: Evaluative Service Unit
                  McLean Hospital
                  115 Mill Street
                  Belmont MA 02178-9106
                  617-844-2000

Beck Depression Inventory / BDI (adult)

Description: Its purpose is to detect possible depression and to
                  assess severity of depression.

Dimensions: Depression (cognitive-affective and somatic-perfor-
                  mance)

Source: The Psychological Corporation
                  555 Academic Court
                  San Antonio TX 78204-2498
                  210-299-1061

Brief Psychiatric Rating Scale / BPRS (adult)

Description: Observer rated scale that provides an assessment of
                  psychiatric status

Dimensions: Florid thinking disorder, withdrawn-disorganized
                  thinking disturbance, hostile depression, withdrawn-
                  retarded depression, agitation-excitement syndrome

Source: Contact for more information:
                  Test Collection
                  Educational Testing Service
                  Princeton NJ 08541
                  609-921-9000

Brief Symptom Inventory / BSI (adult and adolescent)

Description: An abbreviated (53 item) version of the SCL-90 R;
                  see below.

Center for Epidemiologic Studies—Depression Scale / CES-D (adult)

Description: 20 item measure designed to collect symptoms of
                  depressed mood

Dimensions: Depression, depressed mood

Source: The RAND Corporation
               PO Box 2138
               Santa Monica CA 90407-2138
               310-393-0411

Child Behavior Checklist & Youth Self-Report / CBCL YSR (child and adolescent)

Description: Designed to address the issue of defining child be-
               havior problems empirically; reported by parents;
               able to distinguish between children who have prob-
               lems and those who do not.

Dimensions: Social competence (activities, social, school), behav-
               ior problems (internalizing, externalizing)

Source: University Associates in Psychiatry
               c/o Child Behavior Checklist
               One South Prospect Street
               Burlington VT 05401
               802-656-4563

Client Satisfaction Questionnaire / CSQ (adult)

Description: Typically given at discharge and/or at various
               follow-up intervals post-discharge; measures client
               satisfaction

Dimensions: Client satisfaction

Source: Clifford Attkisson, PhD
               University of California
               Department of Psychology
               401 Parnassus Avenue, Box CPT
               San Francisco CA 94143-0984
               415-476-7374

Client Quality of Life Interview / CQLI (adult)

Description: Part of a battery of instruments to assess outcomes
               among persons with severe mental disorders who

were served by the NIMH CSP; general focus on functioning, services, and clinical outcomes.

Dimensions: Essentials of life (food, clothing, hygiene, etc.), job training and education, daily activities and recreation, privacy, social supports, social time, self-reliance, peace of mind.

Source: For more information see:
              Baker, R., and Intagliata, J. (1982). Quality of life in the evaluation of community support systems. *Evaluation & Program Planning*, 5:69–79.

Community Adaption Schedule / CAS (adult)

Description: Self-report measure of subjects relative to the world outside himself; primarily used for measuring groups; for research use only.

Dimensions: Work, family, social, larger community, commercial, professional, affect, behavior, cognition, common question total, total consistency.

Source: Behavioral Publications, Inc.
              (Human Sciences Press)
              233 Spring Street
              New York NY 10013-1578
              212-620-8000

COMPASS / (adult)

Description: Using both patient self-report and therapist ratings, COMPASS assesses patient mental health status, patient perceptions of therapist, and therapist perceptions of patient status and presents the results in the context of national norms for adult outpatients. A unique feature is its capacity to "track" patient progress concurrently with treatment.

Dimensions: Patient demographics, motivation for treatment, presenting problems, subjective well-being, symptoms, functioning, perceptions of the therapist;

therapist rating of patient status, progress, and functioning.

Source: COMPASS Information Services
                 1060 First Avenue, Suite 410
                 King of Prussia PA 19406
                 610-992-7060

Current and Past Psychopathology Scales / CAPPS (adult)

Description: Measures functional impairment from normal to severe; produces a computerized diagnosis using official nomenclature of APA.

Dimensions: Current functioning, past functioning.

Source: Research Assessment and Training Unit
                 New York State Psychiatric Institute
                 722 West 168th Street, Room 341
                 New York NY 10032
                 212-960-2200

Derogatis Psychiatric Rating Scale / DPRS (adults and adolescents)

Description: Psychiatric rating scale designed for use by clinicians trained in psychopathology; companion measure to the BSI or the SCL-90-R; used for initial evaluation or assessment of patient improvement.

Dimensions: Same as BSI/SCL-90-R, plus sleep disturbance, psychomotor, hysterical, abjection-disinterest, conceptual, disorientation, excitement, euphoria.

Source: NCS Assessments
                 5605 Green Circle Drive
                 Minnetonka MN 55343
                 800-627-7271

Denver Community Mental Health Questionnaire—Revised / DCMHQ—R (adult and adolescent)

Description: Designed for use by "non-professional" level case workers; main value is as a preliminary screening

device on the possible improvement in social adjustment following treatment.

Dimensions: Personal distress, alcohol and drug abuse, social
and community functioning, client satisfaction.

Source: James A. Ciarlo (author)
University of Denver
Mental Health Systems Evaluation Project
70 West Sixth Avenue
Denver CO 80204
303-871-2000

Discharge Readiness Inventory / DRI (adult and geriatric)

Description: Rating by social workers of patients' potential for
release and community adjustment.

Dimensions: Community adjustment potential, psychosocial
adequacy, belligerence, manifest psychopathology.

Source: National Educational Consultants, Inc.
5604 Rhode Island Avenue
Hyattsville MD 20781
301-983-4033

Edward's Jefferson Goal Scaling / JGS (adolescent through geriatric)

Description: Client and therapist jointly define the two most
important treatment goals at intake; goals standardized on a 9-point rating scale (+4 to −4).

Dimensions: Environmental, community, legal, work, financial,
education, physical, interpersonal, marital, sexual,
family, affective, mental, general improvement, program attendance, behavioral, drug and alcohol goals.

Source: For more information see:
Mental Health Service System Reports
Assessing Mental Health Outcome Measurement
    Techniques, Series FN, No. 9, United States
    Department of Health and Human Services, 1986.

General Health Questionnaire / GHQ (adult)

Description: Assesses the presence and severity of psychiatric disorder in community and patient populations.

Dimensions: Depression, anxiety, social impairment, hypochondriasis

Source: NFER—Nelson Publishing Co.
              Darville House
              2 Oxford Road East
              Windsor, Berkshire SL4 1DF
              England

General Well-Being Schedule / GWB (older adolescent and adult)

Description: Self-administered self-report questionnaire about symptoms, personal functioning and occurrence of significant problems in a general population.

Dimensions: Overall psychological adjustment and a criterial section assessing more specific instances of psychological distress over past year and attempts to deal with this distress via mental health services.

Source: H. J. Dupuy (author)
              For more information see:
              Mental Health Service System Reports
              Assessing Mental Health Outcome Measurement
                 Techniques, Series FN, No. 9, United States Department of Health and Human Services, 1986.

Global Assessment of Functioning / GAF (adult)

Description: Observer-rated scale that provides an overall evaluation of functioning; typically given at admission and discharge.

Dimensions: Level of functioning (positive and negative), symptoms, social and occupational functioning.

Source: New York Psychiatric Institute
              722 West 168th Street

Room 341
New York NY 10032
212-960-2200

Global Improvement Rating Scales / GIS (all ages)

Description: Assesses general improvement in unspecified areas
of potential change; most require a single global rating of patient's improvement from beginning to
end of treatment.

Dimensions: No specific functional areas assessed; general focus.

Source: Developed from work by L. Luborsky, J. Mintz, and
S. Garfield
For more information see:
Mental Health Service System Reports
Assessing Mental Health Outcome Measurement
Techniques, Series FN, No. 9, United States De-
partment of Health and Human Services, 1986.

Hamilton Rating Scale for Depression / HRSD (adult)

Description: 17 item symptom list administered in semi-structured
interview with client used to assess severity and pattern of depression.

Dimensions: Depression

Source: PAR, Inc.
PO Box 998
Odessa FL 33549
813-968-3003

Inventory of Suicide Orientation / ISO (adolescent)

Description: 30 item screening tool to identify adolescents at risk
for suicide.

Dimensions: Hopelessness, suicidal ideation.

Source: NCS Assessments
5605 Green Circle Drive

Minnetonka MN 55343
800-627-7271

Katz Adjustment Scales / KAS (adolescent to geriatric)

Description: Measures adjustment and social behavior in community; recommended for research use only; ratings from relatives and patient.

Dimensions: Symptoms and social behavior, performance of socially expected activities, free time activities, satisfaction with free time activities, symptom discomfort.

˙Source: Martin M. Katz (author)
Clinical Research Branch
National Institute of Mental Health
Chevy Chase MD 20203
202-619-0257

Kiresuk/Sherman Goal-Attainment Scaling / KS-GAS (all ages)

Description: Intake clinicians set 3 to 5 individualized goals for clients and establish a 5-point scale for each goal (ranging from "best anticipated success" to "most unfavorable treatment outcome thought likely"); at follow-up different interviewers judge client status on each scale.

Dimensions: Individualized.

Source: T. J. Kiresuk & R. E. Sherman (authors)
For more information see:
Mental Health Service System Reports
Assessing Mental Health Outcome Measurement
Techniques, Series FN, No. 9, United States Department of Health and Human Services, 1986.

(Global) Level of Functioning / L-O-F (all ages)

Description: Involves clinician ratings of overall client functioning level on a 7- to 9-point scale; intended to represent an integration of separate judgments of client functioning on several underlying dimensions; also used as a communication tool between clinicians and administration.

Dimensions: General focus.

Source: D. E. Carter & F. L. Newman (authors)
For more information see:
Mental Health Service System Reports
Assessing Mental Health Outcome Measurement
     Techniques, Series FN, No. 9, United States De-
     partment of Health and Human Services, 1986.

Levenstein, Klein, Pollack Outcome Rating / LKP (adult)

Description: Global scale designed to measure patterns of psychiatric and social functioning.

Dimensions: Symptom level, independent functioning and hospitalization over the past year.

Source: The RAND Corporation
PO Box 2138
Santa Monica CA 90407-2138
310-393-0411

Longitudinal Interval Follow-up Evaluation / LIFE (adult)

Description: Assesses the longitudinal course of psychiatric disorders.

Dimensions: Psychopathology, non-psychiatric medical illness,
treatment received, psychosocial functioning and
overall severity.

Source: Boston Massachusetts General Hospital
55 Fruit Avenue
Boston MA 02114
617-726-2000

MHCA Customer Satisfaction System

Description: Two satisfaction tools—one for clients, one for referrers; national aggregation of data with comparison to other users.

Dimensions: Client version: personal therapy perceptions, physical environment perceptions, client/staff interaction perceptions.

Referrer version: services/interaction perceptions, procedures perceptions, communication perceptions, client access perceptions.

Source: Mental Health Corporation of America
2846-A Remington Green Circle
Tallahassee FL 32308
800-447-3068

Medical Necessity Scales / MNS (adult)

Description: Developed to promote effective communication between providers and reviewers; provides guidelines to help trained concurrent reviewers document the psychopathology of hospitalized patients through telephone interviews with providers.

Dimensions: Suicidal behavior, aggressive behavior, levels of functioning.

Source: Dr. William Glazer
Department of Psychology
Yale University School of Medicine
34 Park Street
New Haven CT 06519
203-785-4356

Millon Clinical Multiaxial Inventory—II / MCMI-II (adult)

Description: Based on Millon's theory of personality; developed to parallel and compliment the DSM-III-R.

Dimensions: Scales include schizoid, avoidant, dependent, histrionic, narcissistic, antisocial, aggressive/sadistic, compulsive, passive-aggressive, self-defeating, schizotypal, borderline, paranoid.

Source: NCS Assessments
5605 Green Circle Drive

Minnetonka MN 55343
800-627-7271

Minnesota Multiphasic Personality Inventory / MMPI (adolescent to geriatric)

Description: Developed to be a "complete automated clinician"; Caldwell Report provides an extensive and highly elaborate clinical report; for professional use only.

Dimensions: Hypochondriasis, depression, hysteria, psycho-pathic deviates, masculinity-femininity, paranoia, psychas-thenia, schizophrenia, hypomania, social, question, lie, validity, test taking attitude.

Source: NCS Assessments
              5605 Green Circle Drive
              Minnetonka MN 55343
              800-627-7271

Oregon Quality of Life Questionnaire / OQLQ (adult)

Description: Assess quality of life outcomes among clients served by community mental health programs (especially those developed under the NIMH CSP initiative); self-report or interview versions available.

Dimensions: Psychological distress, psychological well-being, tolerance of stress, total basic need satisfaction, independence, interpersonal interactions, spouse role, social support, work at home, employability, work on the job, meaningful use of time, negative consequences of alcohol/drug use.

Source: G. Brodsky and D. A. Bigelow (authors)
              For more information see:
              Baker, R., and Intagliata, J. (1982). Quality of life in the evaluation of community support systems. *Evaluation and Program Planning*, 5:69–79.

Personal Adjustment and Roles Skills Scale / PARS (adult)

Description: Filled out by significant others regarding personal adjustment and the instrumental performance of adult psychiatric patients.

Dimensions: Interpersonal relations, alienation, anxiety, confusion, alcohol/drug use, house activity, child relations, work.

Source: Consulting Psychologists Press, Inc.
              577 College Avenue
              Palo Alto CA 94306
              415-969-8901

Present State Examination / PSE (adult)

Description: Designed to collect information about psychiatric symptoms.

Dimensions: 140 questions which fall into 3 categories: delusions/hallucinations, behavior/speech, and neuroses.

Source: Cambridge University Press
              510 North Avenue
              New Rochelle NY 10801
              914-937-9600

Profile of Moods States / POMS (adult)

Description: Designed to meet the need for rapid, economical, method of identifying and assessing transient, fluctuating affective states; measures typically reflect anticipated results and thus confirm clinical judgment in a more objective, quantified form.

Dimensions: Tension-anxiety, depression-dejection, anger-hostility, vigor-activity, fatigue-inertia, confusion-bewilderment.

Source: EdITS/Educational and Industrial Testing Service
              PO Box 7234
              San Diego CA 92107
              619-222-1666

Progress Evaluation Scales / PES (child to adult)

Description: Assess the impact of mental health services on client; designed to assist in assessing current functioning, setting treatment goals, and in evaluation treatment outcomes.

Dimensions: Family interaction, occupation, getting along with others, feeling and mood, use of free time, problems, attitude toward self.

Source: Lexington Books
              D. C. Heath & Co.
              125 Spring Street
              Lexington MA 02173
              617-862-6650

Psychiatric Epidemiology Research Interview / PERI (adult)

Description: Designed to investigate dimensions of psychopathology and to conduct psychiatric screening in general populations.

Dimensions: 24 psychopathology scales including 8 scales measuring the dimensions of demoralization of nonspecific psychological distress.

Source: The RAND Corporation
              PO Box 2138
              Santa Monica CA 90407-2138
              310-393-0411

Psychiatric Evaluation Form / PEF (adult)

Description: Interview guide and rating scale of recording scaled judgments of a person's functioning over a one-week period; based upon sources of information such as patient, case records, nurses' notes, etc.

Dimensions: Psychopathology, role functioning, overall severity of illness.

Source: Biometrics Research
              New York State Psychiatric Institute

722 West 168th Street
Room 341
New York NY 10032
212-960-2200

Psychiatric Status Schedule / PSS (adult)

Description: A standardized interview schedule for gathering information from a subject needed to fill out a matching inventory designed to evaluate social and role functioning as well as mental status.

Dimensions: Symptoms, role functioning, summary symptoms and role scales, and supplemental scores.

Source: Biometrics Research
New York State Psychiatric Institute
722 West 168th Street
Room 341
New York NY 10032
212-960-2200

Quality of Well-Being Scale / QWB (adult)

Description: Designed for use in evaluating the impact of medical intervention upon the health status of different groups in terms of years of life it produces/saves.

Dimensions: Mobility, physical activity, social activity, self-care.

Source: The RAND Corporation
PO Box 2138
Santa Monica CA 90407-2138
310-393-0411

Rand Health Insurance Experiment Mental Health Inventory / HIE-MHI (adult)

Description: Designed to assess psychological distress and psychological well-being in the general population.

Dimensions: Psychological distress, psychological well-being.

Source: The RAND Corporation
               PO Box 2138
               Santa Monica CA 90407-2138
               310-393-0411

Rosenberg Self-Esteem Scale / S-ES (adolescent to geriatric)

Description: 10-item self-report assessing self-esteem.

Dimensions: "Self acceptance aspect of self-esteem."

Source: M. Rosenberg (author)
               For more information see:
               Mental Health Service System Reports
               Assessing Mental Health Outcome Measurement
                   Techniques, Series FN, No. 9, United States De-
                   partment of Health and Human Services, 1986.

Schedule for Affective Disorders and Schizophrenia III / SADS
(adult)

Description: Developed to reduce the variance in information
               for both descriptive and diagnostic evaluations of
               research subjects.

Dimensions: Symptoms, level of functioning, lifetime and cur-
               rent problems.

Source: New York State Psychiatric Institute
               Research Assessment and Training Unit
               722 West 168th Street
               New York NY 10032
               212-960-2200

Schedule for Assessment of Negative Symptoms / SANS (adult)

Description: Developed to provide a method for standardizing as-
               sessment of the negative symptoms of schizophrenia
               which have been suggested as predictors of outcome.

Dimensions: Negative symptoms of schizophrenia; there are 30
               individual symptoms constituting measures of 5
               symptom complexes.

Source: The RAND Corporation
                PO Box 2138
                Santa Monica CA 90407-2138
                310-393-0411

SF-36 Health Status Questionnaire / SF-36 (adult)

Description: Generic patient assessment tool; can be applied
                over time to improvement or degradation of health
                in relation to services provided; can be supple-
                mented with diagnosis-specific "TyPE" scales to pro-
                vide symptoms data.

Dimensions: General health perception, physical, social, role
                limitations (physical and emotional causes), men-
                tal health, energy/fatigue, pain.

Source: The RAND Corporation
                PO Box 2138
                Santa Monica CA 90407-2138
                310-393-0411

Sickness Impact Profile / SIP (adult)

Description: Measures impact of illness/health care on daily ac-
                tivities and quality of life; items are phrased in terms
                of performance rather than capacity to perform.

Dimensions: Physical, psychosocial, other independent catego-
                ries (sleep, eating, work, home management, rec-
                reation, pastimes).

Source: The RAND Corporation
                PO Box 2138
                Santa Monica CA 90407-2138
                310-393-0411

Social Adjustment Scale—Self Report / SAS (adult)

Description: Self report measuring social adjustment.

Dimensions: Occupation, family life, economic, health, religion,
                residence, community, and social.

Source: Nathan G. Mandel (author)
           Department of Corrections
           State of Minnesota
           St. Paul MN 55108
           612-647-0020

Service Satisfaction Scale—30 (SSS-30)

Description: Typically given at discharge and/or at various follow-up intervals post-discharge; measures client satisfaction.

Dimensions: Client satisfaction across several dimensions.

Source: Clifford Attkisson, PhD
           University of California
           Department of Psychology
           401 Parnassus Avenue, Box CPT
           San Francisco CA 94143-0984
           415-476-7374

State-Trait Anxiety Inventory (STAI)

Description: Self report measure that provides scores for state anxiety (a variable emotional reaction) and trait anxiety (a personality characteristic).

Dimensions: Anxiety

Source: Psychological Assessment Resources, Inc.
           PO Box 998
           Odessa FL 33556
           800-331-8378

Strauss-Carpenter Outcome Scale / S-C (adult)

Description: Designed as a measure of outcomes for persons with schizophrenia.

Dimensions: Duration of non-hospitalization, social contacts, useful employed, absence of symptoms.

Source: The RAND Corporation
           PO Box 2138

Santa Monica CA 90407-2138
310-393-0411

Symptom Checklist 90 Revised / SCL-90 R (adolescent and adult)

Description: Self-report inventory of symptoms commonly found among psychiatric outpatients.

Dimensions: Somatization, obsessive-compulsive, interpersonal sensitivity, depression, anxiety, hostility, phobic anxiety, paranoid ideation, psychoticism.

Source: NCS Assessments
5605 Green Circle Drive
Minnetonka MN 55343
800-627-7271

Taylor Manifest Anxiety Scale / MAS (adolescent to geriatric)

Description: 55-item self-report measure of manifest anxiety; developed for selecting subjects for research on drive level.

Dimensions: Anxiety

Source: J. A. Taylor (author)
For more information see:
Mental Health Service System Reports
Assessing Mental Health Outcome Measurement Techniques, Series FN, No. 9, United States Department of Health and Human Services, 1986.

Therapy Rating Scale / TRS (adult)

Description: 34 problem-area items on which a therapist rates a client's functioning along a 6-point severity scale; points may indicate areas which will be the foci of treatment.

Dimensions: Psychopathology, interpersonal relations, role functioning, substance use, items pertaining to therapy setting.

Source: R. W. Swindle, Jr., D. Fuqua & G. Gibson (authors)
                     (research done at South Central Community
                     Mental Health Center, Evaluation Research Ser-
                     vice, Bloomington IN)
                     For more information see:
                     Mental Health Service System Reports
                     Assessing Mental Health Outcome Measurement
                     Techniques, Series FN, No. 9, United States De-
                     partment of Health and Human Services, 1986.

OTHER RESOURCES

The RAND Corporation, PO Box 2138, Santa Monica CA 90407-
2138 (301-393-0411).

SUGGESTED READINGS

Baker, R., & Intagliata, J. (1982). Quality of life in the evaluation of community support systems. *Evaluation and Program Planning, 5,* 69–79.

Fisher, J., & Corcoran, K. (1994). *Measures for clinical practice:
A sourcebook, Vol. 1 & 2.* New York: The Free Press.

Kiser, L., et al. (1994). *The AAPH outcomes measurement protocol.* Alexandra, VA: American Association of Partial Hospitalization.

Kramer, J. J., & Conoley, J. C. (Eds.). (1992). *The eleventh mental measurements yearbook.* Lincoln, NE: Buros Institute of Mental
Measurements.

Sederer, S. I., & Dickey, B. (1995). *Outcomes assessment in clinical practice.* Baltimore: Williams & Wilkens.

Touliatos, J., Perlmutter, B. F., & Straus, M. A. (Eds.). (1990).
Handbook of family measurement techniques. Newburg Park, CA: Sage
Publications.

Trabin, T., & Freeman, M. (Eds.). (1994). *Inside outcomes: A national review of behavioral healthcare outcomes management programs.*
Tiburon, CA: CentraLink.

Thanks to John Bilbrey, PhD, for his help in compiling this list.

Appendix C

Internet Addresses

American Psychological Society
    gopher.hanover.edu
    choose:Public
    http://psych.hanover.edu/APS/

An excellent search engine
    http://www.mckinley.com/

Another search engine
    http://www.excite.com/Subject/search.gw

APA PsychNET
    gopher.apa.org
    http://www.apa.org

Behavnet Online
    Telnet behavnet.com
    http://behavnet.com

Cognitive and Psychological Sciences on the Internet
    http://mafia.stanford.edu/cogsci.html

The Complete Guide to Sites Related to Psychology
  (This is an Australian Site)
    http://pegasus.acs.ttu.ade/~civelek/newl/thanatos2.html

Cyberpsych
      http://www.onramp.net/cyberpsych/

Dr. Bob's site
      http://uhs.bsd.uchicago.edu/~bhsiung/mental.html

Dr. John Grohol's great site
      http://www1.mhv.net/~grohol/

Instream Psychology
      http://www.instream.com/psychlink/

Internet Mental Health
   (Canadian site—excellent)
      http://www.mentalhealth.com/p.html

InterPsyche
      http://avocado.pc.helsinki.fi/"janne/ikg/

Larry's Best of the Behavioral Sciences
      http://www.clark.net/pub/\schank/behave.txt

Major Managed Care Site (AMSO)
      http://www.amso.com/

Metuchen Psychological Services
      http://www.castle.net/~tbogen/mps.html

One of best sites if you work with children
      http://www.lloyd.com~pat/k12index.html

Online Psychology
      http://www.onlinepsych.com/

Other Psychology Links
      http://public.sdsu.edu/Psy/psylinks.html

Parenting Points
      http://adware.com/uttm/parent/welcome.html

Psych Support Groups and Newsgroup Pointer
    http://chat.carleton.ca/~tscholbe/psych.html

PSYCHGRAD
    gopher://panda1.uottawa.ca

PsycINFO
    Telnet://cdplus@cdplus.com

Psychology Around the World
    http://rs1.cc.und.nodak.edu/misc/jBAT/psychres.html

Psychotherapy Finances
    Telnet psyfin.com
  Usual and Customary Fee Survey
    http://psyfin.com/tablesur.html

Scholastic Internet Center
    http://scholastic.com:2005/

Very large site
    http://www.mckinley.com/mckinley-
        cgi/focus.pl?behavioral_health

Web links for medical and mental health
    http://www.realtime.net/~mmjw

Web pages for psychologists
    http://psy.ucsd.edu/otherpsy.html

Yahoo Psychology Links
    http://Yahoo.com/science/psychology

(J. Engler, personal communication, November 11, 1995)

References

Alter, G. S., & Currie, P. (1995, March). *Group practice information system: How to cope at different stages of growth.* Paper presented at Behavioral Informatics Tomorrow Conference, San Diego, CA.

American Managed Behavioral Healthcare Association (AMBHA) (1995). *Performance measures for managed behavioral healthcare program.* Washington, DC: The AMBHA Quality Improvement and Clinical Services Committee.

American Psychiatric Association (1994). *Diagnostic and statistical manual of mental disorders,* 4th ed. (DSM-IV). Washington, DC: American Psychiatric Press.

Andrews, G., Peters, L., & Teeson, M. (1994). *The measurement of consumer outcome in mental health: A report to the National Mental Health Information Strategy Committee.* Sydney, Australia: Clinical Research Unit for Anxiety Disorders.

Armor, B. (1994, July/August). At risk contractor: Preparing to deliver what purchasers want. *Behavioral Healthcare Tomorrow, 4*(4), 25–29.

Attkisson, C. C., & Greenfield, T. K. (1994). Client Satisfaction Questionnaire-8 and Service Satisfaction Scale-30. In M. E. Maruish (Ed.), *The use of psychological testing for treatment planning and outcome assessment* (pp. 402–420). Hillsdale, NJ: Erlbaum.

Attkisson, C. C., & Zwick, R. (1982). The client satisfaction questionnaire: Psychometric properties and correlations with the service utilization and psychotherapy outcome. *Evaluation and Program Planning, 6,* 233–237.

Austad, C. S. (in press). *Is long-term therapy unethical? Toward a social ethic in an era of managed care.* San Francisco: Jossey-Bass.

Austad, C., & Berman, W. (Eds.). (1991). *Psychotherapy in managed care.* Washington, DC: American Psychological Association.

Axelson, A. (1995, January/February). Clinicians need standardized procedures and credentialing. *Behavioral Healthcare Journal, 4*, 42–43.

Bahrick, A. S., Russell, R. K., & Salmi, S. W. (1991). The effects of role induction on trainees' perceptions of supervision. *Journal of Counseling and Development, 69*, 434–438.

Balint, M. (1957). *The doctor, his patient and the illness.* New York: International Universities Press.

Ball, M. J. (1995, March). *Where are we headed?: Visioning the computer-based patient record.* Paper presented at Behavioral Informatics Tomorrow Conference, San Diego, CA.

Belar, C. D. (1989). Opportunities for psychologists in health maintenance organizations: Implications for graduate education and training. *Professional Psychology: Research and Practice, 20*, 390–394.

Bennett, M. J. (1984). Brief psychotherapy and adult development. *Psychotherapy, 21*, 171–177.

Bennett, M. J. (1989). The catalytic function in psychotherapy. *Psychiatry, 52*, 351–364.

Bennett, M. J. (1994). Can competing psychotherapists be managed? *Managed Care Quarterly, 2*(2), 29–35.

Bergin, A. E., & Garfield, S. L. (Eds.). (1994). *Handbook of psychotherapy and behavior change* (4th ed.). New York: Wiley.

Bernard, J. (1979). Supervision training: A discrimination model. *Counselor Education and Supervision, 19*, 60–68.

Bevan, W. (1982). Human welfare and national policy: A conversation with Stuart Eizenstat. *American Psychologist, 37*, 1128–1135.

Bloom, B. L. (1992). *Planned short-term psychotherapy: A clinical handbook.* Boston: Allyn & Bacon.

Boland, P. (1991). *Making managed care work: A practical guide to strategies and solutions.* New York: McGraw-Hill.

Borders, L. D. (1992). Learning to think like a supervisor. *The Clinical Supervisor, 10*(2), 135–148.

Bourg, E. F., Bent, R. J., Callan, J. E., Jones, N. F., McHolland, J., & Stricker, G. (1987). *Standards and evaluation in the education and training of professional psychologists.* Norman, OK: Transcript Press (distributed through the National Council of Schools of Professional Psychology).

Bradley, L. J. (1989). *Counselor supervision: Principles, process, and practice.* Muncie, IN: Accelerated Development.

Bradley, J., & Post, P. (1991). Impaired students: Do we eliminate them from counselor education programs? *Counselor Education and Supervision, 31*, 100–108.

Browning, C. H., & Browning, B. J. (1994a). *How to partner with managed care.* Los Alamitos: Duncliff's International.

Browning, C. H., & Browning, B. J. (1994b). *Private practice handbook: The tools, tactics and techniques for successful practice development* (rev. 4th ed.). Los Alamitos: Duncliff's International.

Browning, C. H., & Browning, B. J. (1995). *Bulletproof treatment plans: How to craft written and telephone reports for maximum success with managed care.* Los Alamitos: Duncliff's International.

Budman, S. H., & Bennett, M. J. (1983). Short-term group psychotherapy. In H. Kaplan & B. Sadock (Eds.), *Comprehensive group psychotherapy* (pp. 138–144). Baltimore: Williams & Wilkins.

Budman, S. H., & Gurman, A. S. (1988). *Theory and practice of brief therapy.* New York: Guilford.

Burlingame, G. M., & Behrman, J. A. (1987). Clinician attitudes toward time-limited and time-unlimited therapy. *Professional Psychology: Research and Practice, 18,* 61–65.

Cantor, D. (1993, August). *Will the solo independent practitioner be extinct by the year 2000?* Paper Presented at APA Practice Directorate Miniconvention. American Psychological Association Annual Meetings, Toronto.

Cavaliere, F. (1995). Psychologists as medication advisers. *APA Monitor, 26*(7), 40.

Cummings, J. L. (1989). A psychological autopsy: Case study. In J. L. Cummings (Producer) & K. R. Knight (Director), *A psychological autopsy* [Film]. Dayton, OH: Wright State University TV Center.

Cummings, N. A. (1977). Prolonged or "ideal" versus short-term "realistic" psychotherapy. *Professional Psychology, 8,* 491–501.

Cummings, N. A. (1985, August). *The new mental health care delivery system and psychology's new role.* Invited Awards Address to the American Psychological Association Annual Meetings, Los Angeles.

Cummings, N. A. (1986). The dismantling of our health system: Strategies for the survival of psychological practice. *American Psychologist, 41,* 426–431.

Cummings, N. A. (1988, September). *The future of inpatient and outpatient mental health practice: A series of predictions.* Keynote address to the First Annual Behavioral Healthcare Tomorrow Conference. San Francisco.

Cummings, N. A. (1991). Arguments for the financial efficacy of psychological services in health care settings. In J. J. Sweet, R. G. Rozensky, & S. M. Tovian (Eds.), *Handbook of clinical psychology in medical settings* (pp. 113–126). New York: Plenum.

Cummings, N. A. (1992). The future of psychotherapy: Society's charge to professional psychology. *The Independent Practitioner, 12*(3), 126–130.

Cummings, N. A. (1993). Psychotherapy with substance abusers. In G. Stricker & J. R. Gold (Eds.), *Comprehensive handbook of psychotherapy integration* (pp. 337–352). New York: Plenum.

Cummings, N. A. (1994). The successful application of medical offset in program planning and clinical delivery. *Managed Care Quarterly, 2*(2), 1–6.

Cummings, N. A. (1995a). Behavioral health after managed care: The next golden opportunity for professional psychology. *Register Report, 20*(3), 1, 30–32.

Cummings, N. A. (1995b). Impact of managed care on employment and training: A primer for survival. *Professional Psychology: Research and Practice, 26* (1), 10–15.

Cummings, N. A. & Dörken, H. (1986). Corporations, networks and service plans: Economically sound models for practice. In H. Dörken & Associates (Ed.), *Professional psychology in transition* (pp. 165–174). San Francisco: Jossey-Bass.

Cummings, N. A., Dörken, H., Pallak, M. S., & Henke, C. J. (1993). The impact of psychological intervention on health care costs and utilization: The Hawaii Medicaid project. In *Medicaid, Managed Behavioral Health and Implications for Public Policy: Vol. 2. Healthcare and Utilization Cost Series* (pp. 3–23). South San Francisco, CA: Foundation for Behavioral Health.

Cummings, N. A., & Fernandez, L. (1985, March). Exciting new opportunities for psychologists in the market place. *Independent Practitioner, 5*, 38–42.

Cummings, N. A., & Follette, W. T. (1968). Psychiatric services and medical utilization in a prepaid health plan setting: Part 2. *Medical Care, 6*, 31–41.

Cummings, N. A., & Follette, W. T. (1976). Psychotherapy and medical utilization: An eight-year follow-up. In H. Dörken (Ed.), *Professional psychology today* (pp. 176–197). San Francisco: Jossey-Bass.

Cummings, N., & Sayama, M. (1995). *Focused psychotherapy: A casebook of brief intermittent psychotherapy throughout the life cycle.* New York: Brunner/Mazel.

Cummings, N. A., & VandenBos, G. R. (1979). The general practice of psychology. *Professional Psychology, 10*, 430–440.

Cummings, N. A., & VandenBos, G. R. (1981). The twenty year Kaiser-Permanente experience with psychotherapy and medical utilization: Implications for national health policy and national health insurance. *Health Policy Quarterly, 1*(2), 159–175.

Currie, P. (1994, September/October). Re-engineering the behavioral healthcare industry with information technology. *Behavioral Healthcare Tomorrow, 3*, 71–73.

Currie, P. (1995, March). *How to plan and develop an information system that meets your behavioral group practice need.* Paper presented at Behavioral Informatics Tomorrow Conference, San Diego, CA.

DeLafuente, D. (1993). California groups join for survival: Mullikin Healthcare Partners exemplify trend. *Modern Healthcare,* June 21, 24–26.

Davenport, T. H. (1994, March/April). Saving IT's soul: Human-centered information management. *Harvard Business Review, 72,* 119–131.

Derfler, F. (1995, July). Building the perfect network. *PC Magazine, 14*(13), 224–234.

Disney, J. M., & Stephens, A. M. (1994). Legal issues in clinical supervision. In T. P. Remley (Series Ed.), *The ACA Legal Series, 10,* Alexandria, VA; American Counseling Association.

Donaldson, M. S. (1995, January/February). Confidentiality on the information highway: Balancing the needs of individual patients and society. *Behavioral Healthcare Tomorrow, 4,* 32–36.

Dörken, H., & Cummings, N. A. (1991). The potential effect on private practice of training in targeted focused mental health treatment for a specific population: A brief report. *Psychotherapy in Private Practice, 9*(3), 45–51.

Dörken, H., VandenBos, G. R., Henke, C. J., Cummings, N. A., & Pallak, M. S. (1993). Impact of law and regulation on professional practice. *Professional Psychology: Research and Practice, 24*(3), 256–265.

Follette, W. T., & Cummings, N. A. (1967). Psychiatric services and medical utilization in a prepaid health plan setting. *Medical Care, 5,* 25–35.

Forrester, D. (1994, March). The "physician equity model." *Integrated Healthcare Report,* 1–4.

Frank, J. D. (1984). The psychotherapy of anxiety. In L. Grinspoon (Ed.), *Psychiatry update: The American Psychiatric Association annual review, Vol. 3* (pp. 418–426). Washington, DC: American Psychiatric Press.

Frederickson, L. (1988). *Confronting mitral valve prolapse syndrome.* New York: Warner.

Freeman, M. (Ed.). (1995). *The capitation handbook.* Tiburon, CA: Centralink.

Friedman, S., & Fanger, M. T. (1991). *Expanding therapeutic possibilities: Getting results in brief psychotherapy.* Lexington, MA: Lexington.

Geraty, R. (1995, January/February). Managed care systems require sophisticated data interactions. *Behavioral Healthcare Tomorrow, 4,* 44–45.

Goldman, W., & Feldman, S. (Eds.). (1993, Fall). Managed mental health care. *New Directions for Mental Health Services, 59,* 1–112.

Greenfield, T. K., & Attkisson, C. C. (1989). Progress toward a multifactorial service satisfaction scale for evaluating primary care and mental health services. *Evaluation and Program Planning, 12,* 271–278.

Greist, J. H. (1982, Summer). Conservative radicalism. *Computers in Psychiatry/Psychology, 4*(3).

Hall, C. T. (1995). Customers rate health plans. *San Francisco Chronicle,* October 25, pp. B1 & B8.

Harris, S., & DeMayo, R. (1991). Managed care: Professional roles redefined and re-examined. *Managed Care Outlook, 4*(3), 28–31.

Hill, E. (1995, January/February). Standardized data interchange offers administrative cost savings. *Behavioral Healthcare Tomorrow, 4,* 46–47.

Hoyt, M. F. (1995). *Brief therapy and managed care: Readings for contemporary practice.* San Francisco: Jossey-Bass.

Kardner, S. H. (1975). A methodological approach to crisis therapy. *American Journal of Psychotherapy, 27,* 4–13.

Kent, A. J. (1995, August). *Survey of interns' knowledge of brief therapy and managed care. Presentation 5164.* Paper presented at the American Psychological Association Annual Convention, New York.

Kissick, W. (1994). Working document, President Clinton's Task Force on National Health Reform.

Krul, E. (1994). *The whole Internet user's guide and catalog* (2nd ed.). Sebastopol, CA: O'Reily.

Levenson, H., & Davidivitz, D. (1995, August). *National survey of mental health professionals on brief therapy.* Presentation 4172, American Psychological Association Annual Convention, New York.

Loganbill, C., Hardy, E., & Delworth, U. (1982). A conceptual model for supervision. *The Counseling Psychologist, 10,* 3–43.

Lowe, D. (1995). *Client/server computing for dummies.* Foster City, CA: IDG.

Mann, J. (1973). *Time-limited psychotherapy.* Cambridge, MA: Harvard University.

Martin, S. (1995). APA to pursue prescription privileges. *APA Monitor, 26*(9), 6.

Meichenbaum, D., & Turk, D. C. (1987). *Facilitating treatment adherence: A practitioner's guide.* New York: Plenum.

Michaels, L. F. (1982). *The development of an anchored rating scale for evaluating psychotherapy skills.* Unpublished doctoral dissertation, Colorado State University.

Mirin, S. M., & Namerow, M. J. (1991). Why study treatment outcome? *Hospital & Community Psychiatry, 42,* 1007–1013.

Morrison, D. P. (1991, November). Integrating consumerism into clinical care delivery: The role of the therapist. *Administration and Policy in Mental Health, 19*(2), 103–119.

Morrison, D. P. (in press a). Automating clinical outcomes assessment. In C. Stout (Ed.), *The complete guide to managed behavioral care.* New York: Wiley.

Morrison, D. P. (in press b). Customer service in behavioral healthcare. In C. Stout (Ed.), *The complete guide to managed behavioral care*. New York: Wiley.

Moreland, K., Morrison, D., & Maruish, M. (1995, March). *What role should automated psychological testing have in the evolving era of healthcare reform?* Paper presented at Behavioral Informatics Conference, San Diego, CA.

Mrazek, D.A. (1993). Asthma: Stress, allergies, and the genes. In D. Goleman & J. Gurin (Eds.), *Mind body medicine* (pp. 193–205). Yonkers, NY: Consumer Reports Books.

Nance, B. (1993). *Networking Windows for Workgroups*. New York: Wiley.

Nance, B. (1994). A first step toward client/server. *PC Magazine, 13*(14), 403–408.

Neer, H. M. (1994, July). *The future of occupational medicine*. Address to the National Workers' Compensation and Occupational Medicine Seminar. Hyannis, MA.

Olkin, R., & Gaughen, S. (1991). Evaluation and dismissal of students in master's level clinical programs: Legal parameters and survey results. *Counselor Education & Supervision, 30*, 276–288.

Olsen, J. W. (1995). Big three online services reach out to Internet. *PC Magazine, 14*(12), 37–39.

Orlinsky, D. E., Grawe, K., & Parks, B. K. (1994). Process and outcome in psychotherapy. In A. E. Bergin & S. L. Garfield (Eds.), *Handbook of psychotherapy and behavior change* (4th ed., pp. 270–376). New York: Wiley.

Oss, M. (1993, June). Pro and con: A look at Harvard's new mental health and chemical dependency benefit plan. *Open Minds, 7*, 3–4.

Oss, M. (1995, March). More Americans enrolled in managed behavioral care. *Open Minds, 12*, 1–3.

Overall, J. F., & Hollister, L. E. (1964). Computer procedures for psychometric classification. *Journal of the American Medical Association, 187*, 115–120.

Pallak, M. S., Cummings, N. A., Dörken, H., & Henke, C. J. (1993, Fall). Managed mental health, Medicaid, and medical cost offset. In W. Goldman & S. Feldman (Eds.), *New directions for mental health services, 59*, 27–40.

Pallak, M. S., Cummings, N. A., Dörken, H., & Henke, C. J. (1994, Spring). Medical costs, Medicaid, and managed mental health treatment: The Hawaii study. In N. A. Cummings & M. S. Pallak (Eds.), *Managed Care Quarterly, Vol. 2*. Frederick, MD: Aspen.

Piotrowski, A. (1964). A digital computer interpretation of inkblot test data. *Psychiatric Quarterly, 38*, 1–26.

Powell, D. J. (1993). *Clinical supervision in alcohol and drug counseling: Principles, models, methods.* New York: Lexington.

Poynter, W. (1994). *The preferred provider's handbook.* New York: Bruner/Mazel.

Practitioner (1995, August). Psychopharmacology demonstration program persists despite psychiatry attacks. *Practitioner, 8*(2), 3.

Putney, M. W., Worthington, E. L., & McCullough, M. E. (1992). Effects of supervisor and supervisee theoretical orientation and supervisor-supervisee matching on interns' perceptions of supervision. *Journal of Counseling Psychology, 39*(2), 139–157.

Reis, J., & Trout, A. (1986). *Positioning: The battle for your mind.* New York: McGraw-Hill.

Resnick, R. J. (1995, August). Psychological training in the twenty-first century. *Practitioner, 8*(2), 15.

Rosen, L. D., & Weil, M. M. (1995, Fall). Tips for mental health professionals to merge online. *Treatment Today, 7,* 48–49.

Rosofsky, I. (1993). Psychologists should opt out of health care, says Kovacs. *Practice Management Monthly, 1*(11), 4–6.

Rosofsky, I. (1995). Young doctors support psychologists prescribing. *Practice Management Monthly, 3*(9), 2–3.

Saeman, H. (1996, January/February). Psychologists frustrated with managed care, economic issues, but plan to "hang tough," survey reveals. *National Psychologist, 5*(1), 1–2.

Sattem, L. L. (1989). Suicide prevention. In J. L. Cummings (Producer) & K. R. Knight (Director), *A psychological autopsy* [Film]. Dayton, OH: Wright State University TV Center.

Saunders, R., & Ludwigsen, K. R. (1992). Mental health in New Jack City. *Independent Practitioner, 12*(3), 97–99.

Shueman, S. A., Troy, W. G., & Mayhugh, S. L. (1994). Managed behavioral healthcare. *Register Report, 20*(1), 5–9.

Sifneos, P. E. (1987). *Short-term dynamic psychotherapy: Evaluation and technique.* New York: Plenum Medical.

Silverman, D. (1995, August). Toward a universal library: SGML and the future of electronic documents. *Wired,* 3.08, 62.

Smith, A. R. (1995, June). MIS requirements for managing contracts. *Open Minds, 9*(3), 4–6.

Stearn, S. (1993). Managed care, brief therapy, and therapeutic integrity. *Psychotherapy, 30*(1), 162–174.

Stoltenberg, C. (1981). Approaching supervision from a developmental perspective: The counselor complexity model. *Journal of Counseling Psychology, 28,* 59–65.

Strupp, H. H., & Binder, J. L. (1984). *Psychotherapy in a new key: A guide for time-limited dynamic psychotherapy.* New York: Basic.

Tomsho, R. (1995). At medical malls, shoppers are patients. *Wall Street Journal,* December 29, pp. B-1 & B-11.

Trabin, T., Freeman, M. A., & Pallak, M. S. (1995). *Inside outcomes: The national review of behavioral health care outcomes progress.* Tiburon, CA: CentraLink.

Vieweg, B. W., & DiFranco, B. (1995, January/February). The use of automated assessment with seriously mentally ill clients. *Behavioral Healthcare Tomorrow, 4,* 37–41.

Ward, R. E. (1993, March/April). Information systems support continuous quality. *Group Practice Journal, 42,* 93.

Ware, J. E., Snow, K. K., Kosinski, M., & Gandek, B. (1993). *SF-36 Health Survey: Manual and interpretation guide.* Boston, MA: The Health Institute, New England Medical Center.

Weed, L. L. (1969). *Medical records, medical education and patient care.* Cleveland, OH: Case Western Reserve University Press.

Wilcox, J. (1995, March). *Evolving software technologies to support behavioral healthcare applications.* Paper presented at Behavioral Informatics Tomorrow Conference, San Diego, CA.

Wright, R. H. (1991, Spring). Toward a national health plan. *Advance Plan, 1,* 14–16.

Wright, R. H. (1992). Toward a political solution to psychology's dilemmas: Managing managed care. *Independent Practitioner, 12*(3), 111–113.

Wylie, M. S. (1995). The new visionaries. *Family Therapy Networker, 19*(5), 20–35.

Zimet, C. N. (1994). Psychology's role in a national health program. *Journal of Clinical Psychology, 50*(1), 122–124.

Zinger, G. (1994, July/August). Behavioral health: At risk contracting. *Behavioral Healthcare Tomorrow, 4*(4), 36–39.

Name Index

Allen, W., 17
Alter, G. S., 241
Andrews, G., 224
Armor, B., 191
Attkisson, C. C., 261, 307, 322
Austad, C., 6, 267
Axelson, A., 246

Bahrick, A. S., 109
Baker, R., 308
Balint, M., 8, 12
Ball, M. J., 246
Behrman, J. A., 146
Belar, C. D., 8
Bennett, M. J., 8, 11–12, 14, 17, 125, 262
Bent, R. J., 68
Bergin, A. E., 260, 262
Berman, W., 267
Bernard, J., 97–99, 109
Bevan, W., 27
Bhote, K. R., 219, 267
Bigelow, D. A., 316
Binder, J. L., 124
Bloom, B. L., 8, 11, 124
Boland, P., 149
Borders, L. D., 111
Bourg, E. F., 68
Bradley, J., 98

Bradley, L. J., 115
Brodsky, G., 316
Browning, B. J., 149, 160–162, 169–173
Browning, C. H., xv, 149, 160–162, 169–173
Budman, S. H., 8, 11–12, 14, 17, 124
Burlingame, G. M., 146

Callan, J. E., 68
Cantor, D., 17
Carter, D. E., 314
Cavalier, F., 84
Ciarlo, J. A., 310
Cummings, J., xv, xvii
Cummings, N. A., xiii–xiv, xvi, 8, 9, 12–13, 14, 18, 22, 23, 25, 27, 30, 31, 32, 33, 35, 39, 41, 61, 81, 94, 96, 99, 101, 103, 121, 124, 129, 133, 135, 146, 149, 195, 206, 223, 238, 262, 263, 267, 268, 276, 280, 287, 289, 291, 294, 295
Currie, P., 241, 244

Davenport, T. H., 262
Davidivitz, D., 8
DeLafuente, D., 35
Delworth, U., 105, 109
DeMayo, R., 268

339

Subject Index